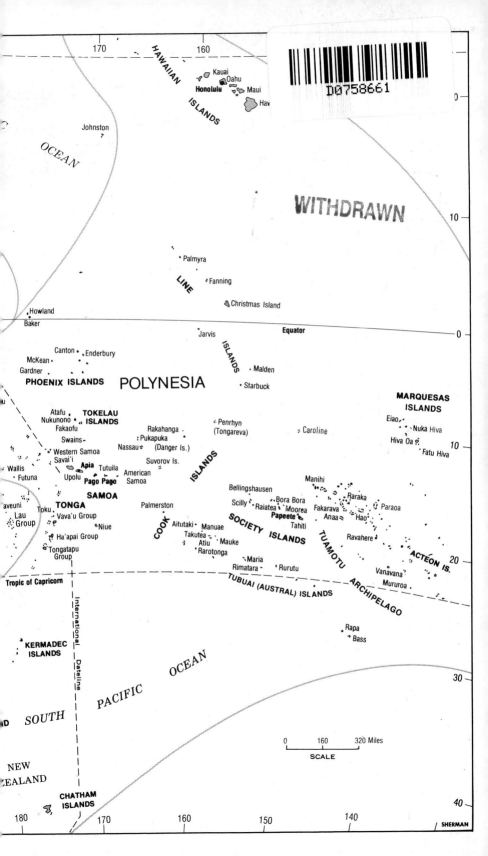

170   160

HAWAIIAN

Kauai
Oahu
Honolulu Maui
ISLANDS Haw

0

Johnston

OCEAN

10

• Palmyra

LINE

Fanning

Christmas Island

.Howland
Baker

Jarvis   Equator   0

Canton • .Enderbury
McKean •
Gardner •
PHOENIX ISLANDS   **POLYNESIA**

ISLANDS

• Malden

• Starbuck

**MARQUESAS
ISLANDS**

Atafu . **TOKELAU**
Nukunono • „ **ISLANDS**
Fakaofu
Swains -
:Pukapuka
Nassau⊐ (Danger Is.)
Western Samoa
Savai'i
Apia Tutuila
Upolu **Pago Pago** American
SAMOA Samoa

Rakahanga .

Penrhyn
(Tongareva)

Caroline

Eiao,.
Nuka Hiva
Hiva Oa ⊝
Fatu Hiva

10

Suvorov Is.

ISLANDS

Manihi

Bellingshausen

Raraka

•Wallis
• Futuna

Toku .**TONGA**
Vava'u Group
Ha'apai Group
Tongatapu
Group

Palmerston

Scilly •. Bora Bora
•Raiatea • Moorea
Papeete
Tahiti

Fakarava
Anaa⊅ Hao

Paraoa

Niue

COOK

Aitutaki • Manuae
Takutea -
Atiu • Mauke
• Rarotonga

**SOCIETY
ISLANDS**

Ravahere

TUAMOTU

20

ACTÉON IS.

Vanavana
Mururoa .

aveuni
Lau
Group

⌐Maria
Rimatara - • Rurutu

TUBUAI (AUSTRAL) ISLANDS

ARCHIPELAGO

Tropic of Capricorn

• Rapa
⌐ Bass

**KERMADEC
ISLANDS**

OCEAN

30

PACIFIC

SOUTH

NEW
ZEALAND

CHATHAM
ISLANDS

180   170   160   150   140   40

International Dateline

0   160   320 Miles
SCALE

SHERMAN

Tin Roofs and Palm Trees

Tin Roofs
and Palm Trees

A REPORT ON THE NEW SOUTH SEAS

ROBERT TRUMBULL

University of Washington Press

Seattle and London

99503

Library of Congress Cataloging in Publication Data

Trumbull, Robert.
    Tin roofs and palm trees.

    Includes index.
    1. Oceanica—History. 2. Ethnology—Oceanica.
3. Oceanica—Social conditions. I. Title.
DU28.3.T78   990   76-49164
ISBN 0-295-95544-9

"Tin roofs, palm trees; palm trees, tin roofs—
that's all you see in the tropics. . . ."

JEAN TRUMBULL, gazing out a
window on a South Pacific island

Contents

Illustrations

ix

Tin Roofs and Palm Trees

ONE

For a New Identity

ROM the eighteenth-century accounts of Captain James
Cook, the British navigator, to the writings of the American novelist James A. Michener, enraptured descriptions
of the Pacific islands have identified the term "South Seas" with
visions of a blissful life in perpetual summer on white beaches
shaded by swaying palm trees. On many an island where such
beaches are commonplace, brown-skinned South Pacific peoples
dream of joining the modern world.

Scenes of haunting beauty abound in the ten thousand islands
of the tropical Pacific, which range in size from mere sandspits
with a fringe of coconut trees to massive formations with towering mountain peaks and broad rivers. Since the arrival of Western
civilization, however, more of the virgin landscapes admired by
Cook and later visitors have sprouted incongruous masonry hotels, and countless palms cast their shade on tin roofs in villages
where metal was unknown in Cook's time.

The graceful palm, the source of much sustenance and many
other needs for people of the islands, shielding a roof of curly,
bare metal from the blazing sun, is a sight that is repeated endlessly in the South Pacific. The stark contrast in the scene neatly
captures the essential ingredients in the story of the South Seas
in two universal symbols. The sheltering palm conveys the feeling of a soothing environment, untroubled by the clashing diversities of a system spawned by harsher climes; the rusting tin roof
(actually corrugated iron, to be precise) suggests the incongrui-

ties resulting from a monetary society parachuted into a communal culture that had evolved in the islands over centuries of isolation from a more competitive, mechanized world.

The Western influx during World War II, followed by an education explosion and the appearance of the ubiquitous transistor radio in the most remote villages, has brought new political awareness to the sun-baked isles between Cancer and Capricorn. Vigorous new leaders, many with university degrees, see themselves as the molders of a new chapter in a history defiled, since the coming of the white man, by loot, enslavement, and disease. They are also the defenders of a gentle culture threatened by the destructive inroads of industrialization and the lure of an unfamiliar money economy. The four million people of the islands, some of whom are still totally unaware of Western civilization, are in a race to catch up with the world.

In the years since the first European incursion into the Pacific by Spanish and Portuguese navigators in the sixteenth century, the South Sea islands have undergone a more drastic metamorphosis, through the magic of technology, than any other part of the world in the same period. Most of it has taken place in the two centuries since the explorations of Cook. The change has been accelerated by the revolution in communications in the middle years of the present century. When I first went to the Pacific as a twenty-one-year-old newspaper reporter, travel was by ship and it took five days to go from the west coast of the United States to Hawaii; today jet planes make the same trip in about five hours and one wide-bodied aircraft carries half as many passengers as the biggest Matson liners on the Honolulu run.

The first Europeans in the South Pacific discovered a culture untouched by the mainstreams of either Western or Asian civilization, with a simple economy based on agriculture and fishing. The islanders were scantily clothed in grasses, leaves, and a cloth-like material made by beating the inner bark of the paper mulberry tree and best known today by its Polynesian name, tapa. Generally speaking, their houses were constructed of poles, reeds, and thatch, sometimes on foundations of stone or chunks of coral, with pebbles or woven mats covering the earth floor. The islanders were skillful builders of canoes and weavers of nets from sennit, and they knew stone-cutting and wood-carving. Their weapons were mainly spears and clubs, and they manufactured simple implements of wood, stone, and marine shells, which now are a source of cash income in the curio markets. Early Western contacts were light; more than 250 years after Magellan's discoveries, Cook's men could still buy love in Tahiti for a nail.

In the absence of written history before the missionaries gave the Pacific people the alphabet, the story of the islands in early times is extrapolated from archeological evidence. In the beginning, mountains rose above the sea. Over the eons, countless tiny marine organisms formed collars of coral around the bases of the volcanic peaks. The so-called high islands, like Tahiti, are the richly overgrown remains of ancient volcanoes and lava flows. Other mountains sank beneath the sea, leaving the coral bands that became atolls as sand and soil accumulated to make islets, which generally form a rough circle enclosing a lagoon. Of a third type are the raised coral islands, the result of successive upheavals in which the coral formation rose and fell and rose again, finally becoming a more or less flat platform of limestone covered with verdure.

The weight of anthropological opinion is that the islands and atolls were populated in a series of migrations from the mainland of Asia. The first migrants in the Pacific are believed to have set out toward the end of the Pleistocene era, or Ice Age, some twenty thousand to twenty-five thousand years ago, from areas of Southeast Asia that later became detached from the continent and formed various islands of Indonesia. The voyagers, using increasingly sophisticated sailing canoes as the centuries passed, eventually peopled New Guinea, the Solomons, the New Hebrides, Fiji, and associated islands. These territories are known collectively as Melanesia, or "black islands," a name derived from their dark appearance on the horizon as they were first sighted by European navigators, and not, as is commonly supposed, from the swarthy appearance of the inhabitants.

Next came the lighter-skinned people who settled Polynesia ("many islands") one or two millennia before the beginning of the Christian era. Traveling in huge, double-hulled sailing canoes, they are thought to have congregated first in Samoa and the Society Islands, from there spreading north to Hawaii, east to Easter Island, and south to New Zealand, forming the great Polynesian Triangle.

The ancestors of the present inhabitants of Micronesia ("small islands") are believed to have migrated from Malaysia through the Philippines to populate the myriad islands and atolls in a broad belt extending from southwest of Hawaii almost to the Asian mainland. The physical appearance of the Micronesians, who are generally lighter-skinned and more Mongolian-looking than other Pacific peoples, suggests a fusion of races.

Contact between one island group and another was inhibited by the vast distances to be traversed in perilous seas, although there are traditions of prodigious voyages by sailing canoe, using the stars and wave patterns for navigation. Micronesian atoll dwellers still travel hundreds of miles by canoe, out of sight of land. Some of the islands were probably settled by castaways blown off course by storms.

The societies that developed in the various groups were distinct but held certain characteristics in common. Matrilineal systems developed simultaneously on many islands. Property was usually held communally. The concept of money—in the form of bits of ceramic in Palau, imported stone disks in Yap, and shells or shell beads in other islands—appeared for limited purposes and still survives in ceremonial exchanges. Authority was in the hands of chiefs, who were not always chosen by heredity and, in any case, were usually responsive to councils and could be deposed. Varying from group to group, there were more or less rigid class systems, sometimes three-tiered with nobles, commoners, and slaves, and even caste divisions along Hindu lines.

The romantic conception of life on a South Sea island envisages a society untrammeled by the conventions of Western existence. In fact, although standards were less rigid in such matters as sex, the Pacific peoples lived under a closely integrated, highly organized, disciplined code of behavior, far from the free and easy style imagined by escapists. Indeed, "tabu" is a Polynesian word.

What seems to be the easygoing nature of the South Sea islander is a product of conditions that discouraged the development of an acquisitive society. The perishable nature of island foodstuffs and other possessions, in the absence of refrigeration and weatherproof storage facilities, made accumulation and saving impracticable. The heavy interdependence of island people dictated a system of sharing material possessions.

Thus the factors conditioning the development of a Pacific personality militated against easy assimilation of Western ways. The evaluation of a person's worth by his ability to accumulate material wealth was a concept strange to the Pacific mentality.

On the other hand, the village communal system prevalent in the islands provided a built-in social security for which Western societies are still striving. As the twentieth century enters its final decades, Pacific societies are struggling to adjust to the Western value system introduced by the white colonial rulers in the century previous. With the colonial era practically ended, the newly free nations of the South Seas find themselves playing by rules formed to suit a culture other than their own.

Against the sweep of history, the colonial era in the South Seas was brief. Spain had asserted imperial claims over most of Micronesia in the sixteenth century, following the discoveries of Magellan and others; but His Catholic Majesty's government exercised little or no authority there in the next three hundred years, except in the tiny, remote Marianas, on or near the sea lanes from Mexico to the Spanish establishments in the Philippines. Intensive colonization in the South Pacific began only in the middle of the nineteenth century with the French annexation of Tahiti, followed by British, German, and American incursions. With the onset of World War II, less than a century later, colonialism went into abrupt decline and is now all but finished.

White contact was haphazard and sketchy following the coming of Cook and other explorers in the latter part of the eighteenth century. Whalers stopped at various islands to provision and refresh their crews. Traders sought sandalwood to barter in China. Runaway sailors, fugitives from justice, remittance men, beachcombers, and adventurers of every kind from all corners of the world appeared in the islands, with dire results for the trusting natives. Besides gunpowder, which added a catastrophic new dimension to the incessant native wars, the whites brought venereal infection and other previously unknown diseases, to which the islanders had no natural resistance. Populations were decimated. Later, however, the islands would suffer from the opposite problem of overcrowding, as new drugs conquered epidemics and lives became longer.

Christian missionaries were in the vanguard of the white influx, coming from Spain, France, Britain, and the United States. The missionaries strove, with some success, to protect the native peoples against the depredations of unscrupulous white men. They also introduced medical and educational programs that the later colonial authorities, always hampered by budgetary problems, were glad to leave to the churches. In recent times, churchmen have fostered political advances; a few, notably the native pastors of the New Hebrides and Papua New Guinea, have led freedom movements.

Against these considerable benefits, the missionaries must be charged with ravaging Oceanic culture. They persuaded the islanders to clothe their unfettered bodies in ugly, unhealthful clothes. They were far from loath to intervene in temporal affairs, and often became virtual dictators through their influence over converted chiefs. Not the least of the transgressions for which the missionaries are held to account was the grafting of Western puritanism onto societies that had been free of prurience.

Some of the earliest white men in the South Pacific deplored the introduction of Western wants into societies that, as Cook wrote in 1770, were "wholly unacquainted not only with the superfluities but the necessary conveniences so much sought after in Europe." "If the advantage of the natives alone were consulted," a New Zealand official declared in the 1840s, "it would be better, perhaps, that they should remain the savages that they are."

Wholesale lawlessness having engulfed many islands as a result of the white man's doing—through the importation of firearms, the entry of the blackbirders, and other assorted villainies—the European powers were beseeched by their nationals and the local chiefs to intervene. The intervention was begun more or less reluctantly, but gathered steam when the entry of the Germans and Americans into the area in the 1880s and 1890s aroused international competitiveness in the acquisition of potentially strategic outposts in the great ocean.

No Pacific territory of any consequence remained fully independent by 1900, although many minor islands seldom saw a white face. With the retirement of Spain following the Spanish-American War, Germany had purchased the Spanish holdings in Micronesia and also ruled Western Samoa, New Guinea, and tiny Nauru. France had expanded from Tahiti to the surrounding islands in what is now French Polynesia, plus New Caledonia and various minor islands, and shared the New Hebrides with the British. Britain ruled a vast collection of islands, including Fiji, Tonga, the Solomons, and the Gilberts. The United States had annexed Eastern (American) Samoa, Guam, and a scattering of small, uninhabited islands, besides Hawaii and the Philippines.

Two world wars brought a reshuffle of colonial spheres with the disappearance of Germany from the Pacific and the short-lived emergence of Japan as an imperial power. None of the wars that touched the South Seas involved issues growing directly out of the affairs of the island peoples whose destinies were to be affected by the outcomes.

World War II underscored the strategic importance of the Pacific islands. For some years, Japan had been quietly converting key islands of Micronesia into an outer defense line that played an important role in the conflict. The Japanese quickly invested numerous South Pacific islands, notably the Solomons and New Guinea, following the successful attack on Pearl Harbor, the Hawaii headquarters of United States defenses in the Pacific. It remained for American forces to install huge bases on still other islands as stepping stones for the drive against the Japanese positions and, eventually, the planned assault on Japan itself. The climactic attack on Japan was made unnecessary by the atomic bombs, delivered from an airfield in the Marianas.

The war was followed by momentous changes in all the colonial territories, including the islands of the tropical Pacific. There, as in Southeast Asia, dark-skinned subject peoples saw the white man humiliated and driven out by a race not so different from themselves. The colonial powers would never recover their shattered prestige. "World War II was the turning point," an American-educated Western Samoan declared at an international conference of Pacific island leaders many years later. "Hundreds of thousands of troops came into the islands, bringing with them a mass of weird and wonderful equipment and supplies. But more important, in the long term, were the new ideas and new ways of doing things."

For the islanders, it was the first contact with Westerners en masse. The experience was a window on a new world. Political sophistication was advanced through contacts fostered by a new postwar organization called the South Pacific Commission, a development organ formed in 1947 at the suggestion of Australia. The original members were Australia, New Zealand, Britain, France, the Netherlands, and the United States, who were the so-called metropolitan powers (colonial rulers, in other words) in the South Pacific. The Netherlands dropped out when Indonesia became independent, but the membership was enlarged later by the admission of Pacific island countries as they became sovereign states. Beginning in 1950, delegates from the dependent island territories met periodically with the commission members in a subordinate body called the South Pacific Conference.

The social and economic development projects of the South

Pacific Commission, limited by an annual budget of around two million dollars maximum, were less significant than the swift political education of the island delegations to the conferences. At first, when the meeting was held every four years, then every two, the island representatives read out stilted papers prepared with the aid of white advisers. In discussions, the islanders were heard seldom, if at all, and with little if any effect on the deliberations. By 1967, when the meetings began on an annual basis, all this had changed.

By then a new breed of island leader had emerged, articulate and outspoken. Usually garbed in multihued shirts, often wearing the comfortable lavalava instead of trousers, they eventually took over the entire running of the conference from the white professionals, who became mainly observers and consultants and wore flowered shirts themselves. One is tempted to attribute the emergence of the island leaders to the mystic quality known as *mana,* a kind of soul force traditionally associated with notable personalities in the South Pacific since early times.

"When we first came to these meetings," the leader of an important Melanesian delegation remarked to me at a South Pacific Conference session in Fiji, "we had to be taught how to wear shoes and use knives and forks." The speaker, a former Papuan villager, later became Sir Maori Kiki, deputy prime minister and foreign minister of independent Papua New Guinea.

At the first two or three of the five South Pacific Conferences that I covered for *The New York Times,* when these gatherings were the closest equivalent of an Oceanic parliament, the seventeen island territories participating were represented by their leading local personalities. The islands were in all stages of political development, ranging from tiny dependencies like the obscure Tokelau Islands, governed by New Zealand, to fully independent states like Western Samoa. Among the delegates were prime ministers, or men who would become prime ministers later, the George Washingtons of their little-known homelands. Others were top civil servants and politically powerful traditional chiefs. Several were all three, like the late Prime Minister Mata'afa of Western Samoa.

One of the most significant political developments from these gatherings was the gradual disappearance from the conference table of the islands' top men and replacement of them by articulate subordinates. This trend did not indicate a downgrading of the conference, which still ranked as the most far-reaching regional activity in the South Seas; rather, it was a demonstration that the island territories were developing administrative talent in depth. Eventually these island men, not the foreign officials, were the determining voices in fixing the South Pacific Commission's budget allocations for development projects in the area.

A historic change in the structure of political relationships in the South Seas followed the establishment of the South Pacific Conference. Until then, island leaders had dealt with their colonial rulers through local administrators, if at all. The different island groups had no direct contact with each other. Decisions affecting the islanders were made in London, Paris, and other metropolitan capitals with minimal reference, if any, to the people most concerned. In the South Pacific Conference sessions, a more sophisticated generation of islanders became accustomed to dealing with their white mentors as a group. Soon they were demanding a new order.

"Change must come, and is coming," a young Papua New Guinea delegate named Oala Oala-Rarua, who was destined to become an ambassador when his country gained independence, burst out at the 1970 conference. "Pacific islanders must take their place in the world today," he declared. Such voices could no longer go unheeded in the postcolonial era.

The evolution of the South Pacific Commission and its adjunct, the South Pacific Conference, into vehicles for political advancement had been far from the intentions of the white founders of these organizations. The white members, especially France, were meticulous in insisting upon the nonpolitical character of both bodies. In fact, critics of the commission cited the agency's parsimonious budget, with its top-heavy allotment of funds to support of the bureaucracy, as evidence that the intent of the founding powers had been to preserve colonialism, not to hasten its departure. The advent of a more liberal outlook in the governments of Australia and New Zealand under the short-lived Labor regimes of the early 1970s, the growing desire of Britain to shed colonial responsibilities in the Pacific, and the hardening mood of the islanders led to a gradual change in the atmosphere surrounding the annual gatherings that eventually accommodated significant structural changes.

A new regional consciousness in the South Pacific found expression in the growing determination of indigenous leaders not only to run their own affairs but also to make their collective views felt on the international scene. One important outcome was the formation of the South Pacific Forum as a vehicle of joint diplomatic pressure by the island states, in conjunction with the sympathetic governments of Australia and New Zealand. Convening in Wellington in August 1971, the founding governments of Australia, New Zealand, Fiji, Nauru, Western Samoa, Tonga, and the Cook Islands (an autonomous state in association with New Zealand) invited other former Pacific colonies to join as they achieved home rule.

The group, meeting yearly or oftener, was described as a vehicle for consolidating the views of the island governments on matters of international concern. Australia and New Zealand agreed to act in the interest of the island states in specific fields such as international trade and communications, besides furnishing various service facilities, while Fiji undertook to be the spokesman for the South Sea states in the United Nations, being the only Pacific island country that was then a member of the world body.

Meeting in different South Pacific capitals in turn, the organization provided an alternative to the South Pacific Commission, which was held to be nonrepresentative of the region because of the strong influence exercised on its deliberations by the "metropolitan powers" through their heavy contribution to the budget. The free island nations also objected to the arrangement under which the Western members were allowed plural voting, casting an extra vote for each Pacific dependency. Eventually, at the insistence of the islanders, the procedure was changed to a system of one member, one vote. The next step would be merger of the South Pacific Commission and its offshoot, the South Pacific Conference, into a single body.

Thus, by various steps in rapid succession, the long-exploited peoples of the South Pacific asserted an identity in the region and the world. Because their territories are small, scattered, and distant from the power centers of the East and West, they remain little known to the world at large. Nevertheless, attention to their needs remains an international responsibility of the bigger countries. Furthermore, it is conceivable that a contentious world might benefit from a greater knowledge of the gentle society developed in the benevolent surroundings of the South Seas.

TWO

Bridging the Ages

APUA New Guinea, the largest and most populous of the newly independent states in the tropical Pacific, defies easy categorization. The ambience is South Pacific, but it is linked geographically to Southeast Asia. Many of the black-skinned people feel a spiritual identity with black Africa, and the fledgling government tends to go to African countries for advisers. The closest political and economic relations remain with the former colonial ruler, Australia.

Michael Somare, the bearded young tribal chief from the East Sepik who became the first prime minister, considered such questions irrelevant. "Papua New Guinea is a country which has been isolated from others until recent times," he once said. "This has meant its people have developed a life-style and attitudes that are wholly Papua New Guinean. Our responsibility lies in finding a modified style that suits itself first to our people, and secondly to the rest of the world. We wish to create an original society. We may borrow from others, but every idea will have a Papua New Guinea application."

General of the Army Douglas MacArthur, when commanding the Allied forces in the Southwest Pacific theater in World War II, once described the island of New Guinea as the most difficult environment in which men had ever been required to fight a war. Soldiers who had served there could be identified by a vivid yellow complexion, known as "Atabrine tan," a temporary condition caused by protracted ingestion of an antimalaria drug. A

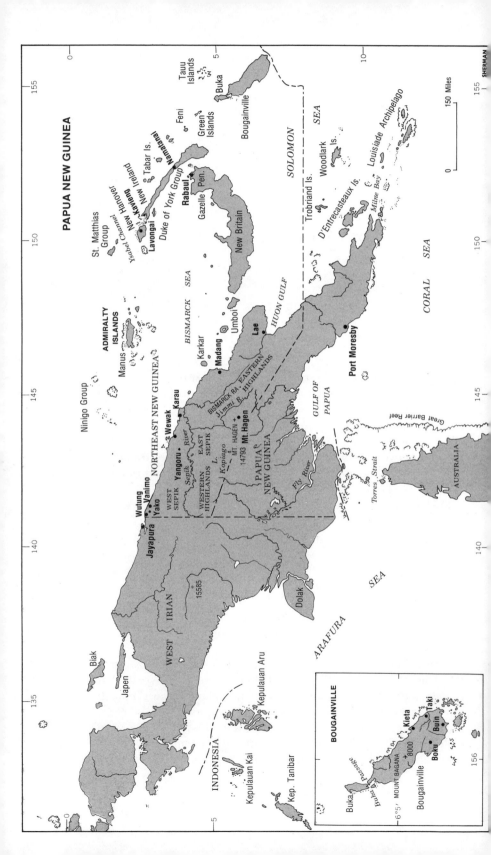

generation later, applicants for visas for the same country, now an independent state, were still being instructed to take antimalaria drugs and to continue the dose for a month after leaving. Improved malaria prophylactics leave no telltale tan, but the medical instructions in the visa office implied a warning of severe cultural shocks to come.

Earlier white visitors to wild, hot, malarious, beautiful New Guinea, the world's second largest island after Greenland, had had it much worse. As if the disease-bearing insects, poisonous reptiles, impassable mountains, stinking mud, dank swamps, endless green jungles, and intolerable heat were not enough, history records that of the first 250 pioneering whites who landed on these forbidding shores between 1885 and 1905, at least fifty were murdered, and probably eaten, by hostile tribes.

Violence has remained a way of life for the majority. Cannibalism also survives. Nowhere is the environment less friendly to modernization. Yet these unpromising surroundings were to be the scene of the most challenging experiment in government to emerge from the changing political climate in the South Pacific following the upheaval of the war.

The first of my many visits to the island of New Guinea was to write for *The New York Times* about the Melanesians who had rebelled against their Indonesian rulers in the former Dutch colony of West Irian and had crossed into Australian territory. The episode marked the turning point in a series of troublesome colonial entanglements involving Germans, Britons, Dutch, and Indonesians on the huge island.

New Guinea, the name of the entire island, also applied to the former United Nations Trust Territory of New Guinea, which had been a German possession until it was taken over by Australian forces in World War I. South of the trust territory lay Papua, a former British colony that had become part of Australia in 1906. Following World War II, Australia combined the two areas under a single administration in Port Moresby, Papua. The new entity, eventually renamed Papua New Guinea, comprised half the huge island. The original name had been Papua *and* New Guinea, but the Australians dropped the "and" in an effort—not too successful—to encourage unity as self-government and independence drew nearer in the twilight of Australian rule.

The other half of the island, called Western New Guinea by the Dutch and West Irian by Indonesian nationalists, had remained under the control of the Netherlands after the successful

Indonesian campaign for independence. The Dutch withdrew in 1962, handing the area over to an interim United Nations administration pending a final disposition of the territory. The Indonesians were placed in control in 1963 on the understanding that the permanent political status of the area would be determined according to the democratically expressed wishes of the eight hundred thousand inhabitants, mostly Melanesians, by 1969.

A callous and corrupt Indonesian administration soon faced armed uprisings by several Melanesian groups. Following sporadic fighting, some six hundred dissidents fled across the border into the Australian half of the island. The embarrassed Australians, who had no wish for a political conflict with the sensitive and belligerent Indonesians, located about four hundred of the refugees on Manus, an outlying island that had been an important American naval base in World War II. The remainder were placed in camps along the jungled border between the Australian territory and West Irian (soon to be renamed Irian Jaya).

The refugees in the frontier camps represented no fewer than thirteen different militant organizations opposed to Indonesian rule. All demanded independence for their homeland, which they called "West Papua" to emphasize their ethnic identity with the indigenes of Australian Papua. Papuan nationalism would later become a threat to the integrity of the new state of Papua New Guinea.

To make contact with the dissidents, I flew from Port Moresby to Vanimo, the administrative center of the largely untamed West Sepik District of what was then called Australian New Guinea, the end of the line for scheduled airlines on the Australian side. The town curved around a crescent-shaped indentation of the Bismarck Sea. A twelve-room hotel, equipped with ceiling fans but no room keys ("Don't need 'em, mate," said the convivial Australian manager), overlooked a beach of smooth gray sand lapped by blue-green ripples. Newly married airline personnel who knew of Vanimo from stopovers sometimes honeymooned in this idyllic spot.

Political intrigue in the South Pacific often involves whites functioning as advisers and interpreters for brown activists on one side or another. Such a man was Adrian Visser, a handsome young Dutchman who had abandoned a prospering lumber business in Jayapura (formerly Hollandia, a one-time MacArthur headquarters) when the Indonesians came and the climate for white enterprisers from Holland deteriorated abruptly. Visser migrated to Vanimo (which is pronounced WAN-ee-moh, the spelling with a "V" being the result of a German mispronunciation). There he opened a well-stocked, efficiently arranged general store that was usually filled with brown-skinned, barefoot villagers carrying homemade shopping bags of woven palm fronds.

Visser, who said he was engaged to a West Irianese girl, kept close contact with the more than one hundred refugees in the tent village set up for them by the Australian authorities in a jungle clearing eleven miles back from the border. Nearby was the charming village of Yako, a place that would have been a perfect set for a South Seas movie. Two long rows of traditional dwellings, with reed walls and thatch roofs, stood along a wide street of snow-white coral sand, with the usual single-room, open-sided schoolhouse at one end. Clean, smiling people dressed in flowered cotton *laplap,* the wraparound garment for both sexes, slashed the tops off green coconuts with a single stroke or two of a machete and offered visitors a drink of the cool, clear liquid.

At the camp, some of the refugees in the green canvas Australian Army tents spoke English. Mostly men, they included teachers, students, and former officials who had left their homes and jobs after the Indonesians arrived. There were numerous stories of thefts, beatings, and even killings by the Indonesian police. They talked of the violence that would break out when the Indonesian takeover became final "and they tell us that we are all Indonesians."

"The Indonesians had three-quarters of the population with them in the beginning," Visser said. Misgivings set in, however, when the Indonesian soldiers began collecting cheap consumer goods from the bazaars to send to their families; the natives had to suspect that economic conditions back home were not healthy. The disillusionment became complete when Indonesian troops began systematically appropriating the villagers' pigs and chickens for food. Sporadic fighting began, and at one point the rebels were reported to hold five airfields. The Indonesians responded with bombing, strafing, and paratroop attacks.

A few days before I arrived at Vanimo there had been a highly publicized incident at Wutung, where the Australians maintained a police border post a few hundred yards from the frontier, on the site of a wartime United States Army camp. The Indonesians raided a rebel bivouac just across the line on their side of the border, then followed the fleeing Melanesian dissidents into Australian territory, firing their rifles at the fugitives as they ran. As the shooting came closer to the Australian post, the Indonesians were confronted by a blue-eyed, bearded young Australian commander named Tony Try, who coolly ordered the intruders to go back to their own jurisdiction. The Indonesians did so, grumbling, and the seventy-nine refugees were safe.

I flew to Wutung in a six-seat Cessna plane with John Wakeford, the friendly district commissioner at Vanimo, whose authority covered sixteen thousand square miles and about one hundred thousand people in the West Sepik. The trip of a few minutes from the coral-surfaced airfield at Vanimo was a fair sample of flying in the wilder areas of Papua New Guinea. A few broken Japanese barges, relics of the war, lay awash in the sun-dappled waters along the coral-fringed coast. Pilot Alan Cheers let the light plane slip sideways, like a scared crab, past a high, wooded headland, then straightened out just before the wheels touched down on a tiny grass strip beneath a chalk cliff.

Tony Try, who had become a national hero in the border incident, greeted us wearing the standard Australian bush uniform of white shirt, blue shorts, and knee-length white socks. He was nonchalant about the confrontation with the Indonesian police. "The Indonesians were probably just trying to force them [the refugees] back into Irian, or farther this way, and simply followed them into Australian territory," he said.

Instead of the expected plebiscite proposed by the United Nations to ascertain the desires of the population as to their political future, Indonesia chose a traditional Malay process known as *musjawarah*, meaning consultation or consensus, with about one thousand representatives of tribal or village councils making the decision for some eight hundred thousand people. Accusations that the Indonesians were predetermining the outcome did not lessen when the result did indeed go in Indonesia's favor. The Jakarta government was anxious, however, to improve its image in the new province and internationally. There were reforms in the administration in Jayapura, and the armed rebellion dwindled into grumbling over "brown colonialism." The expatriates formed a "Republic of West Papua" in exile. (A system similar to the Indonesians' *musjawarah* came into prominence later at the annual meetings of the South Pacific Conference, the organization of all Pacific island territories, and the South Pacific

Forum, the political organ of the independent and self-governing island states. Instead of taking a vote to settle arguments, the delegations discussed the issues until a consensus was reached that could be formally adopted. The Fijian leader Ratu [Chief] Mara, later known as Sir Kamisese Mara, dubbed the method the "Pacific way," a term that became a permanent part of the political lexicon of the South Seas. Unfortunately, the "Pacific way" also has come to mean procrastination and "passing the buck," according to John Carter, the witty Lancashireman who edited *Pacific Islands Monthly,* the outspoken regional news magazine.)

After Papua New Guinea became internally self-governing on 1 December 1973, as a prelude to full independence, one of the first acts of the new government had been to conclude an agreement with Indonesia recognizing the frontier. This imaginary line across impassable mountains and through fetid jungle, made Papua New Guinea the only Pacific island state with a land border. Thus the former Australian territory became a bridge between the South Pacific community and Southeast Asia. Some of the new leaders of Papua New Guinea began to wonder if they were not Southeast Asians themselves, but the attitudes and ambience of the country retained a pure South Pacific character.

Having a land border with the largest and most powerful country in Southeast Asia gave Papua New Guinea special political importance among the Pacific states, including Australia. With a land area of 183,000 square miles—the size of the New England and Middle Atlantic states combined, plus West Virginia —and a population between two and three million, Papua New Guinea dwarfs all other South Pacific territories. With gold, copper, other minerals, and possibly significant oil deposits, it is also by far the richest. The development of the primitive and only partially explored country, however, would require continuing heavy Australian subsidies, which ran between one hundred and two hundred million Australian dollars a year at the time independence was granted (in 1976, Canberra guaranteed to furnish nine hundred thirty million Australian dollars over a five-year period). Australia's cooperation was assured, for the strategic importance of New Guinea to that country had been demonstrated when the island became a springboard for the Japanese advance toward Australia in World War II.

Western-style democratic processes in Papua New Guinea go back only to 1951, when the Australian government instituted the first step toward a modern parliamentary system. The Department of Territories in Canberra, which ruled the combined jurisdictions of Papua and New Guinea through an official in Port Moresby with the title of administrator, set up a Legislative Council consisting of sixteen heads of departments, six members appointed from white commercial, plantation, and missionary enterprises, three elected members from the Australian expatriate community, and three appointed Melanesians. This evolved, by 1972, into a completely elected House of Assembly, or legislature, with a cabinet chosen from its members by the chief minister, who was the leader of the largest party or group of parties in the House. Michael Somare was the first and last to hold the position.

Thus Papua New Guinea had achieved in twenty years, with Australian help, what it had taken Western man centuries to accomplish. The phrase that perhaps describes the achievement most succinctly is the title of the autobiography of Sir Maori Kiki, who rose from the primitive culture of his native village in the Papua jungle to become the self-assured first foreign minister of his country and the recipient of a knighthood from Queen Elizabeth II of England (who, as head of the Commonwealth that links Britain and her former colonies in a free association, is also the sovereign of Papua New Guinea). Sir Maori called his story *Ten Thousand Years in a Lifetime,* referring to his beginnings in Stone Age surroundings. Sir Maori leaped a chasm of ages; for most of his countrymen, however, the Stone Age is the present.

Elections were conducted under the most primitive conditions imaginable, yet it was usual for more than 60 percent of the eligible voters to appear at the polling places to cast ballots. It took a year to prepare for an election in the jungle hamlets and secluded valley settlements, walled off from the rest of the country by mosquito-ridden swamps, impenetrable rain forests, and mountains that had never known the tread of man. Electoral teams crisscrossed the country on foot and in light planes and helicopters to install polling booths of bamboo poles and palm leaves in jungle villages and forest clearings miles from a road. At many of the more than four thousand polling locations, nearly naked tribesmen with tusks and bones through their noses were in charge of the portable ballot boxes.

The turnout on election days, spread over six weeks in the various localities for reasons dictated by climatic conditions or logistical necessities, brought to view a cross section of the fantastically disparate and picturesque population. In the lofty hamlets of the Eastern Highlands District, voters appeared at polling booths above the clouds in country so menacing that only two candidates braved the treacherous jungle trails over humid, insect-infested slopes, beset by frequent landslides and falling rocks, to visit their electorates. The polite villagers assured each in turn that he would get their votes, for it would have been considered rude to refuse.

Some voters, their bodies greased with pig fat, showed up at the polls in a traditional costume of bark jacket with skirts of grass and woven vines, with feathers in the hair and necklaces of bones, dogs' teeth, shells, stones, beads, and bottle caps. The famous "mud men" appeared covered from head to feet in layers of plastered gray clay. Chiefs wore enormous headgear, several feet high, decorated with the prized bird of paradise feathers.

Women came to the polls wearing only bark belts with strings of grass or leaves in front and back. Long bags of woven vines, hanging down the back from a band around the forehead, contained the day's supply of sweet potatoes for the family. Many had painted their faces in blue and red stripes of natural dyes, bore tattoos on their arms and legs, and wore large safety pins in their pierced ears and noses. While some men turned out in cotton *laplap*, shorts, and old military clothing, dwellers in the hidden jungle hamlets often came to the polls wearing only a shell or gourd to protect the genitals. Waiting to vote, they squatted on their heels and rolled cigarettes of trade tobacco and squares torn from old newspapers.

"No one had to walk more than two days to reach a polling place," Simon Kaumi, the bright, thirty-five-year-old Papuan chief electoral officer in charge of the House of Assembly elections in March of 1972 told me proudly. An Australian correspondent called the affair "the weirdest election in the world." The majority of the one and one-half million eligible voters were illiterate, as were many of the winners among the 611 candidates for the 100 House seats. As the names of the aspirants to office were often meaningless to the bulk of the voters, a thumbnail photograph of each candidate was placed after his name on the ballot paper. Many of the electors had never seen a pen or pencil and so did not know how to mark a ballot paper with the strange implement. The rules, however, allowed a voter to whisper the name of his choice in the ear of a polling officer, who would then mark the ballot accordingly and drop it in the box. Observers

from the United Nations called the system the most practical yet
seen for a predominantly illiterate electorate.

Members of a small tribe, the Hewa, whose existence in the
Lake Kopiago region of the lightly explored Western Highlands
District had been discovered only a few months before, "were
enrolled and encouraged to vote," said Kaumi, although they did
not know that there was such a country as Papua New Guinea,
much less how its government functioned. (Less than three years
later, Kaumi would be suspended from government service for
his part in raising a barefoot army to fight for an independent
Republic of Papua.)

Taking the electoral process to remote tribes involved arduous
and dangerous jungle treks, usually led by a young Australian
patrol officer, or *kiap*, with Melanesian interpreters, police, and
medical aides. To the dauntless *kiap* in shorts, knee socks, and
white shirt belonged any credit for bringing the twentieth century
to the wilderness. Trained at the Australian School of Pacific
Administration run by the Australian government in a suburb of
Sydney and in the field, they worked their way through the ranks
of the service in the hope of becoming some day a district commissioner, with virtually absolute authority over a vast area and
looking forward to eventual retirement in Queensland or some
other pleasant haven in Australia. They are now, of course, a
vanishing breed, for the new generation of students at the training school is black.

A *kiap* named Charles R. Brilliante led a prodigious twenty-
seven-day trek into the little-known Blucher Division of the Western District of Papua, near the Indonesian border, to take the
election to a tribe that had never been visited by a government
agent before, although its existence had been known since aerial
observation revealed habitation in the area in 1963. Brilliante
and four companions—an assistant patrol officer, interpreter,
constable, and medical orderly—beat their way through a dense
rain forest to reach the place on foot under conditions he described, in his report to Port Moresby, as "generally perilous to
life and limb."

Daytime temperatures were in the sweltering high eighties,
dropping at night to the bone-chilling low sixties. The humidity
averaged between 80 and 90 percent. Rain—which totaled 200
to 300 inches a year in that region—fell almost constantly. There
were mountains to climb, rushing rivers to cross, and swamps
infested by blood-sucking leeches and insect-eating plants. The

aori Kiki, foreign minister of Papua New Guinea,
office, 1973

Tribesmen at week-end market in Mount Hagen,
Papua New Guinea

en selling shells at the Bung, a public market in Rabaul, New Britain, one of the most colorful bazaars
e South Pacific

Father Bernard Miller with Wal
Salo Gukguk, leader of the forme
"Johnson cult" on New Hanove
which has been converted into th
United Farmers Association, a cc
operative self-help group

Robert Trumbull/*New York Times*

Robert Trumbull/*New York*

Harbor of Kieta, Bougainville, . . . "a heavenly setting"

sequestered tribe was 80 miles from the nearest settlement, and there were no trails. "The area would best be described as very inaccessible," Brilliante, a man given to understatement, noted in his report.

Reaching a clearing, the party came upon a scene from another age. Scattered gardens in the poor soil grew sweet potato, pandanus, taro, and sago, which constituted the entire diet of the tribe except for the rare addition of pork from a slaughtered pig or the meat of slain birds, including the huge, ungainly cassowary, a nonflying, ostrichlike creature. Beside each garden stood one or two decrepit huts, whose walls were adorned with the bones of pigs, cassowaries, and humans, along with the weapons used to kill them. Outside the huts, young women suckled baby pigs.

The simple dress consisted of a breechclout of string made from bark, in front, with the men adding a penis cover from the shell of a large nut; behind, "what was worn varied from nothing to a few strands of string or a handsome cover of fine brown grass," Brilliante stated. Instead of a single tribal structure, the people were divided into eight separate groups, each speaking a different dialect. The economy, the patrol officer reported, was "pure subsistence."

Brilliante, carrying out a standard duty of the *kiap,* took an informal census. "The people appeared pleased with the arrival of the government" and were "friendly and . . . fairly helpful," he said. He counted 200 people, but estimated that 60 or more others had hidden, because of either disinterest, hostility, or fear. They knew nothing of the country beyond the green walls of their jungle settlement. Producing a map of Papua New Guinea, Brilliante explained the existence of mountains and the ocean, and endeavored to describe the constitution of a government by-election. Members of the House of Assembly he compared to tribal leaders, or "big men"—a New Guinea idiom. "Points such as economic development, progress, etc., were never mentioned, as these would not have been understood and would have caused confusion," he wrote.

Without using any names, which would have been "meaningless," he described the candidates who sought to represent this area of Papua New Guinea in the House of Assembly and advised his hearers to expect a polling team "at the time of the next full moon." "I am not prepared to say that most of what they were told was absorbed," Brilliante said. "Interest was shown, but was more than likely the result of extreme curiosity." The *kiap* did feel that his mission had contributed to the advance of civilization in one of the world's last frontiers when leaders of the newly found people assured him that they were prepared to build a proper village.

Another *kiap* discovered a previously unknown tribe of some two hundred fifty people in a jungle pocket less than one hundred miles from Madang, a major seaport with air-conditioned hotels and instant telephone service to any country in the world. The people of the tribe, whom he found to be friendly but aloof, "obviously do not want any outside influence in their serene little valley," he reported to Port Moresby. Politely but firmly, the tribal leaders declined to have anything to do with the government.

As in every other activity, the diversity of languages was a hindrance to the electoral process. According to linguistic authorities working in the area, there are at least seven hundred separate languages in Papua New Guinea, not including dialects. Some are spoken by as few as fifty people in isolated tribes. About six hundred of the languages have been classified and named by a scholarly organization called the Summer Institute of Linguistics, whose people are found making studies in the remotest villages.

The nearest to a common medium of expression is an extraordinary agglomeration of distorted words from several languages, mainly English, called Pidgin ("Don't call it Pidgin English," said the Reverend Francis Mihalic, an expert on the language, warning me against a common solecism of newcomers). Originating in the efforts of early white plantation overseers, seamen, Chinese traders, and others to communicate with the Melanesians, Pidgin abounds in constructions like "me no savvy" for "I don't know," "belong you-me" for "ours." Father Mihalic ("Rhymes with carbolic," he said), a Roman Catholic missionary from Erie, Pennsylvania, devised the officially approved phonetic spelling in which these expressions come out *mi no save* and *bilong yumi.* This system has the virtue of making Pidgin look less like a parody of English, but the sound is usually the same when read aloud. Exceptions are words pronounced with a Melanesian accent, such as *pinis* for "finish."

Over a century or so, Pidgin has acquired a rudimentary but precise grammar, mostly from Melanesian forms. Pidgin-speakers with a talent for oratory can achieve heights of eloquence and imagery in its use; officials who do not know Pidgin thoroughly need interpreters. Missionaries use it: the Lord's Prayer begins "Papa bilong yumi Istap Antap" (Papa belong you me he stop on top) for "Our Father who art in Heaven." It is used on the government radio. A newscast I heard on the Apollo 14 lunar expedition began with "tupela igo daun wokabout long mun"; read aloud, this comes out as "two fella he go down walk about along moon." In the House of Assembly, or Haus Toktok ("House Talk-talk"), the proceedings are interpreted simultaneously in Pidgin, English, and Motu, the principal language of coastal Papua; but most of the debate is in Pidgin, and a member who begins a speech in English is likely to be interrupted by shouted demands to "Tok Pisin!" ("Talk Pidgin!").

Father Mihalic's printing shop in the extensive Roman Catholic mission compound outside Wewak published a twice-monthly newspaper in Pidgin called *Wantok* (from "one talk," the Pidgin term for persons of the same linguistic group or tribe). A reader with little or no knowledge of Pidgin could usually get the meaning of a headline by reading it aloud. A story about the visit of the Australian minister of territories, then in charge of Papua New Guinea affairs in Canberra, was headlined "Basman I Kam," which says clearly, "Bossman he come" (dropping the "h" from "he" is common in less elegant Australian circles). An account of an airplane accident in which four men were injured was headed "Fopela Bagarap," meaning "four fella bugger up," using one of several Australian vulgarisms that have gained respectability in Pidgin (if the victims had been women it would have been "Fopela Meri [Mary] Bagarap," and if they had been killed it would have said "Bagarap Pinis" [finish]).

According to Father Mihalic, the term Pidgin comes from a Chinese word for "business" (old Far East hands often say, "That's your pidgin," "That's not my pidgin," and so on). It has become the lingua franca, with local variations, of the British Solomon Islands and the New Hebrides, a British-French condominium, as well as Papua New Guinea. The vocabulary is derived "79 per cent from English, 15 per cent from Melanesian and 6 per cent from German, French and other languages," Father Mihalic told me. A recognizable German derivation in common use is *rausim,* a word that Melanesian politicians found handy. At a political meeting I attended in a village school auditorium near Port Moresby one sultry night, a speaker was discussing the question of what to do with Australians in senior government positions after independence. A listener shouted, "Rausim ologeta!"—in other words, "Oust them altogether!" The interjector, incidentally, became a cabinet minister with the coming of self-government.

Pidgin is used by an estimated five hundred thousand Papua New Guineans (far more than those who speak English or any other language), and is the mother tongue for thousands of Melanesians who were brought up away from their ancestral surroundings. For many husbands and wives from different tribes who met and married in urban melting pots like Port Moresby, Pidgin is their only common language, and their children often grow up not knowing any other. An old Papua New Guinea hand told me that new arrivals had found that they could learn sufficient Pidgin in two or three weeks for everyday use. He added, however, that there were pitfalls for the careless or unwary novice. For example, there are many meanings for the word *bokis,* from the English "box." *Bokis* used alone could mean "suitcase," but *bokis bilong missus* refers to the female external genitalia.

Scholars like Margaret Mead, the anthropologist, insist that Pidgin has become "a language in its own right," like Swahili and Afrikaans, which also had mixed origins. There have been frequent proposals that Pidgin be officially adopted as the national language of free Papua New Guinea. Opponents of such a move, including United Nations authorities, urge that there be a greater effort to educate the population in English. Race-proud Melanesians contend that the use of Pidgin, with words like *boi* (boy) and *kanaka* for man, *meri* (Mary) for woman, and *pikinini* (pickaninny) for child, is a constant reminder of degrading colonialist racial attitudes. Further, although Pidgin can encompass complex ideas, doing so often requires elaborate and wordy circumlocutions. For instance, the term for "constitution" is *as lo bilong gavman,* or "ass law belong government," a phrase incorporating another sanitized importation from Australia ("ass" in this case means "underlying" or "basic"). John C. Murphy's primer on Pidgin gives a number of other meanings; for instance, a sample sentence concerning a senseless altercation says "Pait nating, nogat as bilongim," or "Fight nothing, no got ass belong him" —in other words, no reason for it.

Official literature, though published in English, is invariably issued also in Pidgin for general dissemination. Government propaganda posters depicting the great cultural diversity of the country, displayed in post offices, schools, and other gathering places in an effort to instill a sense of common national identity among disparate peoples, were headed with the slogan in Pidgin, "Kantri Bilong Yumi" ("country belong you-me" or "our country").

Whatever its shortcomings, Pidgin is a badly needed cultural link. The sudden appearance of Mathias Yaliwan, a "cargo cult" leader, as the most potent vote-getter in the 1972 elections was a jolting reminder to officials of the cultural gulf between the uneducated Melanesian masses and the small, Westernized brown—or black—elite who aspired to lead them to independence.

Yaliwan's tens of thousands of followers believed that untold wealth accumulated by their ancestors was locked inside the summit of Mount Turu, a 3,985-foot volcanic peak near the leader's home village of Yangoru, in the primitive West Sepik District of northern New Guinea. According to Yaliwan, the keys to the hidden treasure were three cement survey markers left by a United States Air Force scientific team in 1962. With the removal of these foreign objects, the people were told, fabulous bounty would burst from the bowels of the mountain.

By the cultural standards of Papua New Guinea, a land ridden with faith in magic and sorcery, the expectations of the Yangoru cult were by no means beyond the realm of reasonable belief. In fact, to the untutored Melanesian, magic made more sense than the intricacies of Western economics, which his background had not prepared him to understand.

Yaliwan and his chief adviser, Daniel Hawina, and several others dug up one of the markers in 1969. For this offense against government property they were sent to jail for a few months. Thus the administration, as had happened often before in official brushes with cargo cults, reinforced the myth by seeming to go to extreme lengths to protect the concealed riches. It was another instance, the cultists reasoned, of white men trying to keep the wealth—*cargo* in Pidgin—for themselves.

So the Yangoru cult thrived and acquired an array of bizarre ritual objects. One was a used flashlight bulb, discarded by a news photographer, whose cube shape was related by the cultists to the four-sided dimensions of the now-sacred markers. One awe-struck member declared that when he put his eye to the cube he "could see the wealth inside the mountain." Another venerated object was the cover of a paperback edition of an Agatha Christie novel, *Evil under the Sun*, with a picture of a doll pierced with pins, voodoo-fashion. According to a report by a university group that studied the cult, one of Yaliwan's aides said he believed "that this persecuted lady is going to be the ruler of Papua New Guinea." Another version was that Agatha Christie would be the ruler, possibly a confusion of the name Christie with Christ.

Yaliwan, who was credited with such supernatural powers as the ability to foretell the future and to hear conversations many miles away, announced that the two remaining markers would be removed amid ceremonies that would include human sacrifices. The sacrifices were canceled when the Australian police authorities showed keen interest in the plan, but thousands of Yaliwan's followers accompanied him to the mountaintop to witness the digging up of the famous markers.

The two-foot-high markers were duly uprooted and carried triumphantly to the cement-block government office in Yangoru, where I photographed them later. Each bore a brass plate inscribed with the address of the Air Photographic and Charting Service, U.S. Air Force; they were part of a system, said an Australian official, "to put Papua New Guinea where it is in relation to the rest of the world." Still the "cargo" failed to appear. The cultists concluded, as had many before them, that the white man had tricked them again. A new story went around that four hundred Boeing 707 jets laden with goodies from the United States would soon land on the mountain—a reflection of wartime memories of American largesse, common in cargo cults throughout the Southwest Pacific.

I met Yaliwan, a short, slightly built man with bare feet, wearing a yellow-checked shirt and dark shorts, at the Western-style house of an associate in Wewak. His eyes burned as he looked up from a thick book with the title *Nupela Testamen* (New Testament) on the worn leatherette cover. The cultist, I knew, had picked up strong religious leanings while working as a handyman at a Roman Catholic mission. He was known as a constant reader of the Bible, an unintended source of many cargo cult beliefs.

Yaliwan, who had just won a seat in the House of Assembly by the biggest majority of any candidate, now believed that he had been divinely ordained to become, as he put it in Pidgin, "Numbawan bikpela long kantri" ("number one big fella of the country," or head of the government). He had joined the new Christian Democratic Party and would work in the Haus Toktok for immediate independence and "brotherhood"—a concept he expressed in the Pidgin phrase, "Ol men iken wok wontaim," "all men he can work onetime [together]."

The cultist, who would cause comment a few days later by arriving in Port Moresby barefoot to take his seat in the House of Assembly, tried in the interview to dispel his cargo cult image. He said he had reorganized his followers into a self-help group called the Peli Association, after a local variety of hawk. Asked how many members there were, he turned to an assistant, who answered glibly, "Sixty-two thousand four hundred and eighty-nine *ologeta ples* [everywhere]." Yaliwan declared that he was now instructing his followers that cargo does not come from *nating* (nothing); he was urging them to develop vegetable gardens and sell the produce, whereupon "moni i kam baimbai" (money he come by and by").

Did this mean that the Yangoru cargo cult was being transformed from a millennial movement into an economic cooperative? I had seen such a thing happen before on the island of New Hanover, an outlying territory of Papua New Guinea in the Bismarck Sea. The story illuminates some of the problems of trying to integrate primitive societies into a modern state, and how an ingenious and enlightened approach may supply some of the solutions.

The main village, in an idyllic setting along a palm-fringed shore of an unspoiled island about thirty miles long and twenty miles wide, was the home of the bizarre "Johnson cult," which tried to hire Lyndon B. Johnson, then president of the United States, to be the ruler of this remote Melanesian jungle domain. The attempt came to the attention of the Australian press and was publicized around the world in the mid-1960s. Years later, I went to New Hanover—reachable by speedboat from New Ireland, the nearest island on an air route—to bring the story up to date.

The leader of the cult, a coffee-colored village notable named Walla Salo Gukguk, was now an influential member of the island's elected Local Government Council, which the cultists had once boycotted. The cult itself had become a cooperative self-help organization, with Gukguk as president, called the Tutukuvul Isukul Association, commonly known by the initials T.I.A. The name is translated into English as United Farmers Association, but the literal meaning of the Melanesian words is something like "let's all get together and plant coconuts," which is essentially what the organization is for. The change in direction from cult to cooperative was the work of a pragmatic, humorous young Roman Catholic missionary, the Reverend Bernard Miller, of Toledo, Ohio.

Walla Salo Gukguk, who spoke no English but attained heights of eloquence in Pidgin, explained that the "Johnson cult" had been the result of a visit to the island by an American military team on a geodetic survey project—possibly the same group that had installed the markers used by the Yangoru cargo cult. It seems that President Johnson had somehow acquired such a lustrous image on New Hanover that his name was placed in nomination for the 1965 elections to the Local Government Council. The slogan "Yumi laikim Johnson" ("We like Johnson") swept the island, and he was elected to the council by the unanimous vote of the one thousand or so electors; it was a bigger landslide, in percentage terms, than Johnson's victory over Senator Barry Goldwater in the United States presidential election.

The cult then raised sixteen hundred dollars for an air ticket to bring Johnson to New Hanover. The sum was sent to the Reverend Alfred Stemper, of Blackhammer, Minnesota, the Roman Catholic bishop of Kavieng, New Ireland, whose jurisdiction included New Hanover, with a request that it be forwarded to the president. Bishop Stemper promptly returned the money, but Johnson's admirers were undiscouraged. "We wanted the Americans to come and show us how to do things," Gukguk said. The American who would fill Gukguk's expectations, albeit in an unexpected way, turned out to be Father Miller. Arriving about that time to take charge of the Sacred Heart Mission at Lavongai village (the name is also applied to the entire island), the missionary saw at once that the cargo cult idea possessed a vitality that could be harnessed and turned around.

"The problem," he explained one morning at breakfast in the mission bungalow, "was to give the people an incentive for self-improvement through their own efforts, and to build up their pride." There were no roads on the island at the time. There was a wharf, but no boat. The natives owned most of the land, which was worked on a communal basis by the matriarchal clans, but the coconut plantations were run down.

Father Miller put his ideas to work on the leaders of the Johnson cult. "You can do things for yourselves, without waiting for the Americans to come," he assured them. He then proceeded to form the T.I.A., charging a ten-dollar membership fee to raise capital. "The time was ripe for a change," said the youthful priest. "Members of the cult had become tired of going to jail for refusing to pay taxes to the Local Government Council [a common tactic of cargo cults everywhere in the Southwest Pacific], so the response was favorable when I insisted that they resume paying taxes as a condition for joining the T.I.A."

The first project of the T.I.A. was to plant more coconut trees in order to expand the output of copra, the dried meat of the coconut, used in soap and chemicals, which was the island's main cash crop. Development in other directions followed. A wholesale change in the island's life style thus flowed from this beginning, founded on the missionary's perception of the useful disciplines inherent in the cargo cult.

By the time I arrived on New Hanover a few years later, the T.I.A. had planted one hundred thousand new coconut trees to produce more copra for the lucrative market in Kavieng, the administrative center of nearby New Ireland. With the aid of cash contributions from the mission, the organization had purchased a bulldozer for building roads on which the copra moved from plantation to wharf; a tractor and trailer had been acquired for bulk transport; a motor-driven vessel had been obtained to carry the copra to Kavieng; a sawmill had been started in Lavongai to turn out lumber for houses and furniture; and the organization had constructed a large cement-block headquarters—the first permanent structure in a community of woven palm leaves and thatch—that also served as a community center. With pooled profits, the T.I.A. was buying stock in the lucrative new copper mine on Bougainville island, the biggest commercial enterprise in the country. The nine thousand or so brown-skinned people of New Hanover, through Father Miller's adaptation of cargo-cult thinking, had turned the corner into the twentieth century.

Gukguk and other former cultists seemed embarrassed when I asked about their early efforts to recruit Lyndon Johnson as their leader. But they were still enamored of the United States. A few weeks before my visit to Lavongai, a United Nations mission had appeared at Namatanai, on New Ireland, in one of a series of public meetings to sound popular opinion on the political future of Papua New Guinea, which then was still an Australian trusteeship. The Melanesian directors of the T.I.A. sent a spokesman to the Namatanai hearing, with a request that New Hanover be transferred to the United States. After Father Miller had pointed out some of the diplomatic obstacles to such a proposal, the board altered the request to ask that *all* Papua New Guinea become an American state, "like Hawaii."

Cargo cults were powerfully affected by the American presence in World War II, when hundreds of thousands of superbly equipped and friendly, gregarious United States service personnel poured into the islands, often coming literally from the sky in great flying ships laden with an awesome panoply of cargo that the G.I.'s shared liberally with the dazzled indigenes. Contact with the efficient Americans also led to enlightening comparisons with the turgid style of colonial bureaucracy. These undoubtedly were the operative factors in the rise of the Jóhnson cult, and the later movement on New Hanover to break away from Australian administration and become part of the United States, in preference to participation in an independent state governed from Port Moresby. The Melanesians of Lavongai had no way of knowing that the American bureaucracy in Micronesia had already demonstrated its own shortcomings in governing distant islands.

The cargo cult concept had originated long before World War II, following the arrival of white missionaries, planters, and traders during the heyday of colonial expansion in the Pacific in the late nineteenth century. The early white men in the islands had brought Melanesians their first acquaintanceship with modern implements, Western clothing and shoes, machines, building materials, and luxuries like tinned beef, cigarettes, and beer. All of this, and more, arrived in the white man's ships, giving rise to the universal use of the word "cargo" as an all-embracing Pidgin term for "trade goods," which the natives equated with wealth.

Naturally, the Melanesians coveted cargo. Efforts to explain the economics of distribution—the manufacturing process, the acquisition of purchasing power through work, and so on— proved entirely unconvincing in the face of clear evidence that the low-paid Melanesian had little chance of accumulating enough money to satisfy his hunger for cargo.

Thus it seemed obvious to the primitive Melanesian that the white man was lying when he linked cargo to money, for no one had ever seen sacks of money being taken aboard ships before the cargo came off. The teaching of Christian missionaries that religion made all men equal also broke down before the realities of the Melanesian's low earning power; nor was baptism in the church followed by a flow of cargo.

The suspicious Melanesians watched closely what the white man did: he sat at a table and shuffled papers; he shouted into a tube with wires attached, while holding another wired tube to his ear; he put on a uniform and marched back and forth in formation, carrying a rifle over his shoulder; he yelled at his black employes: "Hurry up—chop chop—me kickee ass belong you." And the cargo came. Inevitably, the idea dawned that the white man controlled the secret of the cargo through rituals. This made more sense to the Melanesian, against an age-old background of belief in magic and spells, than the white man's incomprehensible explanations.

Missionaries unwittingly bolstered cultist thinking. Bible stories of the miracle of the loaves and fishes, the resurrection of Christ, the manna falling from Heaven reinforced the belief that the secret of the cargo could be unlocked by magic. The problem, it appeared, was to find the effective ritual. So began the cargo cults, which appeared spontaneously in more or less the same form—but independently of each other and at different times—in New Guinea, the Solomons, the New Hebrides, and many other islands.

Cultists imitated the white man as carefully as they could, searching for the right ritual. Some sat at tables and moved pieces of paper around, like the white officials and traders. They shouted—sometimes in a "secret language"—into imitation telephones made of string and old tin cans. It was common for cultists to emulate military drill in makeshift uniforms, with sticks for rifles. In one instance more pathetic than humorous, the marching ritual included shouting in unison, "Me kickee ass belong you!"

A cult's rise was usually accompanied by strong antiforeign agitation, for it was implicit in the cargo myth that the whites were wrongfully keeping for themselves the wealth that rightfully belonged to Melanesians. The cultists have often refused to pay taxes, have kept their children out of the schools, and have turned their backs on the missions. In many cases, fervent cultists have killed their pigs, destroyed their gardens and other property, and thrown their money into the sea to show confidence that the promised riches would soon be theirs. The rituals have also included overt repudiation of tribal traditions, including the breaking of sacred taboos, accompanied by either sexual orgies or rigid abstinence from sex, drinking, and other pleasures, and the observance of severe dietary rules.

Efforts by government authorities to extirpate the cults, because of their often violent antiforeign overtones, have been uniformly counterproductive. Official attempts at suppression merely convinced the cultists that they were, at last, on the threshold of discovering the secret of the cargo because they were clearly causing the white man alarm. After a few disastrous experiences, administrators tried to handle the cults as tactfully as possible, if they interfered at all.

The coming of World War II, with irreversible changes in Pacific societies, brought a strong revival of the dormant cargo cults. Melanesians saw the fulfillment of long-standing prophecies not only in the arrival of cargo in undreamed-of quantities with the Americans but also in the possession of it by black Americans who looked like themselves. Seeing black servicemen enjoying the same luxuries as their white colleagues, apparently on equal terms, was proof enough for the literal Melanesian mind that the dark-skinned people of the islands were being wickedly denied their fair share of cargo by the malevolent whites. Obviously the black American, whom they referred to with respect as *black masta* (master), had discovered the secret still sought in vain by the black Melanesian.

Wartime experiences inspired a new round of cargo cult rituals, based this time on careful observation of American habits. Emulating the American troops, cultists shouted gibberish into simulated radios with tin-can microphones and string aerials. They hacked clearings in the jungle for the expected planes to land in with the eagerly awaited cargo, for which palm-leaf warehouses were built. Lookouts were posted along the shores to watch for the treasure-laden ships from America. And men sat for hours in front of imitation refrigerators made of packing boxes, peeking inside from time to time to see if the tinned beer and snacks had yet materialized, as they had for the Americans. The search for the right ritual was undeterred by continual failure.

Authorities on Melanesian culture aver that cargo cults, representing an unquenchable yearning for social advancement within the framework of experience and traditional beliefs, will continue to exist until an educated generation in the future puts an end to inequalities. An aggregation of social imbalances, separating a tiny native elite class from the primitive masses, posed a constant threat to the tenuous national fabric nurtured by the former Australian administration in Papua New Guinea. "I can never fly over those mountainous New Guinea landscapes without pondering the enormity, perhaps the improbability, of getting any political coherency from the people covered in pig grease who occupy the scattered hamlets below," Stuart Inder, publisher of the authoritative *Pacific Islands Monthly,* once wrote in that fascinating magazine of the South Seas.

Separatist political movements abound. When the new Labor government in Canberra speeded up the timetable for independence, in response to then Prime Minister Gough Whitlam's determination that Australia divest itself of an unwanted "colonialist image," the opposition came not from the conservative expatriate community in Papua New Guinea so much as from apprehensive Melanesians.

"Independence" was a dirty word, in fact, among the eight hundred thousand warlike tribal people of the cool, misty highlands, who feared and resented the dominant political role of the better-educated coastal people. "In some villages, if you mention 'independence' you could be killed," an Australian official told me in Mount Hagen, the principal town and administrative center of the untamed Western Highlands District. "The highlanders would like to stave off independence until education is more general," said Len Aisbett, the Australian acting district commissioner. "Only 22 percent of the highland children of school age are in school, compared to the average of 40 percent for the entire territory. Being realists, the highlanders are for gradual change."

In towns like Mount Hagen, the twentieth century jostles the Stone Age. Said Aisbett, "Where else could you find people who first saw a wheel on the end of an airplane?" Mount Hagen, in jungled surroundings on a 5,000-foot plateau in the shadow of the 13,120-foot mountain for which the town was named, is a bizarre combination of raw frontier and cosmopolitan tourist center. International travelers converge in Mount Hagen to observe the culture of a people whose existence was discovered only in the 1930s by gold hunters, and whose contact with white men in significant numbers goes back only to the 1950s.

The tourists who fly into Mount Hagen for sightseeing sleep in hotels that are comfortable, though of antique design, and shop for picturesque tribal artifacts in a row of neat boutiques. They share the rough sidewalks with painted, mud-smeared tribesmen carrying shields and spears, their only covering being a few leaves or strands of grass hanging from a string waistband.

The spears are often used in the intertribal wars that can spring from such an incident as the theft of a pig.

Violence is instilled in the tribal way of life. Courts tend to be lenient in homicide cases stemming from *payback*, the Pidgin term for revenge killing, which is mandatory under the rigid social code of the jungle villages. Urbanization has brought payback from jungle trails to city streets on occasion; police have fought avenging tribesmen on the outskirts of Port Moresby. Feuds carry on from one generation to the next, until injuries are repaid in kind. Official efforts to deter payback killings, which have accounted for most of the sixty to seventy murder cases brought to trial in Papua New Guinea every year, have had little deterrent effect. Tribesmen accustomed to the rigors of jungle life tend to regard a prison term as a holiday, with food and clothing supplied at government expense. Furthermore, the tribesman jailed for a payback killing returns to the village, having served his time, with his status enhanced by the experience.

Whites are not exempt from payback, either. A young English planter who was driving a vehicle that accidentally struck and killed a tribesman in Mount Hagen was mobbed by the victim's kin and friends; he saved his life by persuading the offended tribe to accept compensation of $1,190 in cash and four pedigreed bulls, which were duly handed over in a public ceremony at the administration office with senior Australian officials watching. That the Englishman had been exonerated of blame in the accident by a magistrate did not matter.

Efforts to introduce legislation upgrading the traditionally subservient position of women were balked by tribal attitudes in the House of Assembly. "Meri i no save pait" ("Women do not understand fighting"), a legislator from the highlands argued in Pidgin, adding: "Wok belongim lukautim pikinini" ("Their work is to look after children"). The reform measure introduced by the lone woman member, Josephine Abaijah, was thereupon voted down.

"This was part of our custom long before Europeans penetrated our country," an educated tribal member of the House of Assembly said of payback during a debate on proposals to increase the prison sentences for such homicides. "Payback is still in the minds of the people of Papua New Guinea. A portion of the present generation is aware of the foreign-introduced law and fears it, but those who have not gone very far away from our traditional activities still carry on with payback killings. Those of us who have known two cultures may try to deny the fact, but it is not very easy for our tradition-oriented people suddenly to drop all traditional ways of thinking and do what modern people do."

Cannibalism still flourishes in remote parts of the country where the tribes have had little contact with modernizing influences from outside. Some highland tribes eat slain enemies, believing that they thereby absorb the courage and fighting qualities of the foe. Others regard human flesh as a practical supplement to a diet chronically deficient in animal protein. "When our children cry for no reason, we parents know that they are hungry for human flesh," a defiant tribal leader in the remote Nomad area of Papua once told a touring Australian official who tried to lecture the tribe on the evils of cannibalism.

Although the Australian government did its best to discourage cannibalism, there was a tendency to take a tolerant view of transgressions. A short time before Australia handed over authority, a man from the Nomad sector was killed with an ax in an altercation. This act called for payback, which the brother of the slain man duly exacted with a bow and arrow. He and six friends then cut up the body of the victim, cooked the flesh, and ate it. (The *Post-Courier,* of Port Moresby, put out a whimsical headline poster on the story with just three numerals, "7–8–1.") There being no law against cannibalism in the Criminal Code for Papua New Guinea, the seven men were charged with "improperly interfering with a corpse."

The case came before Justice William Thomas Prentice of the Papua New Guinea Supreme Court. The Australian judge acquitted the seven men on the ground that "in seeking to construe whether the behavior of the Gabusi villagers here amounted to impropriety . . . ," it was necessary to "look at the average man in the particular community, as it was at the time of these happenings." In other words, the ruling said in effect that cannibalism was not "indecent" or "improper" under the law if custom sanctioned the practice. The decision was widely hailed in Papua New Guinea as an enlightened one. The man who killed the murderer of his brother was found guilty, however, on a separate charge of manslaughter and was sentenced to three years' imprisonment at hard labor.

A decline of cannibalism has been linked by scientists to a striking decrease in the incidence of a strange nerve disease called kuru, which occurs only among the people of the Fore tribe in the Central Highlands. The incurable ailment is also known as the "laughing disease" because of the constriction of the facial muscles that is one of the symptoms. The malady occurred most commonly among the women of the tribe, who had followed a custom of eating flesh from the corpse of a dead relative when pregnant in order to perpetuate the spirit of the deceased in the child to be born. When the practice stopped, the number of cases of kuru lessened.

Like the civil administration, churches in Papua New Guinea have occasionally bowed to local customs. The Synod of Bishops of the Anglican church, meeting in Port Moresby during the last months of Australian rule, tacitly accepted polygamy by annulling a ban on the baptism of men with more than one wife. Various churches dropped their ineffective opposition to the custom of obtaining wives by payment to the prospective in-laws of a "bride price" in cash, pigs, cassowaries, and pearl shells. A number of local government councils decided on their own responsibility, however, perhaps reflecting church pressure, to put limits on the amounts to be paid. In the isolated Jimmi valley, for instance, the council set a maximum payment of two hundred dollars in cash, five pigs, and one cassowary for a "brand new" bride, as the announcement put it; a woman married once before was worth only twenty-five dollars, two pigs, and a cassowary, while one who had been wed more than once was ruled to have "no commercial value."

Doctor John Gunther, the Australian former vice-chancellor of the University of Papua New Guinea and a former high government official in the territory, used to lament that education was widening the gap between the urban minority and the rural masses. The villagers remained 80 percent illiterate, while more and more young town dwellers were enrolling in higher schools. The university, opened in 1966 with 58 students, would soon be graduating a thousand or more each year on the resplendent new campus built over abandoned wartime airfields in the suburb of Waigani, eight miles from Port Moresby. The students took up the fashionable causes of the time, such as Black Power, and liked to boast to visiting foreign journalists that they were "the leaders of tomorrow" in this raw land.

While the highland tribes were suspicious of independence because of the ascendancy of the lowland elite in the black bureaucracy in Port Moresby, the Papuans were apprehensive of the numerical superiority of the New Guineans, who constituted about three-fourths of the population with the highlanders and the people of the attached islands included. Charges that the new government favored New Guinea over Papua gained credence in dissident circles when the national airline was named Air Niugini, using the Pidgin spelling of New Guinea; the omission of Papua from the name set back the cause of unity by years.

Papuans pointed accusingly to the superior road system in New Guinea, and the location of most of the major economic development projects in that area, as evidence that they were being neglected deliberately. At the same time, the Papuans believed that they themselves were intellectually superior to the majority of the New Guineans, who lived mostly in a simple village society, and were convinced that they would progress faster as a separate nation.

Shortly after Australia granted full self-government, at least five Papuan separatist movements appeared. Josephine Abaijah, a London-educated public health worker who defeated six male rivals for the parliamentary seat from a Papuan constituency, led frequent independence rallies on the streets of Port Moresby—a Papuan city, though the population was mixed—under the banner of "Papua Besena," roughly translated as "Free Papua." A separate group proclaimed a "Papuan Provisional Republic," with Simon Kaumi, the former election commissioner, as president. Kaumi raised a barefoot army, which drilled with sticks instead of rifles.

Papuan separatism had been encouraged by the previous status of the Papuans as full citizens of Australia, while the New Guineans were wards of the United Nations. The distinction had been a matter of great pride among the Papuans, although citizenship had not given them the right to travel to Australia proper without a permit, the same as the noncitizen New Guineans. (The document used to be officially titled "Permit to Remove a Native from the Territory of Papua and New Guinea," but the wording was deemed opprobrious and was eventually changed.)

Another major separatist movement, seeking local autonomy rather than the full independence demanded by the Papuans, developed among the relatively affluent and sophisticated people of the Tolai language group on the prosperous Gazelle Peninsula of New Britain island. Half the copra and 28 percent of the cocoa produced by Papua New Guinea was grown in "The Gazelle," as the Australians called the area. Although the Tolai numbered only seventy thousand, they owned half the motor vehicles in the entire country. A handsome, vocal people, passionately attached to their land, they possessed a strong matrilineal social structure in which inheritance traditionally went to a sister's son. Nearly all were Roman Catholics or Wesleyans.

Through the influence of Christian missionaries, who arrived on New Britain in 1875, the proud and progressive Tolai learned to prize education and came to be considered the most Western-ized of all the Papua New Guinea peoples. "We have nine high schools and we need more," said Harry West, the red-haired Australian district commissioner for East New Britain.

The Germans chose the Gazelle as the administrative center and commercial focus of their extensive colonial holdings in New Guinea and the many islands of the Bismarck Sea, first operating out of Kokopo and then, in 1910, moving twenty miles north to the new town of Rabaul to take advantage of a splendid, horseshoe-shaped natural harbor. Rabaul became the business headquarters and social fiefdom of one of the most remarkable women in the history of the South Pacific, the astute and beautiful Emma Coe Forsayth. The daughter of an American consul and a Samoan princess, she became known as "Queen Emma" be-cause of her vast properties, over which she presided regally, on New Britain and the nearby tiny Duke of York Islands. A mural of her stately progress through town in a luxurious horse-drawn coach adorns the main dining salon—appropriately called the Queen Emma Room—of the pleasant Travelodge hotel on the Rabaul waterfront.

Rabaul has had an uneasy history. The town was completely destroyed twice, first in 1937 by a volcanic eruption that drowned the area in hot brown ash and steaming mud, then by American air raids in World War II. Rebuilt after the war in a rectangular pattern with flowery streets, Rabaul became again one of the most attractive cities in the South Seas. Unfortunately, it is still a geologically unstable one, being always threatened by the active volcanoes that ring the harbor and the frequent earthquakes of such violence that, on one occasion, the ground shivered visibly when the tremor hit.

The town lost its political importance before the war when the Australians, disheartened by the recurrent volcanic eruptions, decided to move the capital to Lae, on the New Guinea mainland, in 1941 (the government was transferred to Port Moresby, the principal port of Papua, when the separate Papua and New Guinea administrations were merged after the war). Rabaul figured prominently in the war as a Japanese area headquarters. The bunker used by the Japanese commanders during the frequent American air raids is a tourist attraction in the commercial center of the rebuilt city. After Americans intercepted and decoded a message giving the schedule for a flight from Rabaul to Bougainville by Admiral Isoroku Yamamoto, the Japanese supreme commander, fighter planes ambushed the aircraft in which the admiral was traveling and shot it down in one of the great intelligence coups of the war. The wreckage can still be seen where it fell in dense jungle near Buin, at the southern end of Bougainville, on 18 April 1943—part of the grim detritus of battle that littered many South Pacific islands a generation after the conflict had ended.

When Australian forces expelled the Germans from Rabaul in 1914, foreigners owned 40 percent of the land that had formerly belonged to the Tolai from time immemorial. Bitter Tolai nationalists like John Kaputin, one of the most charismatic and colorful young politicians of the pre-independence period, charged that whites had obtained the land "for a few beads and axes," an assertion with some historical validity. In the most fertile areas of the Gazelle, under the Australian administration, the proportion of foreign-owned land reached 80 percent.

A move by the Australian administration to buy up foreign-owned plantations for redistribution to Tolai families met with resistance from the Tolai themselves, who wished to restore the traditional system of clan ownership. The Australians considered the clan concept incompatible with efficient land management principles. Tolai discontent spilled over when the government instituted a multiracial Local Government Council, giving representation to settlers of European and Chinese stock.

"This is supposed to be a black country, but the institutions are not controlled by us," John Kaputin declared over cool drinks in the air-conditioned Travelodge coffee shop. Kaputin wore his hair cut in Afro style, kept his huge dark sunglasses on indoors, and otherwise emulated American black activists in dress and demeanor. The tall, handsome young Tolai leader had behind him a brief and unpromising career at the East-West Center in Hawaii and an ill-fated marriage to a white Australian teacher; later he would be elected to the House of Assembly and serve a short and controversial term as minister of justice.

Tolai grievances found expression in a political organization called the Mataungan Association, a name derived from a Tolai phrase meaning "Be alert." Led by a politician named Oscar Tammur, who represented the Gazelle area in the House of Assembly, the group denounced the multiracial council and held an election for an all-Tolai body. The Tolai were asked to withhold taxes from the government and to pay them to the new All-Melanesian council. Leaders of the tax boycott were arrested and sentenced to a thirty-dollar fine or thirty days in jail. They chose jail as a matter of Mataungan policy, and a period of confrontation with the police ensued, involving stone-throwing, club-swinging, and tear gas.

Damien Kereku, the slender, earnest young president of the Mataungan Association, and Melchior Tomot, the mild-mannered chief executive of the group's governing council, explained the Tolai objectives in several conversations in the association's offices, a converted frame dwelling on stilts—for coolness and flood protection—along the pleasant seaside road between Rabaul and Kokopo. "We don't want to secede from Papua New Guinea, we just want to control our own affairs and be able to change laws that we don't like," said Tomot. "The Tolai are more advanced than many other tribes, and we resent the direct application of Western law to us." Kereku declared that the association was "not anti-Australian," but, on the contrary, was convinced of a need for Australian expertise in development programs "for years to come." Like other educated Papua New Guineans, they spoke English in neutral accents but used Australian idioms.

Besides its political activities, which resulted later in the election of three Mataungan members to the House of Assembly, the association undertook village improvement programs stressing health education, and invested in economic enterprises based on the principle of self-help. These included what Tomot described as "the first wholly native" development corporation in Papua New Guinea, which was run by John Kaputin. Its showpiece was a small farmers' market that was still a drab competitor for the lively and picturesque public bazaar, called the Bung. The latter offered a seemingly limitless variety of tropical seashells, among many other local wares, in a covered square in the center of the city. Shoppers carrying their purchases in bags made of woven palm fronds stopped to listen to the open court, being held on a breezy verandah for comfort, where well-known members of the Mataungan Association were undergoing trial for refusal to pay taxes to the government.

The strongest separatist movement of all emerged on Bougainville, a large, mountainous island of somber, trackless forests and spectacular active volcanoes, between New Guinea proper and the Solomon Islands, which were still under British rule when Papua New Guinea became independent. Bougainville was a famous World War II battleground for a time, the scene of bloody ground fighting when Australians and Americans combined to drive out the Japanese forces that had occupied the island earlier. Among the Americans who served on Bougainville as a young naval officer was a future president, Richard M. Nixon (two other presidents, John F. Kennedy and Lyndon B. Johnson, had also been navy officers in the Southwest Pacific theater). Bougainville became just another half-forgotten outpost when the tides of war turned elsewhere, but regained prominence a generation later as the site of one of the world's largest copper mines.

Murmurings of independence had already been heard among the eighty thousand ebony-hued Bougainvilleans for twenty years or more when Papua New Guinea became a sovereign state. The islanders had a historic grievance against their white rulers, which they transferred to the government in Port Moresby. Ethnically and geographically, the Bougainvilleans belong to the Solomons. But in 1898, in one of those colonial reshuffles that took no account of the wishes of the inhabitants, Britain transferred Bougainville and Buka to Germany in return for the withdrawal of German claims in the rest of the Solomons chain and Tonga. Britain, in the same deal, also left Western Samoa to the Germans. Thus Bougainville and Buka became part of German New Guinea, and eventually came under Australian rule.

In the general political awakening in the South Pacific following World War II, aware Bougainvilleans began to talk of rejoining the Solomons or, alternatively, of demanding their own independence. The discovery of fabulous mineral wealth on the island gave impetus to the movement. The summary removal of villagers from their long-established homes in the area to be mined, and the brusque overturn of traditional land rights by the Australians, led to violent clashes between Bougainvilleans and police.

Flying down to Bougainville from Rabaul to investigate these stirrings, I found myself deposited briefly on the small island of Buka, separated from Bougainville by a narrow strait called the Buka Passage. Buka had also figured prominently in the hostilities with Japan. The landing strip, a war relic, looked as if it had been carved out of the center of a serene coconut plantation. I recalled an old saying on New Britain, repeated to me by an Australian planter: "If you look after a coconut tree for ten years, it will look after you for the rest of your life."

Buka is known for beautiful and expensive basket work, the finest in the Southwest Pacific. (It is one of the oddities of the Pacific that the famous "Buka baskets" are actually made in Buin, on the south coast of Bougainville.) The plantation workers, the coal-black "Buka boys," also enjoy a high reputation. The Bukans tell a visitor, with great pride, that they are "the blackest people in the Pacific," and speak disparagingly of the less highly pigmented New Guineans as "redskins." The latter retaliate by referring to the Bukans with the explicit Pidgin phrase, "As bilong sospen" ("Ass belong saucepan"). The village of Hahalis on Buka had once been the site of the famous "baby farm cult," devoted to the breeding of a super-race of Melanesians. The cultists, headed by a village couple calling themselves "King John" and "Queen Elizabeth," refused to pay taxes or recognize Australian authority. Local priests were handed a basket of money, with instructions to pay it to the Pope in return for permission to practice polygamy.

The flight from Buka across the gloomy fastnesses of Bougainville to Kieta, the principal town, was enlivened by the sight of Mount Bagana, a majestic, cone-shaped volcanic peak in the center of the island. The boiling crater constantly poured out dense brown smoke in a thick, swirling pillar that reached to a long, flat, dun-colored cloud high in the sky.

A jolting half-hour ride over a pitted coral road, badly in need of repair but magnificently sited between forested hills and the tumbling sea, brought one to the seedy little town of Kieta, the administrative center for the island. Kieta was a sweltering, dismal place in a glorious natural setting, with scabby, tin-roofed buildings sprinkled along a crescent-shaped beach of white sand lined with tall shade trees. A scattering of run-down coastal vessels, a government launch, and a few pleasure craft bobbed at their moorings on the glassy green bay. A crew of sweating convicts, half-clothed in shapeless prison trousers, sloshed buckets of sea water on the unpaved main street to keep down the dust.

The Hotel Kieta was a simple establishment whose management did not bother with keys. With people arriving continually on missions connected with the copper mine, accommodation was in such demand that double rooms had to be shared with strangers; there were no single rooms. In the dining room, the railroad cafeteria decor was redeemed by sprays of spider orchids on the tables.

European patrons of the Hotel Kieta—which included crew-cut American technicians in short-sleeved white shirts, since Australians call all whites "Europeans"—gathered for drinks in a pleasant little patio decorated with tropical plants; the larger "public" bar was patronized by Melanesians. By the time the heavy tropical darkness had settled and the squalor of the grim little town had magically disappeared in the soft light of an outsize moon, the police would quietly park a large patrol wagon nearby, ready to haul away drunks. Drinkers wandered to the beach, which by morning would be littered with empty beer cans to be picked up by a work detail from the town prison.

The public bar was a babble of Pidgin, which virtually all Bougainvilleans spoke. I was told that there were some twenty languages on this island 127 miles long by 49 miles across at the widest point, three of them spoken within a 20-mile radius of Kieta. Sipping a glass of chilled South Pacific Lager, I perused with fascination a slickly printed booklet in Pidgin published by the copper company, entitled *Wei Bilong Kampani* ("way belong company"—meaning, in effect, how corporations operate). It was being used as an economics text in high schools, with teachers comparing modern corporate structure with the familiar operations of trade stores, village markets, and the economics of the *singsing*, or tribal feast, in which all share in providing the pigs.

"Sampela . . . tingting kampani im i samting bilong ol waitman tasol," the booklet said, meaning that some people think the company all belongs to the white man, that's all. After this came a sentence in capitals, "DISPELA I NO TRU"—"this fella he no true," or "This is not so." A chapter explained "rot bilong baiim sare" ("road belong buy him share," or how to buy a share [of stock]). The booklet, distributed in villages with supplementary lectures in the local language, was a text on how to make the leap from a communal system to modern capitalism, a universal problem in South Pacific island societies.

The booklet was not a sales pitch for Bougainville Copper Proprietary, Limited, the British and Australian consortium developing the mine; that would have been illegal. The corporation's offer of a million shares to the Bougainvilleans and other Papua New Guineans, however, was quickly oversubscribed by eager villagers. With this approach the company hoped to defuse nationalist sentiments by involving masses of local people in the ownership of the mine. Furthermore, the government of Papua New Guinea held a 20 percent equity in the enterprise "in trust for the people." In an additional goodwill gesture, the company undertook an extensive program of free apprentice training and scholarships to upgrade the educational and technical competence of the population, and promised maximum "localization" of its permanent staff.

"B.C.P.," as the company was commonly called, had spent $14 million to build a sixteen-mile road to the mine from Kieta. It was by far the finest highway in the Southwest Pacific. Some of the other figures quoted by Cliff Newman, the public relations officer, were staggering. The initial investment of more than $400 million included such items as six huge shovels from Japan, capable of grabbing twenty tons of earth in a single bite, costing $600,000 each, and forty-one American-made 105-ton trucks at $200,000 (Melanesian drivers learned to handle these in nine weeks of instruction). The ore body was estimated at more than a billion tons. The initial output was to be 160,000 tons of copper metal a year, plus gold and silver as by-products. Companies in Japan, West Germany, and Spain had contracted to purchase the entire production for fifteen years ahead. It was the largest single industrial enterprise in Papua New Guinea. Coming suddenly upon the immense open pit, a roughly circular gouge in the earth more than a mile across and hundreds of feet deep, was an awesome experience. "The second biggest hole in the world, next to the Bingham Canyon copper diggings in Utah," said Newman, waving toward the great manmade chasm on the once-serene plateau.

The Papua New Guinea government's revenue from the development was expected to average $40 million annually in the first ten years. It quickly occurred to many Bougainvilleans that the island could keep this money for local projects if it were an independent country. Furthermore, as more Bougainvilleans and other Papua New Guineans pondered the implications of being left in forty years or so with "the second biggest hole in the world" minus any ore, pressure arose to renegotiate the B.C.P. contract upward in favor of Papua New Guinea or Bougainville.

Reflecting upon the ugly scene that had accompanied the Australian government's forcible acquisition of village lands to lease to B.C.P. for the mine, the company was anxious to repair its frayed image among the Bougainvilleans. It set up an elaborate program of resettlement and compensation for the displaced villagers, including payment for fish destroyed by pollution of a river with waste from the chemical treatment of ore. The public acceptance of these overtures was reserved. "Out of the company's profits of $100 million in the first year, $80,000 a year to be divided among some fifty people isn't much money," Barry Middlemiss, an Australian adviser to Bougainville nationalists, said of the rentals and royalties paid to former occupants of the land. I learned elsewhere that these were people to whom a cash income of $150 a year for a family would have seemed affluent before.

I had found Middlemiss simply by passing word that I wished to see him. A friend in the local government radio station put my request on the air—a common way of transmitting messages on this island of sparse telephone service. The Australian, a slender, thin-faced man of about thirty, looked for me at the hotel the same evening. He turned out to be one of the most interesting Australians in all the islands.

A former plantation overseer, Middlemiss had become involved in Kieta politics and assisted a local leader and member of the House of Assembly named Paul Lapun (later to be the first Papua New Guinean to be knighted) in organizing a Bougainville nationalist association called Napidakoe Navitu. The name, Middlemiss said, was a combination of abbreviations for the three languages spoken around Kieta and the vernacular word *navitu,* meaning "unity." The Australian was secretary of the organization and manager of the group's commercial arm, Navitu Enterprises, a holding company for other Melanesian-owned firms that ran a taxi and bus service and had wide-ranging plans in the automotive, tourism, restaurant, and land development fields. He was also a member of the Local Government Council for the Kieta area, secretary of his political party, and managing editor of *The Bougainville News.* "They all pay," Middlemiss said of his numerous jobs, adding: "I'm possibly one of the highest-paid Europeans in Papua New Guinea." And one of the busiest, I thought.

As an Australian who had adopted the cause of Bougainvillean nationalism, Middlemiss seemed to enjoy special exemption from the widespread animosity of local blacks toward Caucasians and Chinese. The Kieta district council, meeting when Middlemiss was away, had passed a resolution forbidding Melanesian girls to marry white men. "You're different," the black councilors assured him later. He was then about to marry a Melanesian girl picked for his bride by the village where he was living. "I had no choice," he said, apparently not displeased with the arranged marriage.

An unofficial referendum run by Napidakoe Navitu was said to have shown the population overwhelmingly in favor of secession from the rest of Papua New Guinea, but Australian officials questioned the validity of the result. Educated Melanesians like John Pippin and Aloysius Sihoto, who worked at the government radio station in the news section, were from widely separated villages and seemed as well informed on Bougainvillean political views as anyone. "Secessionist sentiment is very strong in Kieta and Buin, and is supported by most educated people in Buka," said Sihoto, who came from Buka. "But among the older people, some are against secession and some are just confused." Pippin, from a village near Panguna, thought the Bougainvilleans were divided "fifty-fifty" on the question.

Both young men were opposed to a movement for rejoining the Solomon Islands, though acknowledging that Bougainville belonged there geographically and ethnically. "The Solomons are behind us in almost everything," Pippin said. "We would either have to pull the Solomons up to our standard, or we would be pulled down to theirs. No good."

Organized rebellion broke out in February 1976. Secessionists took over the towns of Buin and Boku in the southern part of the island and proclaimed the "Republic of the North Solomons." Doctor Alexis Sarei, the Bougainvillean district commissioner of the island, defected from Port Moresby to become "interim chairman" of the movement. Somare, who had been heckled by crowds when he toured the island under elaborate police escort before the revolt, managed to work out an uneasy truce with the rebels.

Eventually the dispute was settled by making Bougainville a province, with defined areas of authority in local government and finance that appeared to satisfy the Bougainvilleans' aspirations to autonomy. Doctor Sarei, a former village dweller from Buka who obtained his early education in a mission school and went on to earn a doctorate in canon law at the University of Rome, became the first premier. Somare called the arrangement a triumph of the "Melanesian spirit," which was another way of paying tribute to the "Pacific way" or *musjawarah.*

Thus the Bougainville nationalists lost the game but they won the name, for the island was known thenceforth as North Solomons Province. The change in status set a precedent for other regions with a similarly distinct character, which also became provinces. A native Roman Catholic priest, the Reverend Cherubim Dambui, twenty-eight years old, was elected premier of Somare's own East Sepik Province. The choice was criticized by some as an unhealthy conjunction of church and state; other clerics held elective office, a practice common in other countries including the United States, but Father Dambui was the first to gain the top regional executive post in an important area of free Papua New Guinea, peopled largely by pagans.

Apart from its explosive effect on the Bougainville independence movement, the arrival of B.C.P. on the remote Southwest Pacific island had an immediate and drastic cultural impact on the untutored Melanesians in the villages. To a degree, it was World War II all over again. White men appeared from the sky with vast treasure, which they dispensed generously. Work was offered to thousands of Bougainvilleans at wages that seemed fabulous. Gigantic machines tore at the earth, and where there had been virgin jungle there was suddenly a modern town with amenities such as the Bougainvilleans had never seen before. An enormous industrial plant appeared that included, among other wonders, the largest copper concentrator in the world. A Westernizing process that had taken decades in other parts of Papua New Guinea was compressed into a year or two on Bougainville.

Predictably, the Western incursion with its riches brought a revival of cargo cults. The Melanesian authorities on the island, just becoming accustomed to governing without the Australians, were alarmed. Defiance of the law was built into cultist doctrine. The police, acting on information from the aroused Kieta Local Government Council, made a surprise visit to one isolated village where a cargo cult had been reported, found human bones on an altar, and heard stories of ritual sexual practices.

Meanwhile the white mine workers, finding life on Bougainville sterile and constricting, were also restive. When word got around in the camp of a delightful Polynesian enclave in Papua New Guinea waters, a place as free of conventional restraints as the South Sea isles of the most glowing imagining, a company employee with an entrepreneurial bent conceived the idea of running holiday excursions by chartered vessel to this paradise for lonely miners. Habitués of the Hotel Kieta bar had heard alluring

tales of the good life in the nearby Polynesian atolls from the
bartender, a young man with a tattooed face named Teneke. He
was a prince, being the son of the hereditary chief, of an atoll
250 miles to the northeast, called Nukumanu. This was too far
for holiday trips of the kind proposed, so the promoters selected
an atoll just like it only 120 miles away. This was a ring of coral
islets called Tauu, also known as the Mortlock or Tasman Islands,
after the navigators. The project quickly attracted the unfavorable attention of Bougainville government officials, who dug into
regulations of the former Australian regime to keep the atolls in
their unspoiled state.

As an outpost of Polynesian culture in a Melanesian area, Tauu
was a striking example of the diversity of peoples to be found
within Papua New Guinea, besides proving that the South Seas
of romantic tradition still survive, if only in such fragments. Half
the population of about 450 lived on the main island of their
atoll, also called Tauu, and had preserved there the ambience of
a bygone era in Polynesia. Their only contact with the outside
world was through irregular calls by small trading vessels that
picked up copra, the atoll's only cash crop.

The Tauuans lived like their ancestors in grass houses and ate
mostly coconuts, fish, and taro, the ubiquitous cultivated tuber-
ous root. Authority was exercised through chiefs. In former days,
troublemakers were executed by a blow to the back of the head
with a carved, four-sided club, wielded with two hands. Infanticide, especially of girl babies, had been common in earlier times,
before emigration solved the overpopulation problem. Missionaries were barred from the atoll at the insistence of the chiefs,
who preferred to retain the ancient animistic religion.

Since the atoll was difficult to reach for the ordinary traveler,
tourists were virtually unknown on Tauu. Thus shielded from
contact with germ-carrying outsiders, the Tauuans were completely free of the white man's diseases. There were no mos-
quitoes. And the shapely Tauuan girls were among the most
alluring and friendly in the Pacific. Under native law, an outsider
could marry a Tauuan girl only on condition that if the husband
departed, the wife and any children of the union be left behind.
The Australian authorities, anxious to preserve this classic South
Seas paradise, had made certain that no one visited the atoll
without prior certification, after a careful medical examination,
of freedom from disease. The examiners were especially vigilant
for venereal infection, the great despoiler of South Pacific peo-

ples. The Papua New Guinea government hastily reimposed the Australian restrictions, thus heading off any exploitation of Polynesian tolerance by the proposed excursions for copper miners seeking relaxation among the unspoiled. Australian friends of the island peoples were relieved, if the miners were not.

Australia had handed over the government of this country of a thousand tribes with mixed feelings of relief and apprehension. Many Australians and Papua New Guineans alike were convinced that Canberra was prematurely walking away from the responsibility, assumed when the territory was taken from Germany, to exercise a benevolent guardianship until it was certain that these disparate and quarreling people, in all stages of civilization, were prepared to proceed alone.

Some panic ensued as racial tensions rose in Port Moresby and other towns. Antiwhite manifestations on a small scale were not a new thing, particularly in the dismal squatter colonies where newcomers from the country, lured to the towns by the bright lights and hope of jobs, often wound up penniless and embittered; but such incidents as the throwing of a stone at a passing car with a white at the wheel took on frightening dimensions in the context of the coming independence. Rumors spread that Melanesian extremists had made lists of the houses and cars owned by whites, to be seized and allocated among themselves as soon as the Australian authority departed.

As the time approached for Papua New Guinea to enter the interim period of internal self-government on 1 December 1973, more than fourteen thousand Australians—about 25 percent of the entire expatriate community—left permanently. Many of the three thousand Chinese, mostly successful shopkeepers descended from plantation laborers imported in German times, also packed their possessions and transferred investments. Seats on planes bound for Australia became hard to get.

Independent Papua New Guinea institutionalized racism in the new country's constitution by including clauses restricting the freedoms of whites, in apparent contradiction of a section affirming that all citizens would enjoy the same rights irrespective of color, place of origin, religion, sex, or political opinion. The document specified that, for five years, naturalized citizenship would be available only to those who had been born in Papua New Guinea before Independence Day and had two grandparents born in that country, Irian Jaya, the Solomon Islands, or the Torres Straits Islands. Subsequent legislation provided that only

Papua New Guinea citizens could own land, and that land belonging to noncitizens would be converted into leaseholds. The laws were frankly intended to limit the position of whites, who still owned some 85 percent of industry and held most of the top positions in commerce at the time of independence. "Black Power is as relevant to Papua New Guinea as betel nut," said a Bougainvillean leader, Leo Hannett. "We like to keep Papua New Guinea black, just as Australians want to keep Australia white," said Michael Somare, the first prime minister.

Somare, then thirty-six years old, was aware of his people's limitations, however. When highland chiefs hostile to independence demanded a referendum on the issue, he refused. "Too many people wouldn't understand what they were voting on," he explained.

When I had first met Somare several years earlier in his Western-style frame house in Wewak, the administrative center of his native East Sepik district, he had predicted correctly that internal autonomy would arrive in 1973. He believed that local self-government, contrary to the majority opinion, would be more unifying than divisive. "Under Australian rule, the people relax," he said. "When they have the responsibility themselves, they'll pull together." Nevertheless, Somare was convinced at that time that, following the establishment of internal self-government, there should be an interim period of "six to eight years" before full independence.

Somare had wanted time to heal internecine quarrels and accustom the villagers to the realities of government without white men. With the inflation of the indigenous bureaucracy in preparation for self-rule, Papua New Guineans took over the official homes previously occupied by departed Australian functionaries. The appearance of a new black elite, wearing shorts and long socks and riding in big cars just like their white predecessors, had an effect similar to that of the black G.I. a generation before: there was a sudden renaissance of cargo-cult thinking among the uneducated masses. Somare was aware of the dangers in the cargo-cult mentality. "They think that when we get self-government, everything else will come," he said. The government, uneasy over the risky potentialities in any outburst of public excitement accompanying the formal establishment of self-government, with Somare as the first chief minister, kept the ceremonial aspects of the occasion to a minimum. Somare wore his customary Hawaiian-style flowered shirt at the formalities

—and banned the sale of liquor for three days. None of the feared disorders took place.

Somare had been born to chiefly rank in a clan in which the ability to get along peaceably with others was a proud tradition. "My people believed that almost any dispute could be settled by talk," he said in his autobiography. He was born in Rabaul, where his father was serving as a policeman at the time, but was brought back to his native village in the East Sepik when he was six years old. His first education was in a school run by the Japanese who occupied the area early in the war. Somare and others recalled the Japanese as having been considerate and friendly, a recollection that contributed to the warm welcome accorded investors from Japan by the new government in Port Moresby.

The future political leader continued his education under the Australians after the war. He became a government schoolteacher, then a news reporter and announcer for the administration radio station at Wewak, a job that whetted his interest in politics. An Australian decree freezing the pay of native public servants at about half the amount earned by white expatriates for the same work made Somare an anticolonial activist.

Meanwhile he was assigned to take courses at the Administrative College in Port Moresby, a school to train promising young black civil servants. His nationalism was further sharpened in an informal discussion group called the Bully Beef Club, which took its name from the habit of talking politics late into the night over snacks of tinned meat. Other alumni of the club were the future foreign minister, Sir Maori Kiki, and the first governor-general of free Papua New Guinea, Sir John Guise, who attributed his surname to a French ancestor related to the dukes of Guise.

"We don't hate the white man," Somare once said, "since we have no heritage of slavery in chains." He was determined, however, that the whites remaining in Papua New Guinea would no longer be "little kings," nor would the Melanesians become "black Australians." "We will bring our own social institutions into the law from which they have been ostracized so long," he declared. "This time, the law will be tailor-made for our own society and circumstances." But there was no hurry: a wholesale restructuring of the legal code inherited from the Australians, to adapt it to local customs, was expected to be years in the making.

At the stroke of midnight on 16 September 1975, while fireworks lit the sky over Port Moresby and tribal drums boomed, Papua New Guinea became an independent country and Somare automatically assumed the title of prime minister in ceremonies witnessed by Prince Charles of Britain, representing Queen Elizabeth II as the titular sovereign of the new nation. (In Pidgin, she is known as *missus queen*). Shortly thereafter the new country's flag, red and black with a gold bird of paradise and the stars of the Southern Cross, joined the others in front of the United Nations buildings in New York as Papua New Guinea became the 139th member of the world organization of sovereign states.

While achieving the dignity of political equality among the world's countries, Papua New Guinea clung to its traditions. Many months earlier, Somare made a quiet trip to his home village of Karau, in the Sepik valley. There, in secret, one-month-long ceremonies attended only by males, he formally assumed his inherited rank of Sana, or chief, of his native Saet clan. The clan elders made one modification in the ancient ritual. Because the new chief was to be the prime minister, the customary piercing of the nostrils and ear lobes was waived. Instead, the operations were performed symbolically on a doll.

Robert Trumbull/*New York Times*

...nonese children play in war wreckage on beach at Honiara, capital of the Solomon Islands

...gt. Maj. Jacob Vouza, Solomon-
...e war hero, at age seventy-six

Robert Trumbull/*New York Times*

Public market on Rue Higginson, main street of Vila, New Hebrides

View of Nouméa, New Caledonia

THREE

Out of the Jungle into the World

OING from country to country—or island to island—by fast, high-flying jet plane, a traveler misses the best scenery. In the South Pacific, at a time when many of the civil airfields were still mere coral strips built originally for medium-range bombers and fighter planes, some of the more glorious sights viewed by man were seen through the plexiglass windows of the slow, low-flying DC-3, or Dakota, the sightseeing bus of the air. You might bounce in the erratic tropical air currents, or sweat when the ancient air-conditioning units failed, but the visual treat was worth the discomfort.

Nowhere does a more dazzling vista unroll before the air traveler than the armada of green islands between Bougainville and Guadalcanal on the sparkling waterway called New Georgia Sound, which separates the eastern and western wings of the Solomons. During World War II, when American military planes flew this route under fire from Japanese antiaircraft batteries on the myriad islands, the lovely but perilous aerial corridor was known as "The Slot." For wartime pilots, the scenic splendors of The Slot were marred by countless black puffballs of exploding flak.

On a peacetime flight one day in a shuddering DC-3, the Australian pilot invited me to view the breathtaking spectacle below from the vantage point of the copilot's seat. As he identified the islands slipping past us less than a mile below, the names were a recital of long-forgotten battles in the bitter campaign for the

55

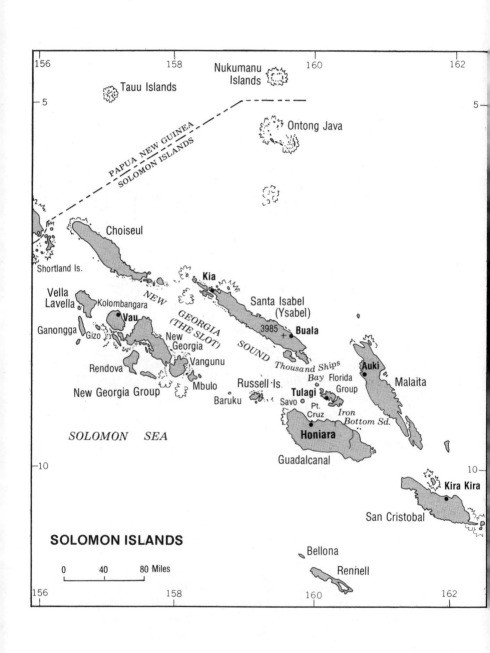

156 158 Nukumanu 160 162
Islands
5 Tauu Islands 5

Ontong Java

PAPUA NEW GUINEA
SOLOMON ISLANDS

Choiseul

Shortland Is.

Vella Kia
Lavella Kolombangara Santa Isabel
(Ysabel)
Ganongga Gizo Vau NEW 3985 Buala
New GEORGIA
Georgia (THE SLOT) Auki
Rendova SOUND Malaita
Vangunu Thousand Ships
New Georgia Group Mbulo Russell Is. Bay Florida
Baruku Tulagi Group
Savo
Pt. Iron
Cruz Bottom Sd.
SOLOMON SEA Honiara
Guadalcanal
10 Kira Kira 10

San Cristobal

SOLOMON ISLANDS

0 40 80 Miles Bellona
Rennell
156 158 160 162

Solomons early in the war. We passed Vella Lavella on the right, then Kolombangara, while ahead lay New Georgia and after that came Savo, where a colleague and friend had lost an eye.

"There's Plum Pudding Island—thought you'd want to see that," said the pilot, pointing out the curved window to a small, round, palm-covered hump among the welter of islands on the blue expanse of sea. This was Kasolo, to give the island its proper name. Here a young naval officer named John F. Kennedy had swum to safety after a Japanese destroyer had run down and sunk his torpedo boat, PT 109, whose profile as reproduced on a metal tie clip became the trademark of the successful Kennedy presidential campaign.

Soon we touched down on the modern runway of Henderson Field, once the object of some of the fiercest fighting in the war. The old American control tower, now abandoned, flashed by and the plane came to rest in front of a neat terminal building. We were on Guadalcanal, described by James Michener, in his *Tales of the South Pacific*, as "that godforsaken backwash of the world." The one-time backwash had become a stop on tourist routes in the South Pacific, and the main island in an emerging black nation with a somber history. But this forbidding island and its mates, steaming in the sun, remained one of the least developed territories in the Pacific.

World War II had given the Solomons, a British protectorate, world prominence. Peacetime brought a new capital, Honiara, and the beginnings of political advances in preparation for independence. The dark-skinned people number fewer than two hundred thousand on a dozen large islands and scores of smaller ones. They are as diversified as the islands themselves, which include flat coral atolls as well as towering volcanic formations. Except for a few thousand Polynesians on some of the smaller islands and atolls, and an enclave of Micronesians resettled by the British from the overcrowded Gilbert Islands, most are of the Melanesian race.

Tens of thousands of American war veterans remember Guadalcanal, named by early Spanish settlers after a small town in their homeland, as a pestilential wilderness. The troops found the inviting beaches patrolled by sharks, and pleasant-looking rivers infested with crocodiles. Besides a brave and resourceful Japanese foe, the unprepared Americans contended with persistent malaria, intestinal parasites, hookworm, filaria, and every kind of skin ailment known to the tropics. The climate is hot, humid, and rainy the year around. Natural conditions and the ferociously hostile native islanders, who practiced cannibalism till recent times, had caused the Solomons to be shunned by white men in previous decades.

A new generation of Solomonese, with more education and knowledge of the outside world, welcomes tourists even on remoter islands like Malaita. Old-timers in the small white community are bemused by the change. The Most Reverend Daniel Stuyvenberg, the Dutch-born Roman Catholic bishop of Honiara, recalled that when he was a young man in the Solomons the crews of mission ships "dared not go ashore" on Malaita.

The Solomon Islands were named by the Spanish navigator Alvaro de Mendaña de Neyra, who discovered the archipelago for the West on a voyage from Peru in 1568. The name, intended to inspire Spanish colonization by association with the wealth of Solomon, was a fraud. The Spanish explorer promised gold, but that metal was not to be found in significant quantities until four hundred years later. The first colonizing expedition was a disaster. After the disappointed pioneers left, hoping for better luck in the Philippines, nearly two centuries would pass before white men laid eyes on the islands again; the next recorded visit was by the British mariner Philip Carteret in 1767. Point Cruz, said to have been named by Mendaña, became the central waterfront area of Honiara.

White colonization was discouraged by the blood-thirsty reception accorded early arrivals. A party of fourteen Roman Catholic priests and lay workers from the French mission of the Society of Mary, landing in 1845 on Santa Ysabel, north of Guadalcanal, and San Cristobal, to the south, make an inauspicious start in efforts to Christianize the Solomons. The leader, Bishop John Epalle, was murdered on his fourth day ashore. His successor died of a fever. After a series of further misfortunes, the mission departed in 1852 and the Marist order did not return for forty-six years. Others murdered by natives in the Solomons in the pre-British period included a Protestant bishop, a commodore of the British Navy, and a wealthy Australian who landed on the northwest coast of Guadalcanal from his yacht with the idea of creating his own tropical kingdom.

White traders and missionaries suffered because of the depredations of the notorious labor recruiters known as "blackbirders." These unscrupulous men rounded up islanders to labor on the sugar and cotton plantations of Fiji and Queensland, and the mines of New Caledonia and South America, in conditions approximating slavery, for a fixed fee per head. The methods of the blackbirders sometimes amounted to kidnaping, and many of the tens of thousands of young men gathered up in the ruthless traffic never saw their home islands again. The anger of the Melanesian chiefs against the blackbirders resulted in the systematic massacre of innocent whites.

The white traders in the Solomons, who numbered around fifty, appealed to Britain for protection. The British government responded by making the southern Solomons a protectorate in 1893. The remainder of the archipelago had been acquired by 1900, some through the treaty that gave Bougainville and Western Samoa to Germany. Labor recruiting had ended by 1910 as the result of British efforts and the establishment of the "White Australia" policy, a measure that has been denounced as racist but which in actuality was intended to protect Pacific islanders against exploitation by white planters.

The coming of British rule was followed by an influx of coconut growers to produce copra for Lever Brothers, the British soap-making firm, and the big Australian trading companies of Burns Philp and W. R. Carpenter, two names that were to become prominent throughout the British sphere in the Pacific (in Papua New Guinea there is a special word in Pidgin, *beepee,* for the ubiquitous Burns Philp shops). The professional colonial administrators who ran the British Solomon Islands Protectorate, as the territory was called, made little or no effort to develop the economy of the place beyond allowing the British and Australian copra interests to acquire vast acreage under coconuts.

Like the other islands in the colonial Pacific, the Solomons were shaken out of their political torpor by the momentous upheaval of World War II. In the protectorate, the impact of the war was most severe on Guadalcanal. It was an indirect result of combat operations that this jungled, volcanic island, eighty miles long by twenty-five miles wide in the middle, and with peaks rising to eight thousand feet, became the site of the future capital of a Melanesian state. Before the Japanese came there was nothing on Guadalcanal, besides the jungle and empty plains, except some coconut stands and a few mission stations. The British administration functioned from a tiny government settlement on the island of Tulagi, in the Florida group about twenty miles north of Point Cruz.

Guadalcanal is a name that shines in the military history of the

United States. It was in that island's fetid jungles that American ground forces came to grips with the valiant Japanese troops for the first time. The American Marines landed on Guadalcanal on 7 August 1942, just a month after the Japanese had arrived and had begun constructing a key air base—later called Henderson Field—on their drive south toward Australia.

The ensuing action, including massive sea and air engagements, lasted until the out-gunned Japanese withdrew six months later, following some of the bloodiest ground action in the war. The island-dotted seaway between the roughly parallel chains of the Eastern and Western Solomons became known as Iron Bottom Sound because of the number of warships of both sides lying beneath those sunny waters. In a series of spirited sea battles, the Allies—chiefly the United States—lost two large aircraft carriers, six heavy cruisers, two light cruisers, and a destroyer, while the Japanese losses were two battleships, a light carrier, three heavy cruisers, a light cruiser, eleven destroyers, and six submarines.

Tourists gazing at Iron Bottom Sound from the broad veranda of the Hotel Mendana, where they are served drinks by barefoot black waiters, often included former Marines who had returned to see what had happened to the island that they remembered as a green hell, and to show their wives and children where Daddy had fought the war. They found the changes unbelievable. Where these grey-haired and portly men had struggled through rain forests in their youth, air-conditioned boutiques now displayed carved wooden heads, colorful seashells, and necklaces of shell money along Mendana Avenue, a broad street shaded by red-flowered poinciana trees. This former jungle path, now paved and bordered by trimmed lawns, had been stained with the blood of some of the 1,600 Americans and 24,000 Japanese killed in the ground campaign.

Sitting at wicker tables in the Mendana, the veterans talked of the spectacular air battles over The Slot, the terror-filled nights when Japanese battleships bombarded the Marine positions for hours with their heaviest guns, and the legendary bravery of the Coast Watchers, the intrepid white planters, colonial officers, and others who reported the Japanese movements by radio, at fearful risk, from jungle hideouts behind the enemy lines.

On the beach next to the hotel, children played in the rotting hulks of wartime barges too far gone to tell whether they had been Japanese or American craft. Old unexploded bombs and shells, covered over with undergrowth, sometimes killed unwary youngsters. The retired Sergeant Major Jacob Vouza, the most famous Melanesian war hero, said that it was not unusual for hikers to find American and Japanese helmets, canteens, and other decaying battle gear in the thickets just outside the town.

Vouza was a living legend. On a scouting mission for the Marines, he had fallen into the hands of a large Japanese detachment that had just landed a few miles from Henderson Field to make a surprise attack on the Marines. When a small souvenir American flag was found in Vouza's possession he was tied to a tree, beaten in the face with rifle butts, and questioned relentlessly about the location and strength of the Americans. He refused to say a word. The furious Japanese bayonetted him twice through the chest and again through the neck, and left him tied up to die. But after the Japanese left the scene later in the day to try to creep up on the Americans, Vouza managed to free himself by chewing through the ropes that held him to the tree. Nearly dead from loss of blood, he crawled back to the American lines and refused medical attention until he had told his story to the Marines.

Vouza's information resulted in the annihilation of the Japanese unit, about eight hundred men, when it attacked the forewarned Marines. Vouza was decorated and became an international celebrity when the war correspondents got the story. After the war, fully recovered, he was given a trip to the United States by the grateful Marines. I found Vouza, white-haired but robust at seventy-five, and wearing his uniform with the row of medals on the chest, amiably allowing tourists to photograph him in the airy coffee shop of a hotel on one of the back streets of Honiara. He was the most famous Solomon Islander that ever lived.

After the war, the British administration abandoned the battered former capital at Tulagi and chose a new site around Point Cruz, which the Americans had conveniently cleared and developed into a sizable camp with Quonset huts and roads. "Honiara" is an abbreviation of a longer Melanesian name for the area, meaning "place of the east wind." Motorists now speed along Mendana Avenue in Japanese cars, ignoring the occasional cenotaph marking the spot where some significant skirmish took place in the battle for Guadalcanal.

Gradually the dusty wartime camp expanded into a sprawling town, with industrial and residential sections flowing toward Henderson Field, ten miles from Point Cruz, and up into the once-embattled Mataniko Valley (which the Marines had called

Matanikau, a misspelling), where the contours of old trenches and foxholes wrinkle the grassy terrain. Nearly all the Quonsets were replaced by standard construction, but one that remained on a hilltop overlooking the town had been remodeled into the Cathedral of the Holy Cross, the seat of the Roman Catholic bishop of the Diocese of Honiara.

The Solomons became one of the last refuges for displaced British civil servants from former colonies in Africa and the Caribbean. They put an unmistakable British colonial stamp on Honiara that undoubtedly will last, at least for a long time, under indigenous governments. Social life, like the machinery of government, the schools, and the judiciary, developed along lines fixed by the British as the colonial era neared its end. Even Pidgin in the Solomons was highly Anglicized, unlike its counterpart in Papua New Guinea. "Tabu for hang around insait sitoa ia," said a hand-lettered sign on the door of a souvenir shop on Mendana Avenue, warning loiterers not to loaf "inside store here."

Honiara was equipped with a nine-hole golf course, which returning veterans would recognize as the former Kukum fighter strip, and not one "Chinatown" but two, for the Chinese community, numbering about five hundred, had a strong hold—if not a monopoly—on small business and retail trade. Like their ethnic brethren on other islands, they formed a solid community.

Government House, the residence of the United Kingdom high commissioner (later governor, when the office of high commissioner was abolished because of obsolescence), was the symbol of the British presence. The gracious building stood in landscaped grounds beside the sea, hidden by tropical foliage from the gaze of strollers passing the impressive gateway fronting on Mendana Avenue. Next door, surrounded by lawns, was the air-conditioned Secretariat Building, where department heads and senior staff conducted the business of government. A circular white building nearby housed the High Court and Legislative Council.

Most redolent, however, of the British colonial connection was the inevitable posh club, on the beach across Mendana Avenue from the spacious sports ground. The higher-caste civil servants came to the Guadalcanal Club from their bungalows on the slopes behind the town, where they enjoyed cool breezes and a magnificent view of the Florida Islands, to relax with their families at the club's swimming pool, tennis courts, and bar. Melanesians patronized a simpler and less expensive establishment, the

Honiara Club, half a mile or so down Mendana Avenue in the commercial district.

A generation after the war, the Japanese had returned to the Solomons in a big way as traders and developers. They were received by the islanders with mixed feelings. "People in the villages are still frightened of the Japanese, remembering the war, but the feeling is beginning to disappear with familiarity," said Henry Raraka, the editor of the first indigenous magazine. "The Japanese tell the people that they aren't here to fight, but are creating jobs. A few Solomonese are starting to learn the Japanese language." Some have misgivings about the large Japanese presence in the Solomons "not because they are Japanese, but because one country—Japan—seems to be getting too strong a hold on the economy," said a British official.

Japanese companies were involved in copra, forestry, fishing, and mineral exploration. Japanese cars and motorcycles formed the bulk of the vehicular traffic on the island's one highway, a coral-surfaced road that ran about fifty miles from Honiara in each direction along the coast. (I was told that the British had rejected an offer by the American forces to extend the road all the way around the island.) The air-conditioned shops along Mendana Avenue displayed a variety of Japanese cameras, optical goods, and electronic items, and many of the cheap consumer articles in the Chinese village stores, such as canvas shoes, were also stamped "Made in Japan." The American presence, once overwhelming, had come down to one small fishing enterprise and a hopeful venture in rice-growing, besides minerals explorations.

Like all the emerging political leaders of the Pacific who had been brought up under colonialism, responsible Solomonese were fearful of foreign control of the economy as the islands moved toward political independence. "Unless the islands are economically viable, independence is meaningless," said John H. Smith, the British finance officer, who had come to the Pacific from Nigeria and later would become the governor of the Gilbert and Ellice Islands. Grants from the British government covered the annual deficit in the budget of the protectorate, but Smith maintained that proper concentration on development programs in agriculture, timber, fishing, and other resources could make the Solomons self-supporting in a few years. "There's no employment problem here, which makes the Solomons unique among developing countries," Smith said. "A third of the available work force are in steady jobs, and the rest are in agriculture. With more development, there could be a manpower problem."

Assisted by a United Nations fisheries expert from Iceland, of all places, Smith worked out the deal whereby the Taiyo Fishing Company, of Japan, gave the Solomon Islands government a 25 percent share in the fish processing plant planned for Tulagi, with an option to raise local participation to 49 percent. An arrangement for a government partnership with Mitsui mining interests to develop the bauxite deposits on Rennell Island, inhabited by about a thousand Polynesians, was pending. "Half the land area of the Solomons is being prospected for minerals," Smith said. The companies involved represented mining interests in the United States, Canada, Britain, and Australia, as well as Japan. Besides bauxite, the volcanic earth of the islands held unknown quantities of gold, silver, copper, iron, and manganese. The Solomons might yet live up to the promise of their name.

The principle, however, that the government was entitled to dispose of mineral rights came into conflict with the strong tradition of attachment to the land, which the people of the Solomons have in common with other Pacific island communities. "There could be serious trouble if the people discovered that they didn't own what lay beneath their land," an elected member of the Governing Council warned his fellow legislators. "All those land laws should be burnt," said David Kausimae, a member for Malaita, pointing to a shelf of books containing the legal code of the protectorate. "It may be necessary to choose between economic advancement and a happy people," said Waita Ben, the member for East Guadalcanal. The outcome of this debate in an air-conditioned hall on the shores of Guadalcanal was in the finest tradition of Westminster: a committee was appointed.

The war had widened the political horizon of the Solomon Islanders. Partly as a result of contacts with the American troops, who tended to be outspoken in their criticism of British colonialism, the end of the war in 1945 was followed almost immediately by the rise of a nationalist movement known as Marching Rule. Tightly organized under various charismatic leaders, and preaching noncooperation with the white authorities, the agitation began on Malaita and quickly spread to other islands, with thousands of adherents. Some Britons associated the name of the movement with Marxism, and concluded that the idea had been picked up from American leftists during the war. Later, it became generally accepted that "Marching" had nothing to do with Marx but was a distortion of the local word *masina,* meaning "brotherhood." By late 1948 the British administration of the Solomons decided that stern measures were necessary, and the principal leaders were arrested.

Suppression by force put an end to the overt defiance of authority, but the underlying nationalist motivation of Marching Rule survived and became an operative factor in the progression toward self-government, which began to move rapidly only in 1970. Until then, advancement had come at a stately pace through various stages from an appointed Advisory Council, which had been instituted in 1921 with four members chosen by the British resident commissioner, who retained all powers. By early 1974 the Solomons were virtually self-governing in practice, with a Legislative Assembly of twenty-four elected members and three top officials serving ex officio, headed by a chief minister. The British governor retained veto powers, but let the legislature set policy.

The leaders of the Marching Rule movement eventually became nationalist heroes (one, Jonathan Fifi'i, was elected to the legislature). Philip Solodia Funifaka, of Malaita, a former schoolteacher who had studied for the priesthood and was known for independent views, stood up in the legislative chamber one day and asserted that he and his colleagues might not be sitting where they were had it not been for the efforts of Marching Rule in an earlier time, for the movement had given the impetus toward self-government. "They were courageous men who had started a movement which was one of the best things to happen in the Solomon Islands," he said of the Marching Rule organizers. Another cabinet member, Gideon Zoloveke of Choiseul Island, defended the colonial power. "Members should appreciate the British government for having taken government in the Solomons to this stage," he asserted. The advances in self-rule "had been made possible by the United Kingdom's imposition of order and control in days past," he declared.

The first chief minister, Solomon Mamaloni, was a bushyhaired young man whom I had noticed in the Solomons delegations to meetings of the South Pacific Conference. A former clerk to the Legislative Council, the forerunner of the Assembly, he had attended a Maori college in New Zealand and became the elected head of the government at the age of thirty-two. As a legislator from his native Makira island in the Eastern Solomons, he was the author of an important new law giving greater powers to the eighteen elected local councils. A highly centralized government for 175,000 people living on scattered islands and speaking dozens of mutually unintelligible languages is "ridiculous," he said. "Solomon Islanders are proud of the differences," he declared. "At the same time, they want to feel proud of their country."

As chairman of a committee on local government in the old Governing Council, the predecessor of the Legislative Assembly, young Mamaloni had drawn up a statement of official policy toward customs and traditions (later adopted) that could serve as a model for other island governments with the same problem. The keynote was respect for established customs and traditional systems of leadership in the process of introducing changes needed for the development of the country. "All of us have felt at some time a sense of loss, insult, or sadness when the government, or some foreign influence, has struck a blow at our traditional ways through ignorance, thoughtlessness, or a deliberate attempt to change something old and trusted into something new and glittering," he said.

The determination to respect the cultural identity of the Solomons was set forth in a paragraph on religion. While praising the contribution of the Christian churches to advancement in the islands, the passage also affirmed "the right of pagans to follow their religions and religious practices" as well. The statement was supported by a New Zealand Anglican missionary, the Reverend Peter Thompson, the only white member of the legislative body, who cited church condemnation of the custom of paying a "bride price" as an example of unwise interference that had caused "great distress to the people" on Malaita. "Solomon Islanders do not want to develop into white black men," said Ashley Wickham, a mixed-blood member from Honiara. (His great-uncle, Alec Wickham, is said to have made sports history when, as a dental student in Australia, he introduced a stroke known as the "Roviana crawl," used by swimmers in the Roviana lagoon of New Georgia Island, which then became the "Australian crawl" and was adopted around the world for free-style swimming.)

Traditional attitudes played an operative role in politics. For instance, the fact that Chief Minister Mamaloni and the leader of the opposition, Benedict Kinika, were both from Makira made it impossible for Kinika to continue in a post that would automatically bring him into public contention with his fellow islander, thereby giving rise to feuds and unrest at home. Kinika resigned and the job went to another member of the opposition party, Philip Solodia Funifaka, the Marching Rule admirer from Malaita. Tom Russell, a veteran British administrator, remarked on the problem legislators had in being kept from their constituencies by their time-consuming duties in Honiara, which seriously damaged their prospects of being re-elected. "We're counting on the Melanesian concept of loyalty to 'big men' to make up for the loss of personal contact," he said.

The administration thought it had found a way to blend the traditional concept of government by consensus—"the Pacific way"—with British parliamentary forms in the Solomons. Each department of the government was placed under a committee of legislators. The chairman, also a legislator, functioned as a minister in carrying out his committee's policy decisions, but only after these had been endorsed by the entire legislature. Everybody was on at least one committee, and everybody had a chance to vote on the recommendations of all the committees. Each committee had a majority of elected members that could overrule the British officials participating. Each chairman had a British expert as adviser, but his advice was not binding and was sometimes rejected. The complete involvement inherent in this system was supposed to keep everybody happy—or all the Melanesian members, anyway—and perhaps it did. But it did not work.

"Too cumbersome," a British official explained when I returned to Honiara to see how government by committee was faring, only to find that it had been abandoned. "Couldn't get anything done, you know. Works all right in a Melanesian setting, but not in combination with Westminster," he said.

The experiment had served a purpose of historic importance, however, as an indoctrination in government for the Melanesian participants. The involvement allowed latent talents to surface and created a pool of experienced men from whom future cabinets would be drawn. "The chairmen were an extraordinary bunch of men, very impressive in committee," said Tom Russell, who after more than twenty-five years in the Solomons later would be transferred to the Cayman Islands to govern a colony peopled by blacks of a different race.

The political achievement in the Solomons deserved more publicity than it got. Considered against the historical background of the islands, the progress was remarkable. The time between the inauguration of virtual self-government after the demise of the committee system, though the British were nominally in charge, and the agreement in London on a timetable for independence in 1977 was only five years. This was a rapid maturing for a country so sparsely developed that the chairman in charge of public works, Gordon Siama of Choiseul, came from an island that had no roads—only an airfield.

Gordon Siama was typical of the young new leaders of an emerging Pacific island country. He came from an island with only eight thousand people on it, but they spoke eight different dialects, and he could remember when people from different villages fought each other on sight. In his air-conditioned office in the Secretariat Building, crisply disposing of telephone calls at a businesslike desk with in-out baskets, he was all efficiency. Off duty, he changed from trousers and shirt to a flowered *laplap*.

Like Chief Minister Mamaloni and other leading politicians, Siama was a product of mission schools. As in other island territories, there was a movement to transfer the control of education from the churches to the government, not in opposition to religion but for the sake of uniformity in administration. The missions, lacking funds to meet the rising demand for more and more schools, were glad to cooperate.

At that time, about half of the Solomonese children of school age were in classes (according to the 1970 census, 45 percent of the population was under fifteen years of age). The paucity of higher education impeded political awareness. "We have only three university graduates in the whole population," said Francis Bugotu, a senior official of the education department. But the number would increase rapidly; more than sixty Solomonese students were attending the universities in Fiji and Papua New Guinea, and the government hoped to be sending double that number in future years.

The Solomons, though the least advanced of the major South Pacific territories, played the most progressive role of all in efforts to reconcile the needs of a modern state with traditional concepts. Guidelines for foreign investment policy and land use were made the subjects of long-range studies. A committee, on which Mamaloni served until his governmental duties became too demanding, undertook a broad review of educational policy in the light of local needs. "I have a feeling that we are losing a battle which most of us don't even realize is going on," Mamaloni, then the chairman of the legislative committee on local government, told the legislators. "Here in this air-conditioned house, with our strange clothes, you would never know it," he added, "but it is so."

Leaders throughout the South Pacific were deeply concerned with the contribution of the schools to the erosion of the indigenous society. For convenience, pupils from widely scattered villages were brought to boarding schools far from their homes. The curricula had little, if anything, to do with the realities of village life. Teaching was entirely in English, which led to the decline of the local languages and all that they meant in preserving traditional culture. Returning home, the youngsters found themselves alienated from their families and surroundings; they had been trained for a different kind of life, which existed only in the towns.

The education review committee in the Solomons went about its assignment with astonishing energy. In a few months the group traveled more than 4,500 miles, mostly by boat, to 93 locations throughout the islands and talked to more than 8,000 persons—11 percent of the entire adult population, more than the most scientific opinion poll would cover. The members found overwhelming dissatisfaction with the schools, and a vocal demand for changes.

In its report, the committee recommended an entirely new approach to education, designed to equip youngsters for life in the village as well as the town, instead of merely preparing them for higher schooling. Specific proposals included kindergartens in villages, with specially trained teachers, and abolition of boarding schools except where there was no alternative. The local language—or Pidgin, if necessary—would be the medium of instruction in the first three years, during which English would be taught; after that, English would be the medium. The elaborate King George VI High School, nicknamed the "Honiara Hilton," which tended to separate its students from the rest of the population because of its higher standards, would be changed to a preparatory school for teachers and university entrants.

Early doubts of the political maturity of the Solomonese leaders were dissolved in the proceedings of the legislature, where the behavior of the Melanesian members belied the colonial image of an irresolute people relying on expatriate advisers. Nor did the predicted fractiousness materialize from the incompatibility of the disparate social systems on various islands, such as the patriarchal order on Malaita compared to the matriarchy prevailing in the villages of Guadalcanal. "The ability to handle independence usually comes when you get it," said Francis Bugotu, the education officer.

Responsible leadership at the top often failed, however, to percolate down through the ordinary population. "Land and women are the basis of life here, and everyone wants them," Mamaloni told a visiting newsman. "The Solomons has to make itself a much more unified nation. Politically, we have been under an umbrella. We have had a slow rate of economic growth, but we need economic development for true independence."

The Mamaloni government quietly dropped the words "British" and "Protectorate" from the name of the territory, which then became just "The Solomon Islands." Full internal self-government came inauspiciously on 2 January 1976, with tear gas instead of trumpets when police tried to prevent a striking labor union from marching along Mendana Avenue in defiance of a ban on demonstrations. In the ensuing melee, shop windows were broken. The marchers were said to have been confused over the reason for the turnout, some believing they were marching for higher wages, while others thought they were protesting against self-government.

The incident was followed by second thoughts among the Solomonese leaders on early independence. Britain had proposed that full sovereignty be conferred upon the islands around the middle of 1977. A new government elected in the summer of 1976, with a thirty-three-year-old district official and former school teacher named Peter Kenilorea replacing Mamaloni as chief minister, asked London to postpone the step at least until 1978 to allow time for a campaign to educate village-dwellers on all the islands in the exercise of self-rule. Unless the meaning of independence was understood by all the people, a member of the legislature said, sovereign status would have real meaning only in towns like Honiara.

FOUR

Pacific Pandemonium

$\mathscr{S}$ OUTH Pacific punsters have long referred to the British-French Condominium of the New Hebrides as the "pandemonium." The old joke reflects a standard view of the many conflicts and overlaps built into the joint rule of these eighty-odd flamboyant, underdeveloped islands by colonial bureaucracies of London and Paris acting in tandem.

A group of towering volcanic formations, the New Hebrides archipelago forms a huge, lopsided "Y," 450 miles long, in the sun-heated waters southeast of the Solomons, between Fiji and New Caledonia. The exotic human mix on this hot, humid, and beautiful scene inspired Michener's classic *Tales of the South Pacific* when the author was an obscure World War II naval officer in the area. Residents accept that Aoba island in the New Hebrides was the model for Michener's Bali Ha'i.

Most of the nonofficial foreigners, planters, and businessmen whom I met on several reporting trips through these jungled islands assured me that the average brown-skinned Melanesian villager was oblivious to politics. Independence, they said, was hardly an issue except among a limited circle of educated protagonists in the towns, of which there were only two. An exception was a young French resident journalist, Jean-Eudes Barbier. "When anyone says that the villagers are without politics, it means that he has no contact with Melanesians," he said. Every Melanesian I met agreed with Jean-Eudes, who was to be proved right by subsequent events.

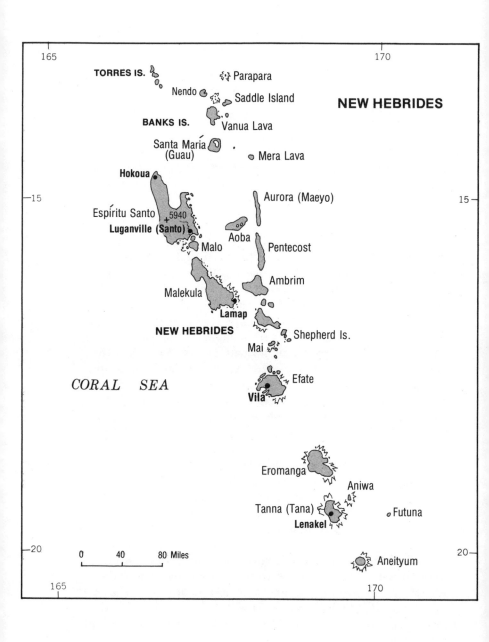

165   170

TORRES IS.

           Parapara

Nendo

       Saddle Island

NEW HEBRIDES

BANKS IS.

     Vanua Lava

Santa María
(Guau)

     Mera Lava

Hokoua

—15   Aurora (Maeyo)   15—

Espíritu Santo   +5940

Luganville (Santo)

     Aoba

   Malo

     Pentecost

     Ambrim

Malekula

Lamap

NEW HEBRIDES

     Shepherd Is.

Mai

     Efate

CORAL SEA

Vila

Eromanga

     Aniwa

Tanna (Tana)

Lenakel   Futuna

—20   20—

0   40   80 Miles

                                         Aneityum

165   170

"Melanesians are a shy people, and tend to tell whites what they think they want to hear," said Kalpakor Kalsakau, a Melanesian employed by the British branch of the dual administration and a leading member of the fledgling New Hebrides National Party, the pioneer political organization in the archipelago. So it was not strange, he said, that many white residents remained wholly unaware of the true Melanesian political views.

The British and French officials, being experienced and competent professionals, were fully sensitive to the political currents swirling around them. As often happened, however, in the dual administration of the condominium, the two partners in the tandem government operated at cross purposes politically. The British, who yearned above all to be out of the onerous and expensive business of running overseas territories, encouraged the acceleration of political maturity. The French, wishing to hold onto their Pacific connections for national aggrandizement and profit, applied brakes to forward political movement until a late stage. In contrast to the turgid flow of events at the official level, political awareness among the people set its own pace.

The government of the New Hebrides is correctly described as the only functioning condominium in the world, although Britain and the United States have an agreement for the joint administration of two tiny islands, Canton and Enderbury, in the Phoenix group. The difference is that the British-American arrangement does not actually function, for the United States runs Canton exclusively for military purposes and Enderbury, apparently useless, is deserted. The curious situation in the New Hebrides originated in bloodshed and intrigue during a lurid period in Pacific history. The two ruling powers entered the islands with reluctance, their main interest being to keep a third power out.

The history of the New Hebrides is similar to that of the Solomons. The explorer Pedro Fernandes de Quiros discovered the largest island, and called it Espíritu Santo, in 1606. An early Spanish colony was abandoned after discouraging experiences with malaria and hostile natives. The next known European contact was by the French navigator Louis Antoine de Bougainville in 1768. It remained for Cook to name the chain New Hebrides a few years later.

All of the early Western intrusions had violent consequences. The establishment of the sandalwood trade in 1825 by an Irish seaman named Peter Dillon began an era of bloody clashes be-

tween the unwanted whites and resentful Melanesians. The first
two missionaries in the New Hebrides were murdered by tribesmen the day after they landed on Eromanga in 1839. Later missionaries were slaughtered following an outbreak of measles,
which the islanders rightly blamed on contacts with white men.
After the demise of the sandalwood traffic when there were no
more of the valuable trees left, the notorious blackbirders arrived
and enticed away thousands of young men, many of whom never
returned. Those who did return often brought back Western
diseases that decimated the population.

Meanwhile, British and French planters bought up vast tracts
of land—"for a few axes, bolts of calico, and bottles of gin,"
according to an Australian expert on the Pacific, Robert Langdon
—and began the important copra industry. The land grabs also
laid the foundation of political unrest in a later generation. Planters urged France to annex the chain, but Paris demurred. There
was another movement, organized by Presbyterian missionaries
and based in Australia, for annexation by Britain.

After years of consultations and temporizing, Britain and
France formed a Joint Naval Commission to keep order in the
untamed islands. The members of the commission consisted of
two British and two French officers from naval vessels of the two
powers in Western Pacific areas, with the chairmanship alternating between the two nationalities. The absence of a joint code
of laws, however, made the arrangement ineffective. The New
Hebrides remained a collection of independent tribal areas ruled
by their respective Melanesian chiefs, until Germany showed an
interest in the chain.

To keep the Germans out, Britain and France came to terms
on a joint civil administration in the islands. The condominium
was established by an agreement signed in 1906, which stipulated
that the New Hebrides would remain "a region of joint influence,
in which the subjects of the two signatory powers shall enjoy
equal rights of residence, personal protection and trade. . . ."
Disputes were to be adjudicated by a joint court, with a neutral
president appointed by the king of Spain (the position has been
vacant for many years, as was the Spanish throne during the
Franco dictatorship).

The arrangement evolved into a three-pronged government—a French administration for some 3,500 French nationals,
a British one for about 1,500 Britons or Commonwealth citizens,
and a jointly administered condominium government for the

80,000 New Hebrideans. In the condominium establishment, each department was headed by either a Briton or a Frenchman, and by convention a department chief of one nationality would have a deputy of the other. "French law is enforced by gendarmes and British law by constables, but either one can arrest a Melanesian," a sardonic Australian resident observed.

The British resident commissioner headed the British government, the French resident commissioner the twin French establishment; the two men functioned together, with equal status and powers, at the head of the condominium administration. Everything was dual. French and English were official languages for all functions, so postage stamps read "New Hebrides" and "Nouvelles Hebrides," the post office was also a *bureau de poste,* and every place name had English and French versions; for the French, the capital was Port Vila on Vate island, while the British called it Vila, Efate. To communicate with the bulk of the village New Hebrideans, who speak dozens of languages, both sides used New Hebrides Pidgin, an English-French hybrid that produced such forms as the imperative *allez-go.*

Two currencies were in daily use, a special New Hebrides franc for the French and the Australian dollar for the British. For the British civil servant paid in dollars and his French counterpart paid in francs, the duality was meaningless as long as the currencies remained interchangeable, with a fixed exchange rate of 100 francs to one Australian dollar. One purchased Scotch whiskey at the Burns Philp store, bought French wine at Magasin Alice, and shopped for souvenirs at Shu Hing's, paying either in 100-franc notes or dollar bills, or a mixture of the two, and getting change in both currencies. This insouciance ended when international exchange rates fell into disarray, and francs and cents were no longer one-to-one. Life became more complicated for people with an income in one currency and charge accounts at shops that operated in the other. "You never know what you're paying for anything bought on credit, since accounts are calculated at the rate of exchange on the day the bill is made out at the store," a British matron explained. Meanwhile, inflation brought the untimely demise of the fifty-cent crêpe suzette at Hotel Rossi, a waterfront establishment whose terrace restaurant was one of the pleasanter memories of Vila.

New French residents automatically came under the French legal system, while Commonwealth citizens were subject to British law. Nationals of other countries taking up residence in the

New Hebrides were required to opt for one system or the other. Most chose to "live French," I was told, because of a more permissive attitude in the French Residency on matters concerning immigration and business. The Melanesian population came under condominium law. This was enforced by the New Hebrides Constabulary, which was divided into British and French sections. British and French agents took turns presiding over the Native Courts, for Melanesians.

Under the agreement between Britain and France, the indigenous Melanesians were specifically excluded from acquiring citizenship under either of the powers and thus were people without a country in their own land. They traveled abroad with a document resembling a passport but containing the arms of Britain and France and the signatures of both resident commissioners. Juridically, the New Hebrides were a country in which there was no such thing as territorial sovereignty.

Nature cooperated with the condominium concept by providing two pleasant knolls of equal height behind Vila, a tacky little town that spills along the shore for several miles. By establishing themselves separately on these hills, the British and French maintain equal identity, with neither headquarters at a higher elevation than the other, although the French site offers a superior view of the town and harbor, where ships and yachts ride on waters of multiple shades of green and blue. The construction of the headquarters buildings of the two administrations seemed to reflect their different philosophies of government in the New Hebrides. The British occupied temporary-looking wooden structures, with unglassed windows for cross ventilation and storm shutters propped open with sticks. A grassy parade ground, a towering flag pole for the Union Jack, and the stately colonial architecture of the cottagelike building housing the resident commissioner's office exhibited the majesty of empire in low key. The French, on their separate hill, were ensconced in a somewhat grander building, comfortably air-conditioned, to which they were adding a two-story concrete annex the last time I was in Vila. The resident commissioner at the time, a professional with much experience in former French African colonies named Robert Langlois, acknowledged with a smile that the new construction might indicate French expectations of being in the islands for a considerable time to come.

Appropriately, under the circumstances, the joint condominium government with its complement of British and

French officers in equal numbers, and Melanesian staff, was quartered on the steaming flat along the waterfront on Rue Higginson, the main street named after an early British land-grabber. This branch operated the general services, such as the postal system, communications, and public works. Routine functions were carried on efficiently enough, I was told, but important decisions required the concurrence of the two resident commissioners, and really big questions might have to be referred to London and Paris. Under these conditions, inaction was built into the system. An example was the impasse over a Japanese proposal to build a second fish processing plant. The French wanted it, but the British balked on the advice of their experts on the region's marine resources, who disagreed with the French experts.

My first visit to Vila in 1970 coincided with the official opening of an Australia New Zealand Bank branch, the first to break the monopoly long held by the Banque de l'Indochine. Soon half a dozen banks were operating along Rue Higginson, and lawyers, accountants, and general business agents filled the condominium's first multistory, air-conditioned office building. The reason for the sudden expansion was the rush of business registrations in the New Hebrides to take advantage of the absence of taxes on individual and corporation income. The growing fame of Vila as a tax haven attracted many companies away from the taxless islands in the Caribbean as disturbing political changes overtook that area. American investment companies in Vila conveyed an impression, in their advertising brochures, that social unrest in the New Hebrides was unlikely in the foreseeable future. This was an assessment with which I could not agree unequivocally.

The sudden American interest in what had been mostly a French plantation community quickly changed the ambience of Vila, a town that had been known throughout the South Pacific for its Gallic flavor. American-style subdivisions and apartment buildings sprouted on the lush landscape. Busloads of American tourists appeared at Le Lagon, a suburban resort complex in which the Tokyu hotel chain of Japan had acquired a sizable equity. There were traffic jams on Rue Higginson, and a general air of bustle began to replace the old tropical languor. These developments were welcomed by the French administration, possibly because French nationals would benefit most from expansion. The British, who had never become so well entrenched commercially as the French, grumbled that the place was in danger of "being over-run by the Americans," and kept strict curbs on the granting of residence permits to newcomers. "We don't intend to impose a multiracial culture on the New Hebrideans," said a British official, adding that the British considered themselves "trustees for the New Hebrideans until they can decide their own political future."

Educated young New Hebrideans to whom I talked in the islands felt a cultural dichotomy. A majority of the village children attended the British schools and learned to speak English, a holdover from early missionary days when Presbyterians from Britain got in first with a vigorous education policy, supported later by the British government. There were also, however, a substantial number of youngsters in the French-language government and missionary schools. Consequently, said my New Hebridean friends, a language barrier was appearing in the rising young educated generation that promised complications in a future self-governing New Hebridean society.

Political views were aired by local people at sunset in the cool, open-air bar of the Hotel Rossi, a favorite rendezvous overlooking the picturesque welter of small islands and sailing yachts in the broad harbor. There I met two articulate young New Hebrideans who worked for the British administration on Efate and Tanna, and were rising stars in the budding nationalist movement. Both were members of the Advisory Council, a quasi-legislative body over which the two resident commissioners presided in turn. The eight Melanesian members were elected by local government councils; three British and three French representatives were chosen by the Vila Chamber of Commerce, and the rest of the thirty members were nominated by the resident commissioners. This body debated legislative and budgetary matters, but its powers were only what the resident commissioners chose to give it. It did have what amounted to a veto, however, since the French and British authorities avoided taking actions to which the council was known to be strongly opposed. *Pacific Islands Monthly* referred to the system as "the last bastion of the colonial Pacific."

"We New Hebrideans look forward to having our own government," said twenty-five-year-old Iolu Abbil, a senior inspector of cooperatives and representative from Tanna island on the Advisory Council. "It is difficult to say what form self-government would take, but most people are talking about independence. Meanwhile, we should have more say in our own affairs." His friend George Kalkoa, a thirty-three-year-old assistant administrative officer in the British service, was troubled by the divisiveness in the dual government. For example, he said, the British and French schools taught "not only different languages but different philosophies and ideologies" to the younger generation of New Hebrideans. He feared that the result, among the new educated class, would be the psychological disarrangement known as "split personality."

"The British are training the New Hebrideans to take on more responsibilities in the administration, but the French seem to concentrate on bringing up our children as little brown Frenchmen," he said. Using himself and a counterpart in the French establishment as examples illustrating the different approaches, he added: "I can sign papers in my boss's absence, but my colleague in the French service can't."

Several years later, I watched with profound sympathy as condominium protocol's requirements put George through moral agonies at a meeting of the South Pacific Conference in a lavish Hilton Hotel on Guam. Like all the English-speaking delegates, George wished passionately to vote in favor of a formal protest by the conference to the secretary general of the United Nations against the French nuclear tests at Mururoa Atoll, a perennial target at these meetings. The delegates from the French islands and the French half of the condominium administration, well indoctrinated by their mentors from Paris, made themselves absent while the vote was taken. George, unable to vote in the absence of his French associate in the two-headed New Hebrides delegation, was a stricken man as he announced his abstention. The protest passed.

Political stirrings in the New Hebrides went back to the appearance of the strange and once powerful cargo cult, known as the John Frum Movement, around 1940 on the island of Tanna. On a visit to Tana I found that the cult remained widespread and active, although political leadership had passed to other hands and adherents were divided among three branches of the original grouping. I encountered the distinctive emblem of one branch, a crude wooden cross painted red, on walks along the beaches and jungle trails. The crosses denote the belief that the original John Frum, thought by this branch to have been a sergeant in the U.S. Army Medical Corps stationed on the island in wartime, will return one day with planeloads of cargo for all.

John Frum was the classic Messiah figure in cargo cults.

Whether he was really an American soldier, if he existed at all, may never be known. But somewhere there is a former G.I., possibly dead, whose field jacket with a sergeant's stripes and the red cross of the U.S. Army Medical Corps on the sleeve is a sacred object on Tanna, displayed by the John Frum cult on special occasions. John Frum is described as a small, light-haired man with a high voice, wearing boots and a solar topee or sun helmet—not unusual wartime gear for American servicemen in the Pacific. In another version of the story he wore a hat that was half white and half red, which might describe one of the baseball caps commonly worn by the Americans. Some say that the name is a reversal of "from John," and refers to John the Baptist; but Sam Tocuma, a middle-aged cultist I met on Tanna, had a different explanation.

Sam, a lightly built man in a blue-and-white striped shirt and tan shorts, was the chief of three villages and a former teacher in a Presbyterian mission school. He said that his father had been one of the first chiefs on Tanna to make contact with the mysterious white man. Sam referred to the Messiah simply as "John." The name Frum, he said, is a common corruption of "broom," and came from John's order to the villagers to sweep their houses every day, a command that is still faithfully carried out by the cultists.

"John sat between my father and another chief, shook hands, and said he would lead our people out of the wilderness, like the children of Israel, to the promised land flowing with milk and honey," he related. "The Presbyterians had stopped the people from dancing and kava drinking, forbade idols and made circumcision tabu. John said God had only ten commandments, but the missionaries put in more. He said they lied to us, so we should let them take our school away. So we drank kava and left school."

"John commanded us not to steal or swear, to observe the Ten Commandments, do good works, and follow only what the Bible says," Sam continued. "He told us to look toward the sea, and by and by the things would come. He promised us planes and trucks, and said he would be coming back some time, but he didn't promise when. Then the war began, and everything in the stores was finished. And then the Americans came, and gave us clothes to wear. I could believe John then. He was right."

According to another version, John Frum appeared to the villagers only at night. Some authorities surmise that he originated in a dream, or vision, and was given a material identity later. For him to become an American soldier at a later stage was a logical development after the New Hebrides became an important logistics base on the route to Guadalcanal and other South Pacific battle areas. At that time, I was told, the United States forces gave employment to virtually every able-bodied male New Hebridean who wanted work, and the generosity of the troops was legendary. The dazzled cultists proclaimed that John Frum was really "King of America" and that the promised cargo was coming from the United States. An American officer was taken on a tour of Tana to assure the villagers that the United States had never heard of John Frum, but he was not believed.

Sam said he had helped to clear two landing areas for John Frum's plane. Bamboo sheds were constructed for the expected treasure. As time went by, it was assumed that the Messiah was waiting for a message from the island, so a large imitation radio was built, with a rope aerial and tin-can earphones, in an attempt to make contact. There was still no word nor sign from John, but his thousands of followers were steadfast in their faith that he would eventually return with cargo.

After the war, when all the Americans had left, the cult split into three major factions in different areas of the island. One group still holds Friday night musical gatherings, with what an Australian resident called "a poor imitation of Western dancing" and the singing of the latest American popular songs learned from records.

Another group formed what it called the "Tanna Army," with American-style khaki uniforms with "Tanna-U.S.A." embroidered on the shirts, and drilled with wooden rifles. At this point an alarmed administration ordered wholesale arrests, and white residents carried pistols for protection.

The militant phase passed, and with it the government's attempts to suppress the movement, and the cult continued to flourish. Sam Tocuma returned to the Presbyterian church and became an elder, but remained a follower of John Frum, like many other churchgoers on the island. "They go to church on Sunday and venerate John Frum all week," said the Australian, a widely known planter and entrepreneur named Bob Paul. I asked Sam if he really believed, after so many years, that John Frum would return to Tanna. Sam smiled gently and answered in a soft voice, "People have waited two thousand years for Christ—we can wait a few more years for John."

A more sophisticated movement called Nagriamel, with some

cultish aspects but mainly devoted to agitation for land reform, appeared on Espíritu Santo about the middle of the 1960s and spread throughout the islands. Led by a charismatic personality named Jimmy Stevens, whose followers gave him the title of Chief President Moses in the belief that he—like John Frum— would lead them out of the wilderness, the organization was the nearest approximation of a political party for some years.

Jimmy Stevens was one of those people, found all over the world, who are destined to be venerated by some and denounced as a charlatan by others. He was a guru and an organizer, respected for his ideals and at the same time criticized for high living. His personal background was extraordinary: he had a white grandfather, an English seaman and trader who married a relative of the royal family of Tonga, and one of the half-English, half-Tongan sons of this union married a New Hebridean and produced Jimmy.

When I met Jimmy by appointment one afternoon in the open-air lounge of the Hotel Rossi in Vila, he was a well-built man of about forty-five, dressed in white shirt and slacks. A young wife held a small baby on her lap. Jimmy's light tan complexion and long, patriarchal beard, shot with gray, distinguished him from the dark-skinned, usually clean-shaven Melanesians in his following, which at that time was said to number about ten thousand, mostly in the northern part of the chain.

Jimmy preferred to converse in Pidgin, his mother tongue, although he could also speak English. He had little formal education, but had learned several skills while working for the American forces on Espíritu Santo, and had been at various times a bulldozer operator, master of a Burns Philp trading vessel, Roman Catholic church caretaker, and vegetable gardener. His travels to Fiji, New Caledonia, and Australia had given him sufficient knowledge of the world to impress his influential but untutored Melanesian associates. He had once been jailed briefly for having fleeced some followers out of a sum of money, but he had not been incarcerated long before the same people who had laid the complaint were petitioning the government for his release. He was unquestionably a hero to thousands of New Hebrideans.

The Nagriamel movement led by Jimmy stressed the resumption by villagers of ownership of unused land, cooperative development of these plots, and a return to customary ways. The name of the organization was taken from the New Hebridean words for two plants whose leaves figure in village ceremonies and customs—the *nagria*, a variety of croton, and the *mel*, or cycad palm. The plants, pictured on the Nagriamel flag, also symbolize the universal male-female, death-and-renewal principle, Jimmy said.

Land resumption was a powerful issue in the New Hebrides. A British official told me that few New Hebrideans, accustomed to regarding all undeveloped jungle tracts as communal property, had been aware of the vast extent of the foreign land holdings until 1959. In that year, he said, a disastrous hurricane had crippled the copra industry, the mainstay of the economy. The French coconut planters thereupon turned to cattle-raising to recoup, and began to open previously unused areas for grazing. A group of about twenty chiefs in the bush villages of Espíritu Santo, startled to find the French encroaching upon land that they had considered clan property, organized to resist.

Stevens and a number of cohorts, taking up the land issue in the name of Nagriamel, quietly occupied a large tract of vacant land owned by the French company Société Française des Nouvelles Hebrides—better known by the initials S.F.N.H.—at Vanafo, about fifteen miles north of Luganville, the administrative headquarters on Espíritu Santo and the only other settlement besides Vila that is classified as a town. There Stevens directed the development of a model agricultural community with neat garden plots and houses grouped around a large, open square with a huge banyan tree and a tall flagpole flying the banner of Nagriamel.

S.F.N.H., on the advice of the French administration, decided to ignore the takeover of the Vanafo property. The company, which had acquired the enormous holdings of the pioneer British entrepreneur John Higginson around the turn of the century, and thus became by far the largest landowner, later transferred the bulk of its undeveloped tracts, amounting to thousands of acres, to the French authorities for redistribution to New Hebrideans. As Nagriamel agents planted the organization's signs on other properties around the island, however, smaller owners brought trespass charges and the courts handed out a few mild jail sentences to Stevens and others.

Unconcerned by official actions, Stevens and his associates made Vanafo into such a showplace that a reception center for visitors was established by the central square. Volunteers came to work on the gardens for varying periods, after which they returned to their home villages to spread the doctrine of Nagriamel. New permanent settlers were allotted living quarters and garden space. There was a calendar of periodic community feasts, one of which included the annual election of a "Miss Nagriamel." Peanuts were planted as a major cash crop, and as funds piled up Vanafo became a going business with an Indian legal representative in Fiji who, among other services, drew up a petition to the United Nations asking for "an act of free choice," under international supervision, on the question of independence for the New Hebrides.

The activities of Nagriamel, and the coincidental appearance on the scene of a real estate developer from Hawaii with elaborate plans for an American-style subdivision in a sequestered beach area, gave Espíritu Santo more prominence than that island had known since World War II, when the place was a key base for a time with the code name "Buttons."

The town of Luganville is mistakenly called Santo, after the name of the island, more often than not. The normally somnolent marketing center was a teeming place during the war, with more than fifty-five thousand American servicemen present at a time, and a resident told of having once counted 120 ships in the beautiful harbor. On their departure after the end of the war, the Americans regretfully dumped millions of dollars' worth of vehicles and other equipment, much of it still in the original crates from the factory in the United States, into the Segond Channel, a narrow belt of water between Luganville and tiny Aore island. The administration had declined an offer to sell the material at fire-sale prices; nor would the colonial government have the stuff left with the New Hebrideans, on the ground that the sudden affluence would "upset the local economy." On the other hand, it made poor economic sense to the Americans to take shiploads of war equipment all the way back to the United States. So into the sea it went, paving the bottom of Segond Channel with jeeps and trucks. A landspit opposite this graveyard of untold wealth is still known as Million-Dollar Point.

As on many South Pacific islands, traces of the war abound. The principal hotel at the time, the twenty-two-room Corsica (since burned down), was remodeled from a pair of Quonset huts. Broad rectangles of concrete where other Quonsets had stood were being used as basketball courts and playgrounds. I shopped nostalgically in a general store owned by a woman who was widely believed to have been the prototype of Michener's character, Bloody Mary, in his *Tales of the South Pacific* (a distinction also attributed to at least two other women whom I have known elsewhere in the South Pacific). Driving across the island on a road built by the Seabees, neglected and crumbling but still serviceable, one passed numerous abandoned small airstrips that had once played a brief and soon forgotten role in South Pacific history, and were being reclaimed by the jungle.

In spite of the political stirrings, Espíritu Santo dozed in a lovely tropical lassitude. "We don't see two hundred genuine tourists in a year," said Alen Brown, the Australian manager of the Hotel Corsica. "This is the way we like it, so we can stay the way we are," he added. Although there would be one or two new hotels in Luganville soon, Espíritu Santo would probably be spared a tourist inundation. I drove thirty miles to the American real estate development at Lokalee—formerly called, less romantically, Hog Harbor—and found a jewel of a hotel in a grove of palms overlooking two smooth, white beaches lapped by warm surf, a view of offshore islands, and an occasional whale spouting in the varicolored water. At the time, I was the only guest.

The one tourist attraction in the New Hebrides that is known everywhere is the amazing annual land-diving ritual on Pentecost, an island at the northeastern extremity of the chain (the French pronounce it "pont-coat"). In a ceremony associated with the yam harvest, young men dive headlong from a platform at the top of an eighty-foot tower of tree trunks lashed together with vines. Vines attached to their ankles halt the plunge just in time to stop the divers from crashing into the earth and almost certain death. The custom, considered a proof of courage, is said to have originated in the legend of a young couple who jumped from the top of a palm tree to commit suicide; the girl, so the story goes, was saved because she had thoughtfully bound her ankle to the tip of a coconut frond, which broke her fall. The performance, which takes place at a time when the strength of the vines and various omens are considered just right, is supposed to insure that the yams planted in that season will produce a good crop. The spectacle has been seen around the world in South Pacific travel films and television programs.

It is said that injuries have been all but unknown in the Pentecost land dive. A demonstration for Queen Elizabeth II and her party, however, during a royal tour of the South Pacific in February 1974, was held out of season and went tragically wrong. One young diver's restraining vines broke when they took his weight, and he smashed into the ground. The youth, named John Tabi, suffered spinal injuries that resulted in his death two days later.

An investigation by a local British official determined that the vines selected for Tabi had been of insufficient strength because of a misjudgment by the New Hebridean supervisors of the event.

The villagers had more elaborate explanations that illustrated the tenor of traditionalist thought in the remoter areas of the chain. According to these views, the ceremony was held on ground that had been rendered tabu by a death in the area many years before. One of the intending divers, who withdrew because of an ailing knee, violated another tabu by neglecting to dismantle the tower he had built for his jump. Finally, the villagers said, Tabi had broken still another tabu by using the abandoned tower instead of building his own, as required by custom.

According to less imaginative accounts, Tabi's real mistake had been in using the vines prepared for the other man, who was of lighter build. And, perhaps out of consideration for the queen's feelings, the villagers chose not to inform the British investigator that vines cut in February, instead of in the usual diving season between September and November, have a higher moisture content and break more easily. Tabi's fate was not a surprise; members of his family wept as he climbed the platform, although he had performed the dive successfully twice before.

The British queen's visit provided the occasion for a show of political spirit new to the condominium till then. On her arrival in Vila, banners appeared saying: "You are not *our* Queen—We are stateless—We are unprotected—We are fed up." As the British community cheered when she and her party landed on Espíritu Santo, Jimmy Stevens and his followers watched in utter silence. The feeling among the New Hebrideans generally was one of curiosity rather than warmth. In the aftermath, nearly a year later, two young independence agitators strode into a British private club in Vila and were refused service at the bar. One of the youths then ripped the queen's picture from the wall and hit a British policeman with it. The young man, a student at the University of Papua New Guinea, received two weeks in jail for assault.

Christian missionaries spearheaded the movement for self-government and eventual independence. The role of the churches emerged publicly in 1971 with the formation of the National Party, the first modern political organization in the condominium, under the leadership of a Melanesian cleric of the Anglican faith, the Reverend Walter Lini. The Reverend Gerard Leymang, a Roman Catholic priest and a Melanesian elected

Robert Trumbull/*New York Times*

fic on Boulevard Pomare, main street of Papeete, Tahiti, in 1969

Robert Trumbull/*New York Times*

ists at an ancient *marae* (temple ruins) on Moorea, French Polynesia, an important archeological
evealing part of Polynesia's past

Robert Trumbull/*New York Times*

A road on Tahiti is a tunnel through the trees

Robert Trumbull/*New York*

The Government Buildings at Suva, Fiji, reflect the colonial past

member of the Advisory Council, consistently championed New Hebridean causes in that body and once publicly branded the British-French covenant governing the condominium as a document that "oozes from every pore the stench of an antiquated colonial policy." And in 1973 the General Assembly of the Presbyterian church, which claimed the allegiance of more than half the population, formally asked the United Nations to assist in preparations for independence (the appeal was fruitless, but made good propaganda).

"Independence is not the only solution," the French resident commissioner, Robert Langlois, told me in a conversation in his spacious office. "There may be other forms," he said, adding that the French were "well aware that more and more people want political progress." Wherever people talked politics in the South Pacific, it had long been assumed that the French outlook was conditioned by the convenience of the New Hebrides as a permanent labor pool for the huge, French-owned nickel mines on the nearby island of New Caledonia, another "overseas territory" of France. The strong, wiry Melanesians were good workers, though inclined to take life lightly in the delicious island way. The high wages paid by Société le Nickel, the French monopoly, enabled some fifteen hundred New Hebrideans employed in the mines to remit more than half a million dollars a month to their families at home, an official said.

To the surprise of many politically conscious New Hebrideans, as well as the fossilized French and British plantation and business communities, progressive new governments in both London and Paris turned official attitudes in the condominium almost completely around in late 1974. Following a bilateral conference in Paris, it was announced that a legislative assembly would replace the Advisory Council, a single currency would be established, the criminal code would be unified, land reforms would be undertaken, and the two administrations would encourage a steady drift of authority over domestic affairs to the condominium government. Although independence was not mentioned in the announcements, clearly the era of nineteenth century colonialism—and "pandemonium"—in the New Hebrides was being overtaken by the new political currents sweeping the South Pacific. The dream of a sovereign state in the New Hebrides, once considered a fantasy in the minds of a few patriots, rapidly approached reality. A new French resident commissioner in 1976, Robert Gauger, stated publicly that the future of the islands would be "neither French nor British." The two Western powers, he added, would work together in the condominium to "lead it . . . to independence. . . ."

Developments moved rapidly once the new government in France had decided upon a policy of decolonization. New Hebridean political leaders were invited to Paris in July 1977 for talks with Britain and France, after which the two governments issued a joint statement offering internal autonomy to the condominium in 1978, with independence to follow. The ensuing elections brought out a complexity special to these islands mentioned to me earlier by George Kalkoa. Politics tended to polarize around the division between the Melanesians educated in English and those who had been schooled in French, giving the New Hebrides a problem that Canada had failed to solve in more than two centuries of conflict between the English and French linguistic communities.

Thus one more colonial foothold gave way before the determination of a subject people to assert an equal place in the expanding political horizons of the South Pacific. For the New Hebrides, the road ahead would be rough but the goal was in sight.

FIVE

Nickel-plated Paradise

---

*L*IFE proceeds with charming tropical drowsiness in French Oceania. The torpor that normally envelops Nouméa, the capital of New Caledonia, was interrupted by American briskness for a few years during World War II, when the town was headquarters for United States naval operations in the South Pacific theater. Early war correspondents on the scene were astonished to find the easygoing French authorities unwilling to open the one telegraph office on weekends for transmission of news dispatches. Frustrated Americans sometimes asked each other if the main enemy in the area was Japanese or French.

On visits to Nouméa many years later, I found the venerable Hotel Sebastopol—irreverently renamed the Cesspool by the correspondents who made it their headquarters—still flourishing but no longer Number One, having been upstaged by the glittering rank of tourist traps along beautiful Anse Vata beach, Nouméa's Waikiki. But traces of the old languor remained. A typewritten notice glued to my bathroom wall advised that water service was subject to curtailment at times because of some technological emergency. The date on the notice was three years old. I went to the front desk to cable a story to *The New York Times*. It was Friday evening. "The telegraph office is closed till Monday, monsieur," the French clerk murmured. Suddenly I felt an overpowering nostalgia for the war.

When Captain Cook landed on this long, cigar-shaped island between the New Hebrides and Australia, he caused a notice of

89

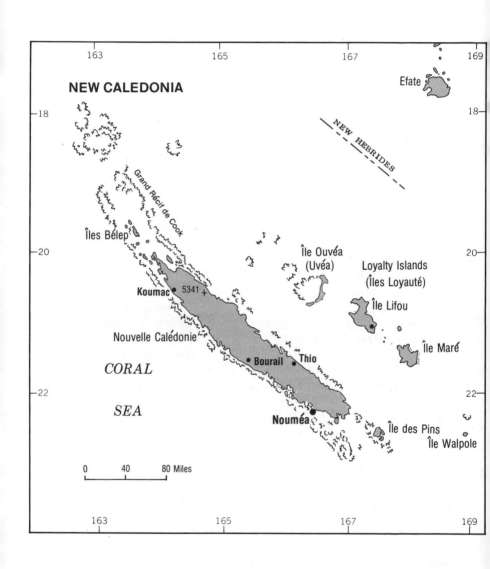

NEW CALEDONIA

163   165   167   169

18   18

NEW HEBRIDES

Efate

Grand Récif de Cook

Îles Bélep

20   20

Île Ouvéa
(Uvéa)

Loyalty Islands
(Îles Loyauté)

Koumac 5341 +

Île Lifou

Nouvelle Calédonie

Île Maré

CORAL

Bourail Thio

22   22

SEA

Nouméa

Île des Pins

Île Walpole

0   40   80 Miles

163   165   167   169

his arrival on 12 September 1774 to be carved into the trunk of a large tree to show that he had been there first and then he formally annexed the place in the name of the British crown. Later he called the island New Caledonia, for reasons that can only be surmised. One theory was that its appearance from the sea reminded him of Scotland (he had been away a long time), another that he was following his habit of naming discoveries after areas of the British Isles—like New Britain, New Ireland, and the New Hebrides in the same South Pacific quadrant. The tree has disappeared, no doubt reclaimed by the rich earth whence it sprang, and the British claim to New Caledonia, never followed up seriously, has become an obscure footnote in the political history of the South Pacific. But the name bestowed by Cook has endured, although the present rulers of the island spell it Nouvelle Calédonie.

Under any name, the native urge for self-determination on this richest of all the South Sea islands has been an endless and sometimes bloody trial for the French overlords. Cook, who seemed to have an innate liking for native peoples and was there-fore liked in return, formed a favorable impression of the indige-nous Melanesians whom he encountered on the northeastern coast of the island. (Cook's testy behavior in Hawaii four and a half years later, which resulted in his death at the hands of the islanders, appears to have been the result of a lapse in his normal understanding of natives.) Later white visitors were received less hospitably.

Missionaries began to appear in 1840, first British Protestants, then Roman Catholics from the Marist order in France, the latter arriving incongruously in a French warship. The discovery of sandalwood on New Caledonia and its smaller appendage, the Isle of Pines, later to become an international vacation resort, brought more whites. White fishing bases and trading posts proliferated along the coasts. With familiarity came an enhanced interest by Britain and France in the strategic value of this large island on the approaches to Australia, which by that time was carrying on a growing trade with Europe.

Many of the newcomers were accorded an unfriendly welcome, however, by the Melanesians, who rightly saw the white incur-sions as a threat to their way of life. A few missionaries were killed and eaten. Relations sagged irretrievably after a punishing out-break of previously unknown diseases following the arrival of a large party of shipwrecked sailors. Blaming the missionaries for this catastrophe, which wiped out a third of the local population, the embittered Melanesians forced the French missionaries to retreat to the Isle of Pines.

Meanwhile, French ambitions were sharpened by a desire to set up a penal colony on the island, in emulation of the British in Australia, as an alternative to the notorious prison settlement in Guyana. Agitation for annexation flared in Paris when France learned that the entire crew of a French survey ship had been killed and eaten. Furthermore, there was apprehension that the British might seize the island first. Finally, on 24 September 1853, a French admiral named Despointes raised the Tricolor over New Caledonia and proclaimed the island French. This was a declaration, repeated five days later on the Isle of Pines, that successive French officials would have to keep reiterating from time to time through the ensuing decades of uneasy French rule.

There was much British resentment of the French penetration to the threshold of Australia, virtually under the noses of a survey party aboard a British naval vessel calling at the island. London seethed over this Gallic effrontery, but did nothing. France was to remain unchallenged, except by the natives and eventually some of her own people, on the most valuable mineral property in the entire Pacific, except Australia itself.

The new French domain consisted of an island about 250 miles long and 30 miles across at the widest point, plus the Isle of Pines and the outlying small Loyalty and Huon islands. New Caledonia proper, sometimes called Grande Terre by the French, is divided into two distinct regions by a central spine of rugged, deeply eroded mountains rising to more than five thousand feet, with many sequestered valleys and plateaus. The rainier eastern side of the range—which, unfortunately, most visitors to Nouméa never see—is a typical lush South Pacific scene, with palm groves, coffee gardens, white sand beaches, and serene villages of thatched huts. The dry western side resembles the inner core of Australia, with rocky hills of red earth covered with scrub brush and gum trees. On the mountainsides, traces of ancient terraces are evidence of a vanished native agricultural society.

The somber hills turned out to be a gigantic treasure chest of nickel, chrome, iron, cobalt, manganese, gold, copper, antimony, mercury, silver, and lead. The island was found to have the third largest known nickel reserves in the world, after Canada and the Soviet Union, and shipments of the metal—mainly to France and Japan—have constituted 99 percent of the French territory's exports. "We can start on the other ores when we run out of nickel," a French mining man told me, adding that he did not expect the end of the nickel deposits to be reached for centuries. With its huge open-pit strip mines, the refinery that converts the ore to ferro-nickel, blast furnaces that light the night sky with sunset colors, warehouses and loading machinery on a desert of reddish slag (all belonging to Société le Nickel, or S.L.N., a Rothschild enterprise with a near-monopoly on the treasure chest), New Caledonia is by far the most industrialized island in the tropical Pacific. There is the usual land despoliation and pollution; but, along with their desecration of the clear South Pacific air (the purest in the world, according to a United Nations finding), the French have preserved the South Seas flavor in the rural areas and brought an appealing Gallic insouciance to the lifestyle of Nouméa, including characteristic French political intransigence.

Initially, France had concentrated on transforming the unspoiled island into a prison colony for criminals and political offenders. The first consignment of 246 convicts, arriving in 1864, were quartered in stone barracks on the tiny island of Nou, in the harbor, which still serves as a prison. The place soon became notorious for brutality and vice. It is said that many inmates, sentenced to death for rebelling against sadistic guards, welcomed the guillotine.

About thirty thousand prisoners were shipped to New Caledonia in the thirty years of the penal colony's existence. It was they, working under military command or under contract to private employers, who built the foundations of present-day Nouméa (the town was first called Fort de France, but was renamed after the prison island to avoid confusion with Fort de France in Martinique), constructed highways, and installed the infrastructure of a profitable colony. Among the less grisly relics of convict days is the fashionable open-air Théâtre de l'Isle, on Nou island, where popular plays are staged against a stone backdrop remodeled from the prison chapel. A grimmer reminder is the old guillotine, still kept ready for use. According to local legend the device was the one used to behead Marie Antoinette.

To promote white settlement, the naval regime installed well-behaved prisoners on ten-acre plots of farmland in the interior. Many of these intermarried with Melanesians, creating a new class of mixed-bloods whose descendants have more or less blended into the present middle class on the island (one mixed blood, Edouard Pentecost, became the colony's leading entrepreneur and occupied the most elaborate home in Nouméa at the time of his death in 1974). Political offenders exiled to the colony provided an intellectual element in the new population. To offset a shortage of white women, the government imported French orphan girls and female prisoners; they and their convict spouses became the progenitors of prominent families in a later era.

Melanesian tribes resisted French encroachments on their land from the beginning. To protect settlers and missionaries, the government was forced to install military posts in the interior and on outlying islands. These became the focus of native revolt.

The thoughtless French policy of arbitrarily pre-empting native lands for allocation to convict settlers, coupled with callous desecration of sacred burial sites and general neglect and abuse of the indigenous people, led to an organized rebellion by the Melanesians in 1878 under the leadership of a chief named Atai. After the French forces killed Atai in an ambush, the natives lost cohesion; they continued a widespread guerrilla warfare, however, that kept the white population in a state of terror. Some two hundred Caucasians and an unknown number of Melanesians were killed, and there was severe destruction of property in the fighting, which lasted a year.

In French history, the outbreak is still known as the Kanaka Revolt. The word "kanaka" was an opprobrious term applied by whites to all Pacific islanders from New Guinea to Hawaii until recent, more enlightened times. (The term "native," though out of favor in white circles, is used by many Pacific island people, without self-consciousness, in referring to themselves.) It is conceivable that Melanesian nationalists in New Caledonia, following precedents elsewhere, some day will enshrine the 1878–79 rebellion as a milestone in their freedom struggle and adopt Atai as their national hero by hindsight.

New Caledonia is one of two Pacific island territories (Hawaii is the other) where the indigenes are outnumbered by aliens, if the approximately twenty thousand Polynesians, Vietnamese, and immigrants are added to the French population, which is approximately equal to that of the Melanesians. As in Hawaii, where the sugar planters imported Orientals, Puerto Ricans, and Portuguese to make up for a shortage of native labor in the fields, the French brought in cheap Asian labor to work the mines. The government also encouraged an influx of French settlers, who developed the coffee and cattle industries, among others.

The Melanesians, with nobody except the scattered missionaries much concerned about their welfare, were left to subsist on limited reserves allotted to them by the French authorities. Native holdings became progressively smaller as more French settlers arrived and persuaded a willing government to set aside choice areas for the newcomers' plantations and cattle herds, in total disregard of native rights and the traditional attachment of the tribes to ancestral lands. French petty officials assigned to the rural districts undercut the authority of the chiefs, who had already lost their former status as spiritual leaders following the wholesale conversion of the tribes to Christianity. Meanwhile, disease reduced the Melanesian population to about thirty thousand, perhaps half the number in pre-European times. Some French officials confidently predicted the total extinction of the race, without regret.

Pent-up resentment of French mistreatment and neglect burst forth in the tribal uprising of 1917, in which eleven whites and some two hundred Melanesians were killed. Again, as in the revolt of 1878, the emergency faded away following the death of the leader, a chief from the northwestern part of the island.

As in other South Pacific territories, World War II accelerated the advancement of the native people. The effect would be historic. At the outset of the war, the French population rejected the collaborationist Vichy regime of German-occupied France, and opted to go with General Charles de Gaulle. This was an early indication of the independent attitude among the island French, as well as the Melanesians, that was to cause anxiety in Paris long afterward, in another context.

The Vichyite governor, Georges Pélissier, was forced to leave the colony by a show of force by the Free French majority in Nouméa, augmented by seven hundred or so *broussards* (rural settlers) who came to the city ready to fight the governor and his supporters with shotguns. Earlier, the elected council in Nouméa had passed a resolution demanding autonomy for the territory, at least till after the war; Pélissier succeeded in keeping the document from being transmitted to the French government.

Pélissier was replaced by the popular Henri Sautot, the French representative in the New Hebrides condominium and a Gaullist. De Gaulle then sent out the anachronistic Admiral Thierry d'Argenlieu, a haughty autocrat whose dictatorial behavior so incensed the local French civilians that they mounted mass demonstrations and a general strike, eventually forcing him also to leave the island. The same d'Argenlieu, a Carmelite monk as well as a naval officer, was named French high commissioner in Saigon after the war; and there his high-handed relations with the Vietnamese contributed significantly to the dissatisfactions that eventually lost all Indochina to the Communists.

Meanwhile, American troops under General Alexander Patch arrived in March 1942, to protect New Caledonia and its rich ores against any Japanese attack in the enemy's southward drive toward Australia. The American presence temporarily changed Nouméa from a sleepy tropical ore port to a bustling city teeming with work opportunities for the Melanesians, who received fair wages and considerate treatment for the first time in the long, sad history of their contact with whites.

Although Washington had reassured de Gaulle that the United States fully recognized French sovereignty on the island, in practice the American military ran the place in every way that mattered. The troops constructed key roads that are still in use, if neglected; they developed the future international airport at Tontouta, thirty miles northwest of the capital, and demonstrated to the conservative local French—to say nothing of the Melanesians—what efficiency and modern equipment could accomplish when used intelligently. Again, as was happening on other islands at the same time, exposure to the open-handed ways and liberal ideas of tens of thousands of friendly American servicemen was changing the entire outlook of the native people. And the white New Caledonians were also learning from the Americans that a higher standard of living was possible even on a remote Pacific island. The social atmosphere would never be the same again.

After the war, the French removed regulations that had prevented Melanesians from leaving their reserves except under special circumstances—for instance, to work. Full of heightened expectations and no longer reconciled to struggling for a meager living on the reduced and inferior lands left to them by the French, thousands of Melanesians drifted from their villages to Nouméa and other towns, where they congregated in slums that soon became hotbeds of alcoholism, prostitution, and disease. An energetic French communist element took over the political guidance of the depressed Melanesian community. There was soon a rival effort fostered by the alarmed missionaries, both Protestant and Roman Catholic. The result was a rapid growth of political awareness among dissatisfied Melanesian youth.

Meanwhile, in the postwar years, the decline in the Melanesian population was reversed. At the time of Cook's arrival in 1774 it is believed that there were between 50,000 and 70,000 natives on the main island. An official estimate exactly 200 years later put the number of Melanesians at 53,500, and with a constant rapid growth at the extraordinarily high birth rate of just under 3.9 percent. By the same estimate, there were 53,250 "Europeans," about 15,000 Polynesians, and 4,000 "others"—Vietnamese, Javanese, and so on—on the island. The French, alarmed by the growing preponderance of nonwhites in this outpost of the republic, offered inducements to new immigrants from France. For instance, young men contracting to work in New Caledonia were excused from compulsory military service, as I learned from a young white waiter at the Chateau Royal, the posh, very French hotel at the southern end of Anse Vata.

Despite the Melanesian influx, Nouméa remained a city predominantly of French-speaking whites and mixed bloods. A generation after the war, the only conspicuous monument to the once overwhelming American presence was the five-winged building—called "Pentagon West" by the troops—that had housed the American command at Anse Vata's other end, about three miles from the city center and across the road from a popular section of the beach. The structure was extensively remodeled as the headquarters of the postwar South Pacific Commission, whose international staff determinedly functioned in both French and English.

Travelers around the Pacific, though seldom made to feel particularly welcome on an island that can afford to be indifferent to the tourist industry, frequently express delight with the special character of this city of more than fifty thousand inhabitants. The tree-shaded streets, laid out in a neat grid pattern with a square park in the center, bear the names of French national heroes and famous battles. Visitors are charmed by the little blue minibuses that provide cheap public transportation with admirable regularity.

It is a cosmopolitan scene, with bronzed mine laborers from the Polynesian islands and the New Hebrides, earning four to five times as much money as they could make at home, snapping up expensive French imports in the smart shops and boutiques. No income tax drains off excess cash—but the prices do, for the system of heavy indirect taxation makes goods and services come high. But everybody makes plenty of money, or could if he cared to, and the chic clothes on the well-groomed women shriek "Paris!"

In the thoroughly Gallic ambience of the city, little of a purely Melanesian flavor intrudes except the riotous tropical foliage and the hilarious female cricket matches, played by hefty, tea-colored matrons and girls clad in loose gowns of flower-patterned cotton, with frangipani blossoms in their dark, frizzy hair. It is a spectacle seen nowhere else; the English game thrives in its peculiar form on this French-Melanesian soil because of the long interchange with nearby Australia.

To the distress of the brisk French foremen in the nickel mines, the benevolent economic system fosters leisure. A payroll tax of 25 to 30 percent, paid entirely by the employers except for a small part of the tax share allotted to old-age pensions, supports a comprehensive social security program. Bosses complain that many Melanesians choose to work only the eighteen days a month required to qualify for monthly child support payments and other benefits.

Under the placid surface, political unrest has smoldered. Reforms promised by the French after the war stopped far short of the complete local autonomy demanded by a majority of the white, part-white, and Melanesian voters, who united across racial lines against the strong-willed, but slow-moving, establishment headed by starchy officials from metropolitan France, called "metros" by the local people. Although elements of Black Power surface ominously in political demonstrations, the opposition to the direct rule from Paris has vocal leaders among the locally born French, who call themselves "Caledonians." Young whites as well as disgruntled Melanesians participated in outbreaks like the major riot of 2 September 1969, which was touched off by the arrest of a chief's son on charges, later dropped, of having attempted to organize a coup d'état.

During a visit to Nouméa in January of 1975 by the then French minister of overseas territories, Oliver Stirn, anti-French slogans appeared overnight on the walls of the legislative chamber where the minister was to meet with officials, and a crude explosive device was found on the desk of the Melanesian president of the Territorial Assembly. Slogans demanding "independence," going beyond the usual call merely for local self-government, or *autonomie interne,* bore the signature of a militant political organization calling itself the Kanaka Liberation Front.

Some said that the French authorities found the occasional

relatively harmless shows of racial unrest not unwelcome, for they demonstrated to the peaceable citizenry that the firm hand of France, with her gendarmerie and paratroops, was indispensable to protect the whites against lurking black militancy. The Caledonians were reminded continually that they represented French culture in the Pacific, and should never forget it. Some Caledonians maintained, however, that Melanesian racial feeling was directed less against local whites than toward the Polynesians and other outsiders whose presence among the nickel workers prevented a Melanesian monopoly of the New Caledonian labor market.

Although there was a façade of local self-government in the elected municipal bodies and the Territorial Assembly, the supreme authority was vested in the governor appointed in Paris. The governor customarily acted in consultation with a Governing Council, or cabinet, chosen from the Assembly, but he was under no compulsion to accept the council's advice. The governor also served as French high commissioner in the Pacific, with responsibility for the interests of France in the New Hebrides and the French Territory of Wallis and Futuna, two groups of Polynesian islands northeast of Fiji and west of Samoa. "We are still a colony," a fiery young Caledonian member of the Territorial Assembly, who later left the territory in disgust with the system, told me with passion.

The authority of Paris was sometimes exercised in ways that seemed whimsical to the islanders. Bourail, a major town, was forced to proceed with the construction of an elaborate municipal swimming pool during a period of severe water shortage: the project had been authorized in Paris, and there was no bureaucratic way to divert the funds to the more needed improvement of the town water supply. When Paris adopted daylight-saving, tropical New Caledonia had to follow suit; when the islanders complained of having to go work in darkness, the governor was unable to reset the clocks, but he could—and did—order a change in the working hours on the island.

While many New Caledonians may have been anti-French, however, few were anti-France. In 1958, citizens of all the French overseas territories were called upon to vote on President de Gaulle's new constitution. An affirmative vote meant acceptance of permanent membership in the French Union; territories rejecting the constitution would be given independence, and no more French economic aid. Fewer than a thousand of the 27,028 persons who went to the polls in New Caledonia voted no. Few of the New Caledonians related home-rule to independence, the overwhelming majority cherished their French citizenship, and were proud to be sharers of the French language and culture in a part of the world where the working language of most people was English, usually with a British or Australian accent.

Despite the emotional attachment to French citizenship and culture, which may well keep New Caledonia and the other French territories of the South Pacific permanently tied to France, the yearning for local self-government never stopped growing. Nor did Paris show a disposition to relax the metropolitan grip on New Caledonian affairs. On the contrary, the French government strove for greater control over the disposition of the island's vast mineral resources. A request for local autonomy within the French Union, adopted by the Territorial Assembly in 1968 and carried to Paris by a special delegation, was summarily rejected. "It must be remembered once and for all that New Caledonia, despite its distance from France, is part of the national territory," said General Pierre Billotte, the French minister for overseas departments and territories at the time. "This situation, which conforms to the wishes and interests of the population, will not be brought into question again," he added stiffly.

But the question was to recur continually. In 1974 the leading champion of direct rule by France, a conservative French lawyer in Nouméa named George Chatenay, resigned from the Territorial Assembly with a dramatic announcement that he had changed his views, having become "fed up" with the French government's disdain for the political aspirations of the New Caledonians. Perhaps symbolically, the assembly seat that Chatenay had held for eighteen years as a spokesman for France went to a young Melanesian. "The tide of history is irreversible," said Chatenay.

SIX

Flawed Eden

OLITICS in the benign climate of Tahiti and the associated paradisiacal islands of French Polynesia—of which Papeete, on Tahiti, is the capital—were even more turbulent than in New Caledonia. At least no Caledonian activist had ever been accused of trying to burn down the capital, as the anti-French nationalist Tahitian leader Pouvanaa a Oopa allegedly did in Papeete.

Tahiti. The very sound of the name brings visions of romance. It was there that the legend of the South Seas, personified for a generation of movie-goers by Dorothy Lamour in a sarong, was born in the latter half of the eighteenth century. The first glowing reports by Captain Samuel Wallis, who discovered the island in 1767 and claimed it for Britain, captivated Europe.

"An island such as dreams and enchantment are made of," the late New Zealand expert on the Pacific, J. C. Beaglehole, wrote of Tahiti. He added: "On the day that Wallis discovered it, the knell of Polynesia began to sound." "I thought I was transported into the Garden of Eden," Bougainville said of his arrival in the next year. Unaware that Wallis had already been there, Bougainville proclaimed French sovereignty and named the island New Cytherea, after the birthplace of the Greek goddess of love. The name failed to stick, but the association with Aphrodite did.

Cook arrived in the following year with a scientific expedition to observe the transit of the planet Venus across the face of the

101

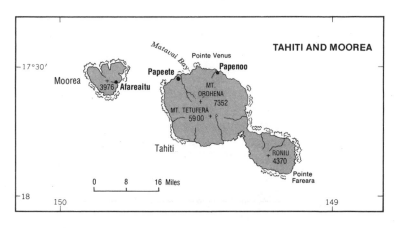

sun, Tahiti being in an ideal location for the purpose. Cook also reported the passage of many a brown Venus on the beach (the place still retains Cook's name, Point Venus), and his account excited the imagination of the Western world. Twenty years after Cook's visit, it was the beauty—or rather, beauties—of Tahiti, more than any cruelties of Captain Bligh, that caused the celebrated mutiny on H.M.S. *Bounty.* Two American residents of Tahiti, the writing team of Charles Nordhoff and James Norman Hall, described the episode in a famous trilogy whose filming later, by a huge, free-spending crew from Hollywood, briefly lifted the sunken economy of the island.

Early contact with whites left the usual heritage of disease and the rapid erosion of a distinctive way of life. Two centuries after Wallis, guidebooks were still warning visitors that fraternization with the sociable Tahitian *vahine* could be a danger to health. But the beauty of the landscape remained, as did the unquenchable spirit and beauty of the Polynesian people.

Yet, perhaps three out of five visitors to Papeete whom I have polled personally had come away disillusioned by the comparison of the reality to the dream. Travelers responding to a questionnaire disseminated by the Tahiti tourist authorities a few years ago called the picturesque French-Polynesian town "dirty," "tawdry," "smelly," "over-rated," and "over-priced." The last is a criticism with which anyone must agree, although the thoughtful French have carefully avoided contaminating Polynesian culture with the practice of tipping, and there is no income tax for residents (it is virtually impossible, however, under current regulations to become a permanent resident without French

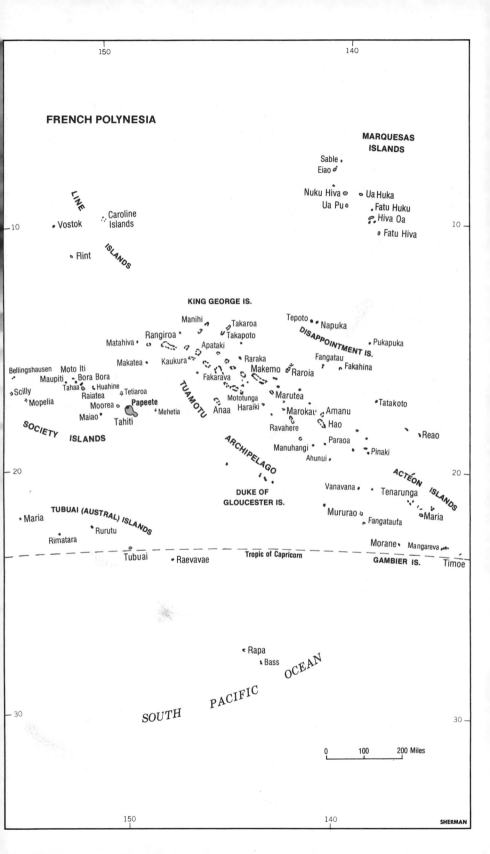

citizenship; others are permitted to stay no longer than six months in any one calendar year).

"It is sad to see Papeete becoming a modern city," Alfred Teraireia Poroi, a leading politician and businessman, remarked one day in his air-conditioned office, which shared a downtown building with the local agency for Fiat cars, one of the many Poroi enterprises. Yet Poroi, a friendly man of mixed French, English, and Tahitian ancestry, was proud that the reconstruction of Papeete from a tin-roofed semislum had been initiated in the latter part of his own twenty-five-year tenure as the town's mayor, an office he left to become the elected senator for French Polynesia in the National Assembly of France. Tourism being Tahiti's leading indigenous industry, the design of the project was entrusted to the Tahiti Tourist Development Board, whose decisions in its area of responsibility had the force of law. One of the board's rules was that no new structure should be taller than the average height of a mature palm tree.

Under the board's direction, the former drab waterfront scene of seedy shops and rowdy bars was transformed into a blown-up approximation of a Polynesian village along part of the curving harborside street, which was widened, divided by a strip of parking, and renamed Boulevard Pomare, after the former royal family. The handsome new buildings of simulated traditional architecture, housing tourist services and an exhibition hall for local arts and crafts, made a fitting companion piece to the stunning view of Moorea, the sister island across the harbor, whose towering blue peaks are perpetually festooned with wisps of white cloud. But the local people on the street retain the old, appealing character—looking, as someone else has said, like a Gauguin painting come to life on a motorbike. Seen from the deck of an arriving cruise ship, Papeete probably looks more Tahitian today than at any previous time since the port was moved there from Matavai Bay by early traders.

A casualty of the civic beautification program, mourned by many old Tahiti hands if not by architects and the clergy, was the rickety old frame and bamboo building of the original Quinn's bar. Quinn's was unquestionably the most famous saloon in the South Pacific, aptly described in the *Official Directory and Guide Book for Tahiti* as "the most picturesque place with the best music and most fascinating people" in the South Seas. "Uninhibited" was the word for Quinn's; jollity was unconfined, and the ambience reflected the untrammeled spirit of Tahiti. The photo in an

American picture magazine of a famous author in a *pareu* doing the *tamure*—the super-erotic Tahitian version of the hula—on a tabletop decked with frangipani was not an untypical scene. The location across the street from the piers made Quinn's the natural gathering place for the sailors and merchant seamen of a dozen countries, Foreign Legionnaires of divers nationalities, tourists likewise, and gregarious Tahitians of both sexes.

Mountains rise behind the town in green majesty, and the paved highway around the island is lined endlessly with a wild variety of flowers. One day on a drive my wife began a census of plant life along the road: she wrote down "ginger (white and red), frangipani, hibiscus, allemanda, bougainvillea, croton, breadfruit, mango, pandanus, poinciana, coconut palm, travelers' palm, hau, casuarina, banana, papaia, oleander (pink and white), be-still tree," then stopped.

Papeete is believed to be the oldest town in the South Pacific. The early navigators anchored in Matavai Bay, to the east of the present capital, but later callers preferred the more sheltered harbor and the easier access to fresh water on the adjacent site of Papeete. A village of a few hundred Polynesians had grown there by 1827, when Queen Pomare decided to make the place her capital. When the French took over in the 1840s, Papeete automatically became the administrative center of the new government. But the capital remained a seedy little trading settlement until the 1960s, when the French nuclear tests and the coming of large-scale tourism changed the atmosphere as well as the appearance of the place.

Wallis, Bougainville, Cook, and later arrivals found Tahiti and the nearby islands ruled by a number of chiefs. The cluster of which Tahiti is a part is divided into two subgroups, the Windward Islands (Tahiti, Moorea, Tetiaroa atoll, and Maiao) and the Leewards (Huahine, Raiatea, and Bora Bora). Cook named the whole collection the Society Islands—not in honor of his sponsor, the British Royal Society, as some have believed, but because, as the navigator stated in his journals with his own peculiar spelling, "they lay contiguous to one a nother." One chief, who had been a friend of Cook, gained some ascendancy over the others and became known as King Pomare I, monarch of Tahiti, Moorea, and a few other islands, and founder of the Tahitian ruling dynasty. His son, Pomare II, was at least the nominal ruler over most of the six sprawling archipelagoes—the Society Islands, Rapa, the Tuamotus, the Australs, the Gambier Islands, and the Marquesas—that eventually were brought under the control of Paris under the collective name of French Polynesia.

An event of significance, leading to other events that contributed indirectly to the end of the French monarchy and nearly brought on war between Britain and France, was the arrival of the first missionaries, eighteen Congregationalists of the London Missionary Society, in 1797. While the early explorers had been critical of such customs as human sacrifice, it was the sexual mores of the Tahitians that most appalled the missionaries. With sound political sense, they began the project of totally altering Tahitian moral values by first converting the king. Under missionary influence, Pomare II promulgated laws forbidding not only human sacrifice, infanticide, and polygamy but also adultery. In a few years the missionaries had converted virtually the whole of the population, and the Westernization of Polynesia through Christianity had begun. In the realm of morals, however, it was a flawed success: in Tahiti, as elsewhere throughout the South Pacific, sexual freedom and prayer coexist. (Pomare was a poor exemplar: he simultaneously loved two sisters, marrying one but continuing an affair with the other, and died of the effects of alcoholism.)

Having been first on the scene, the Protestants gained a dominance that they never lost. Royal favoritism toward the British Protestants over the French Roman Catholics led, however, to the establishment of a French protectorate and the abolition of the Tahitian throne. Following the expulsion of the Catholic missionaries by Queen Pomare IV in 1836, a French naval vessel arrived off Papeete. The commander, Rear Admiral Abel du Petit-Thouars, extracted an indemnity of two thousand dollars from the queen after threatening to bombard the town. Later, in 1839, another French naval commander named La Place similarly forced the queen to sign an agreement that French citizens could enter Tahiti freely and propagate Catholicism. Admiral du Petit-Thouars appeared again in 1842, protesting against alleged mistreatment of the French missionaries who had arrived under the previous concession. In the absence of the queen, who was on a tour of her domain, he forced her ministers to sign a document placing Tahiti and the subordinate islands under a French protectorate. The queen later repudiated the action of her ministers, whereupon the admiral returned—this time with three ships —and took formal possession of the Tahitian territory for the

French crown. As noted before, this event in 1843 was the beginning of European colonialism in the South Pacific.

Affairs in Tahiti did not escape attention in far-off Europe. The French blamed a former British missionary named George Pritchard, who had become a merchant and British consul in Papeete, for having instigated the expulsion of the Catholics. When the French admiral proclaimed the protectorate, Pritchard appealed to Britain to intervene but was ignored. London took notice, however, when the French arrested the consul in 1844 and sent him off the island in a British navy ship. This action was to have far-reaching results in London and Paris.

While the British had been loath to become involved officially in a quarrel centered around rival missionaries and the dusky queen of a distant South Pacific island, they reacted strongly to the treatment of their consul. France finally cooled British ire by paying Pritchard an indemnity. This in turn aroused the sensitive emotions of the French public, and there was an outcry for the resignation of the minister who had authorized the payment. But King Louis Philippe refused to dismiss the official, an action that added to the monarch's unpopularity and helped speed his personal downfall and the abolition of the monarchy. After the crisis between London and Paris had subsided, Britain formally recognized the French protectorate and Pritchard was reassigned as the first British consul in Samoa, where the name is still carried on by mixed-blood descendants of some prominence.

Meanwhile, the French were having trouble in Tahiti, where followers of Queen Pomare staged an unsuccessful rebellion. France appointed a chief named Paraita as permanent regent for the queen, who remained in exile on the sacred island of Raiatea until her death in 1877. The London Missionary Society, seeing the futility of resisting the French determination to eliminate British influence, handed over to a French Protestant group and left for friendlier fields. In 1880 the late queen's heir, known as King Pomare V, ceded the kingdom to France in return for a guarantee to respect Tahitian customs, plus certain privileges and a pension for himself. Thus ended the Tahitian monarchy— but not Tahitian nationalism.

France proceeded to extend her authority over other Polynesian groups as far south as the Austral and Gambier islands, which are south of the Tropic of Capricorn, and east to the Marquesas. French acquisition of South Pacific territories was not completed until 1930, when King Victor Emmanuel of Italy arbitrated rival claims between France and Mexico over isolated, uninhabited Clipperton Island in favor of Paris. (Clipperton, named for the British pirate John Clipperton, who had made it his base in 1705, is also one of forty-eight Pacific islands claimed by the United States under the Guano Act passed by the Congress in 1856. The legislation authorized the United States to take over all uninhabited Pacific islands with deposits of the accumulated bird-droppings called guano, a valuable source of fertilizer. Although the American claims have been largely forgotten and have not figured in recent South Pacific affairs, maps of the National Geographic Society still show the United States as a claimant to small territories that have long been incorporated into other jurisdictions, such as the northern Cook Islands and the Tokelau group, a cluster of atolls administered by New Zealand.)

Early in her Tahitian tenure, France introduced substantial numbers of Chinese as plantation laborers. Their descendants have become prominent in every field except politics, and the prevalence of interracial mating between Chinese and Tahitians shows in the faces seen on the streets of Papeete today, with the Chinese strain refining the heavier Polynesian features and adding an exotic tilt to the eyes.

Papeete remained a slumberous South Seas port, in which the big occasions were the "boat days" when cruise ships arrived, until the 1960s, when two developments—a big international airport and a nuclear testing center—had a profound effect on the life of Tahiti and French Polynesia.

With the imminent closure of the phosphate workings on Makatea island in the Tuamotus, long the mainstay of the French Polynesian economy, the territory faced an unpromising future of dependence upon the generosity of the finance ministry in Paris (the mining operation, which at its height had produced an average of 300,000 tons of phosphatic rock a year, ended in 1966 when the depleted resource ceased to be profitable). The islands were completely lacking in commercial assets save coconuts, mother-of-pearl shell, and vanilla. Without the phosphate, a valuable ingredient of fertilizer much in demand by the farmers of Australia and New Zealand, the prospective imbalance of imports over exports posed an unpleasant problem for the French treasury.

As mentioned earlier, the making of the motion picture *Mutiny on the Bounty* in 1961–62 temporarily inflated the economy. An offshoot of that enterprise destined to have a lasting, if limited, significance for at least a few Polynesians was the purchase by Marlon Brando, who played Fletcher Christian in the *Bounty* film, of a large section of Tetiaroa island in the atoll of the same name twenty-six miles north of Tahiti. Tetiaroa had long been associated with chiefs and contained numerous temple sites, archery platforms, and other traces of royal occupation of interest to archeologists. The atoll had once been owned by the Pomare family, which used it for recreation and as a refuge when the fortunes of war with rival chiefs were adverse. Brando converted the main island into a resort for affluent travelers and had associates studying various possibilities of economic development, such as fisheries, to supplement coconut cultivation. The actor also permitted the Bishop Museum in Honolulu to bring in a team for a complete archeological survey.

An obvious, if controversial, avenue for economic improvement of all French Polynesia lay in tourism, which had undergone vast expansion in the Pacific with the coming of jet planes. The opening of the Faaa international airport, on filled-in Faaa lagoon land west of town, to big jets early in 1961 was duly followed by the hoped-for stream of visitors, which grew from year to year. Swiftly, hotels proliferated along the shore on both sides of Papeete, spread into the lush Tahitian countryside, and sprang up on the islands of Moorea, Raiatea, Bora Bora, Huahine, and Rangiroa. '

While improving the economy of the islands, the tourist wave brought permanent changes that destroyed some of the old charm, especially on Tahiti. The expansion of foreign investment, encouraged by the Tahiti Tourist Development Board with inducements such as capital loans and tax rebates, swelled the population of Papeete with the addition of many businesslike *popaa*, as the Tahitians call Caucasians. "It's a new South Sea town," one of the long-established American settlers, Bernard (Bert) Covit, the publisher of the encyclopedic *Official Directory and Guide Book of Tahiti*, wrote me when the tourist flood had passed the 100,000-a-year mark. "When I go down daily to pick up my mail, if I see two or three faces that I know it's unusual, whereas I remember when I knew everyone in sight, Tahitian, Frenchman, American. . . ."

Far more controversial than tourism, not only in Tahiti but throughout the South Pacific and in other countries as well, was the nuclear program initiated in the South Seas by President de Gaulle when the independence of Algeria ended the French tests in the Sahara. The Centre d'Expérimentation du Pacifique, or C.E.P., was installed in a sprawling complex of laboratories, staff housing, a hospital, and other facilities in the Papeete suburb of Pirae and beyond, east of the town center. Along with the new buildings came a horde of French scientists and other personnel. The famous Foreign Legion furnished a permanent security force of 2,500 men, which rose to 10,000 when the explosive devices were actually being tested. Again the character of Papeete, and to some extent all French Polynesia, underwent change.

The actual explosions, which began in 1966, took place in the air over the uninhabited Mururoa atoll, 800 miles southeast of Tahiti in the Tuamotu chain, also known as the Low Islands or the Dangerous Archipelago. De Gaulle himself journeyed out to witness part of the first test series.

Each series of explosions was accompanied by a flurry of protests in Australia, New Zealand, and the Pacific islands. Critics of France charged that the tests poisoned the seas and atmosphere with radioactive material, destroying marine life and threatening the health of humans as well. Reassurances by the French were met with reminders that the American tests at Bikini atoll in the Marshall Islands had exposed islanders and Japanese fishermen to damaging radiation, resulting in serious illness and death, despite the earlier conviction of the scientists that the explosions would pose no danger.

"We learned from the American experience," Colonel Paul Gambini, the C.E.P. spokesman, said when I visited the test headquarters with a French official of the Tahiti government in 1969. "Control is much more certain now. We have the tests in the Southern Hemisphere winter months of May, June, and July, when the trade winds are steady and their course can be predicted in advance for several weeks. In any case, the winds from Mururoa blow northeast across four thousand kilometers of empty sea." To demonstrate how safe the tests were, the then French minister of defense, Michel Debré, and half a dozen aides swam in the Mururoa lagoon six hours after one nuclear blast.

The critics were unimpressed. Australia brought a case against France in the International Court of Justice in The Hague, charging that the tests violated international law by imperiling health in noninvolved countries. Australian unionists refused to handle

French goods, and postal and telecommunications workers banned mail, telephone calls, and cables to France.

Feeling ran high in New Zealand, which officially supported the Australian actions. A Canadian pacifist group sailed a yacht from New Zealand to the prohibited sea area around the test site and was chased out by the French Navy. Protests by the official representatives of non-French islands at successive meetings of the South Pacific Conference disrupted the sessions, with the French delegates walking out each time the subject was raised. In Tahiti, the Territorial Assembly passed a resolution prohibiting the introduction of radioactive material into French Polynesia, but the measure was nullified by the French Supreme Court.

There was relief all around when France announced that the atmospheric phase of the nuclear experiments had been completed and that further tests would be underground. These began in June of 1975 at Fangataufa, an atoll twenty miles south of Mururoa, where France had maintained a forward observation station for the aerial operations. (Later, the underground tests were returned to Mururoa.) By that time, most French Polynesians were either indifferent to the uproar over possible dangers from the tests or enthusiastic supporters of the program because of its beneficial spinoff in roads, airfields, water supply, port improvements, and other significant contributions to the territory's previously neglected economic infrastructure, besides supplying much badly needed employment.

The establishment of the C.E.P. in French Polynesia greatly enhanced the importance to Paris of maintaining a favorable political climate in the islands for a permanent link to France. For this France was willing to pay. Accordingly, the French government publicly guaranteed that substantial economic aid would continue as long as needed. This promise was coupled with an ambitious French-sponsored development program stressing food production—more farms in the interior, more cattle-raising —and light industry. When I last visited the islands, the plan was showing visible results. American investors, for instance, were looking beyond the tourist-hotel scene and were getting into such job-creating activities as fruit canning and the manufacture of products ranging from a meat tenderizer to resort clothes.

With the combination of the C.E.P. stimulus, tourist-related employment, the fresh input of developmental assistance, and foreign investment in a variety of fields, the people of Tahiti acquired a standard of living far above the average for South Pacific islanders. Tin roofs sprouted television antennas all over the island, most houses had washing machines, and there was a car parked in nearly every yard.

French generosity was rewarded when the political parties demanding an autonomous government for the islands lost their majority in the Territorial Assembly in the 1972 elections. But, as I learned from many conversations on Tahiti and other islands, Polynesian nationalism was far from dead.

Historically, enthusiasm for continued political association with France has risen in bad times, when the prospect of losing the French subsidy became frightening to the islanders. Conversely, with the lessening of economic stresses the agitation for local autonomy, or even independence, increased. Thus, when I toured several of the islands at the height of the newest wave of affluence, it was not surprising that a rural coconut grower should refer casually to his plans for expansion "when the French leave," as if their eventual departure was a certainty.

Nevertheless, on the basis of many other conversations and interviews, I had to assume that the coconut grower who looked forward to an independent Polynesia represented only a small minority of nationalists, most of whom were to be found in the Leeward, Austral, and Gambier groups, still strongly traditionalist and remote from the sophisticated political thinking of Papeete. Bora Bora, Raiatea, and Huahine in the Leewards, 80 to 140 miles northwest of Tahiti, cherish the tradition of having resisted absorption into the French empire until forced to yield before superior strength. On these islands one can still see the ancient stone temple platforms, or *marae,* some of which have been restored by the Bishop Museum, where once human sacrifices were offered in rites of a vanished Polynesian religion. Raiatea is considered to be one of the islands from which the great Polynesian migrations started. Bora Bora, with its squared-off central peak jutting toward the sky like a giant green smokestack, is James Michener's choice as the most beautiful island in the Pacific.

Huahine has the historical distinction, among others that go farther back in time, of having been the birthplace of the preeminent Tahitian nationalist Pouvanaa a Oopa, who might have been the Gandhi or Jomo Kenyatta of an independent Polynesia had his designs succeeded. Pouvanaa, as he is called, was an extraordinary political figure in the South Pacific. His ancestry was part Danish, as revealed by his blue eyes and light complexion, but his indomitable spirit and insouciant personality were pure Polynesian. A carpenter and a veteran of World War I with the French forces, he was a firm Protestant with strong fundamentalist views, contentious, xenophobic, and indifferent to detail.

The future nationalist leader was forty-five years old when, in 1940, he first attracted public attention by starting a movement for various economic reforms, including the closing of liquor shops. In the following year he sponsored an agitation against Caucasian and Chinese control of the economy, which he thought should be in Polynesian hands. By that time the colony, as it was then, had entered World War II on the side of General de Gaulle, like New Caledonia and the French in the New Hebrides. After the Japanese attack on Pearl Harbor had brought the United States into the conflict, the Gaullist administration permitted the Americans to establish an air base on Bora Bora. These events significantly influenced future Tahitian politics and the course of Pouvanaa's budding career as an anti-French gadfly.

The decision to support de Gaulle, made by a referendum in which the vote was overwhelmingly on the side of the Free French, sharpened old personal animosities that were to figure in postwar politics. The alliance also resulted in the introduction of a prominent British and American presence in addition to the long-standing consular representation. The enhanced contact with outside elements inherently sympathetic to liberal causes tempted the Tahitian nationalists to seek foreign support.

France had never been comfortable with foreign influence in her colonies, especially that of the British and Americans, whom the French lumped together as "Anglo-Saxons." The wartime governor attempted to keep the American troops apart from the Polynesians on Bora Bora, and his lack of success in this endeavor can be measured by the number of villagers on Bora Bora today with lighter-than-average skin. Eventually, some years after the war, de Gaulle ordered the American consulates out of New Caledonia and Tahiti, and refused permission for a United States satellite tracking station and private scientific studies in the islands.

Meanwhile, Pouvanaa lost no time in seeking the aid of the wartime British and American consuls, to whom he sent a petition outlining his desires on behalf of the Polynesian community.

For this he was exiled to his native Huahine, the first of several times he was banished from Tahiti for political activity.

Almost immediately after Japan surrendered, ending the war, the Free French administration rewarded the colony for its wartime support by giving the people a voice, though not much power, in the island government through an assembly elected by adult suffrage. At the same time, French citizenship was extended to all native-born residents except the Chinese, who still could become French citizens only through naturalization and continued to suffer various kinds of discrimination in the tax system.

In 1946 the Établissements Français de l'Océanie—generally called, naturally, the E.F.O.—officially ceased to be a colony and became an Overseas Territory, a change that entitled the islands to a senator and a deputy in the French parliament. A decade later, the assembly's mostly nominal power was enlarged when that body was empowered to elect a council from among its members, which would function as a cabinet and participate in executive decisions with the French-appointed governor. The old name of the territory, which to the islanders had an odious colonial association, was changed officially to Polynésie Française—French Polynesia.

None of these steps soothed the agitators for real authority over local affairs, since the ultimate power remained with the governor. That official, chosen in Paris, not only functioned as the chief executive of the territory and president of the council elected by the assembly but could also exercise a veto over decisions of the elected representatives. The French governors managed cleverly to exert virtually absolute authority without coming into open confrontation with the council. A member of one of the councils, whom I met when he headed the French Polynesian delegation to a meeting of the South Pacific Conference in Suva, Fiji, explained how the system worked.

"Legislation passed by the assembly goes to the governor, who has the function of putting it before the council for approval," said the councilor, a thirty-five-year-old part-Tahitian named Romuald Allain, who held the portfolio of public works in the territorial executive body. "Therefore, the governor decides what will be discussed at the weekly meetings. If he doesn't like a law, he simply doesn't put it out for approval. If asked about it, he says it is 'under study.' The council has no power to demand that the legislation be submitted."

One example, he said, was a demand for self-government

passed by the Territorial Assembly in repeated sessions over several years, but never placed before the council for approval. Allain, and others in the French Polynesian delegations, who spoke against policies espoused by France during the five successive sessions of the South Pacific Conference that I covered for *The New York Times* never appeared on the list of delegates a second time.

French insensitivity to Polynesian political ambitions produced extraordinary turbulence in Papeete. Pouvanaa, finally permitted to return from his exile on Huahine in 1945, was a leader in numerous disturbances. This man, who ran a cafe on the Papeete waterfront before becoming a full-time politician, was perhaps the territory's greatest orator in Tahitian, a musical language given to floridity. His followers called him *Metua*, a Tahitian honorific comparable to the *Bapu* (father) applied to Gandhi by his adherents. Pouvanaa also acquired a Gandhian aura of martyrdom after he had been jailed for participating in a demonstration in 1947 in which three officials sent out from France were prevented from leaving their ship until they were escorted ashore by armed soldiers sent by the governor. Pouvanaa and several associates were acquitted, however, when witnesses to the episode were unable to agree on what had actually happened.

At this time Pouvanaa's efforts were directed mainly toward economic issues, including the advancement of Tahitians in the civil service and curbing the commercial power of the Chinese residents. His nationalist phase, in which he advocated full independence for the islands, came later. Meanwhile he lost two bids to join the French Parliament. He was defeated in his first attempt, receiving only forty-four votes. On the second try he won the election but was barred from taking office because he was in jail again. The leading campaigner for political change in the islands at that time was Mayor Poroi, an advocate of autonomy in local affairs, whose party defeated Pouvanaa's group in the 1947 municipal elections. Pouvanaa finally went to Paris upon winning a by-election in 1949 following the death of the deputy from the islands. It was the first of many political successes for the old warrior.

Pouvanaa's advocacy of complete separation from France backfired in 1958. Clearly, a majority wished to retain the French link while agitating for self-government at home. His party's downfall came when it pushed a bill through the Territorial Assembly instituting an income tax. An enraged mob gathered at the assembly hall and threw stones at Pouvanaa when he appeared at a window. The tax was subsequently repealed.

Four months later, when French overseas dependencies were called upon to decide by referendum whether or not to remain within the French Union, Pouvanaa campaigned for a negative vote—which would have meant independence, but also an end to French economic assistance. He lost by 14,818 votes to 8,467, an outcome that put an end to significant agitation for independence in Tahiti—but not to the movement for internal autonomy.

The bizarre episode in which Pouvanaa was accused of trying to burn down Papeete followed two nights later. Convicted on 28 October 1959 of attempted murder, arson, and illegal possession of firearms as a result of the incident, he was sentenced to eight years in prison and fifteen years' banishment from the islands. After an appeal failed, he was sent secretly to France to serve his prison term and exile. Also, he was expelled from the French Parliament.

Pouvanaa insisted that he was innocent, and a demand that he be freed and returned to Tahiti became a standard political rallying cry in the islands. An amnesty was granted late in 1969. He returned to a hero's welcome at the airport, and shortly was re-elected to the French Parliament as a senator.

Pouvanaa's final appearance in the Territorial Assembly, in which he served concurrently with being a senator in Paris, was characteristically dramatic. As the oldest member, he had the honor of opening the session of October 1972, in the presence of the French governor, Pierre Angeli (most governors sent to Papeete were Corsicans, for reasons that never came through to me, but which appeared ironically appropriate when an autonomist movement also erupted on that island). Although the official language of the assembly was French, Pouvanaa insisted on delivering a caustically antigovernment autobiographical speech in Tahitian, defying the furiously protesting governor.

A week later, seventy-seven years old and in failing health, the living symbol of Polynesian political aspirations resigned from the assembly, to be replaced by a younger man with similar views, though Pouvanaa remained in the French senate. The leadership had already passed, years before, to men like Poroi; John Teariki, a landowner, ship operator, and chief of Moorea; and Francis Sanford, a former schoolteacher and mayor of the Faaa municipality, whose surname came from a Bostonian ancestor.

Teariki and Sanford, strong advocates of autonomy, had both

served as deputy for French Polynesia in the parliament in Paris. Though the two men had been electoral rivals, they marched together under the banned flag of the Tahitian monarchy in a demonstration protesting against the refusal of a visiting minister of overseas territories to discuss the autonomy issue with political leaders in Papeete in 1970.

In succeeding years, the old royal flag of Tahiti became the defiant standard of a new, younger generation of activists. Though new faces appeared in political circles, they belonged mostly to the large mixed-blood community—called *demis*—from which the leadership had traditionally come in Papeete. And the remoter islands, which benefited least from prosperity on Tahiti and suffered most from official neglect, continued to supply the more extreme agitators against French rule. The French, maintaining that to grant full local autonomy would somehow cast an aspersion on the capability of France to govern in the Pacific, allowed only minor constitutional changes.

"Either Polynesia will be an independent state or Polynesia remains part of the French Republic," the responsible French cabinet minister, Olivier Stirn, proclaimed in an interview with the editor of a French-language newspaper in Papeete, *La Dépêche,* in 1975. "Independence," he added, "is a position that could have been admitted if it had been wanted, which was not the case. . . ." This pronouncement followed a request by the Territorial Assembly for a change in the government charter permitting the president of the executive council, a position now held by the French governor, to be elected at large.

The rigid French position was challenged immediately with an implied threat by the president of the Territorial Assembly, a French-born former sailor named Frantz Vanizette, who had settled in Papeete as a young man and entered politics early. "It must be clearly pointed out," Vanizette declared in a press conference, "that independence is not on the agenda, but definitely will be if the statute [governing the council] does not conform with what we wish."

Political unrest in Papeete surfaced again on 10 June 1976, in an anti-French demonstration that was considered a landmark in the continuing struggle for autonomy. The outbreak developed from a challenge by Vanizette, Sanford, and others to the election of Gaston Flosse, the leader of a pro-French faction in the Territorial Assembly, to the presidency of that body in place of Vanizette. About twelve hundred angry autonomists, led by Vanizette, prevented the new French governor, Charles Schmitt, from entering the assembly building to open a legislative session. As a further token of defiance, the anti-French signs carried by the protesters ("French Colonialism Go Home") were nearly all in Tahitian and English. The demonstrators continued to occupy the assembly premises for some time, allowing only sympathizers and journalists—who were often the same—inside the gates.

Classic South Seas colonialism under the French flag, though dignified and disguised by the title Overseas Territory of France and the election of a senator and a deputy in the French parliament, survives in the lonely, backward Polynesian islands of Wallis and Futuna, two small groups about 120 miles apart, some 200 miles west of Samoa.

France acquired the Wallis islands in the 1840s—they were named for the British navigator who discovered them in 1767, the same year he discovered Tahiti—and annexed the Futuna group in 1888. As the colony of Wallis and Futuna, they were administered first from Tahiti and then from Nouméa till they became an Overseas Territory in 1959. Although theoretically on a par politically with New Caledonia and French Polynesia, the top official is called "administrator," not governor, and below him the authority rests in practice with the Roman Catholic missionary establishment and the traditional chiefs.

Uvea island, in the Wallis group, was an American air base during World War II, but was far from the scene of action. Without commercial assets except coconuts, the territory is supported by grants from Paris. The best-known export from Wallis is a well-regarded young painter named Alois Pilioko, who lives near Vila, in the New Hebrides, sharing a combined salon and living quarters with his mentor, the Franco-Russian artist Nicolai Michoutouchkine. Restless young Wallisians, as the people of the territory are called collectively, migrate mostly to Nouméa, where they are looked down upon by the Melanesians and form a compact, depressed community of laborers.

France has discouraged contact with Wallis and Futuna by outsiders other than Frenchmen. After an unfavorable report on health and hygiene in the islands by a team from the South Pacific Commission, no further visits by the commission's staff were allowed. An archeologist from the Bernice P. Bishop Museum in Honolulu, studying early Polynesian migrations, was refused permission to carry on research on Wallis and Futuna. Although the six thousand or so people of the two islands have been consid-

board royal palace at Nuku'alofa, Tonga, with royal chapel at left

street of Nuku'alofa, capital of Tonga

Robert Trumbull/*New Yor*

Tongans wearing the *ta'ovala,* or waist mat, at the Tongatapu airport

Robert Trumbull/*New York Times*

King Taufa'ahau of Tonga
uniform at left) reviews troop
independence celebration, v
his brother and prime minis
Prince Tu'ipelahake, at right

ered friendly to France, which supplies funding for essential services, the local leaders are anything but servile; in 1974, public
protests forced the removal of an unpopular French administrator. This event was followed by a visit to Paris by the hereditary
Polynesian "kings" of the islands, who were entertained by
French President Valery Giscard d'Estaing.

The long struggle by Pouvanaa, Sanford, and their colleagues
came to a triumphant conclusion in July 1977, when the French
Parliament passed a statute granting full control of internal affairs to a new Government Council. Sanford, as acting premier,
opened the historic first meeting on 22 July 1977 with an emotional tribute to Pouvanaa, who had died, as Sanford said, "on
the eve of victory."

Thus the new political stirrings following World War II inevitably reach the remotest backwaters of the South Pacific sooner or
later. In the French sphere, the remaining question is whether
tiny, economically dependent islands like Wallis and Futuna,
should they find independence a nonviable ambition, willingly
continue the direct link with Paris or, alternatively, seek association with a larger sovereign or autonomous state developing out
of the nationalist spirit sweeping Tahiti and other Polynesian
territories.

SEVEN

Knights and Cannibal Forks

HILE the French outposts in the South Pacific may seem anachronistic in an era of emerging former colonial states, the British or former British territories have been in the vanguard of constitutional progress in the islands. Fiji, where the sun rose first on the British Empire every day because of that colony's proximity to the International Dateline, became an independent nation barely a century after a Christian chief prohibited cannibalism. The light blue flag of sovereign Fiji unfurled for the first time over the broad greensward of Albert Park in Suva on the humid, sunlit morning of 10 October 1970, in ceremonies dating from pagan times. The proceedings involved the presentation of roasted pigs and yams on banana leaves to the chiefs, and the ritual drinking of *kava,* performed with the same rigid punctilio as in the formal partaking of Japanese tea in a Buddhist temple.

Exhibiting the polyglot nature of the population, there were Asian ethnic dances by tiny Indian girls in chiffon saris and willowy Chinese maidens in embroidered silks, spirited Fijian dances by bare-chested young men with garlands of flowers around their sinewy brown necks and kilts of leaves over their undershorts, and the Fiji armed forces band, clad in military tunics and white skirts with jagged hemlines, performed a stately drill to British martial airs.

The thousands of entranced watchers at this colorful spectacle were a picturesque assemblage. The official representatives of

120

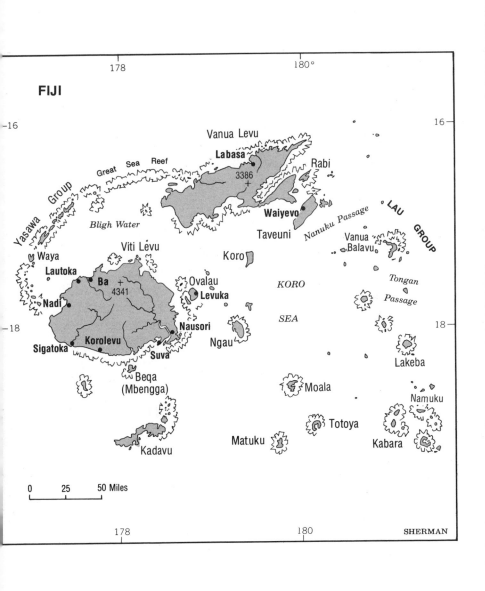

FIJI

foreign countries included a Maori knight from New Zealand and an American who had been to the moon. Crown Prince Charles of Great Britain, whose great-great-great-grandmother, Queen Victoria, had accepted these islands from a former cannibal chief in 1874, was there to hand them back ninety-six years later to the day.

And among the Fijian chiefs sitting cross-legged on a huge mat in front of the grandstand was Ratu (Chief) George Cakobau, great-grandson of the man who had ceded Fiji to the British crown. A necklace of boar's teeth and other exotic regalia indicated the exalted rank of "Ratu George" as the Vunivalu of Bau, the foremost among the six "paramount chiefs" of Fiji. Nearby sat a well-built, handsome man wearing a blue *sulu,* the Fijian version of the *lavalava,* blue suit jacket, and red necktie. This was Ratu Sir Kamisese Mara—"Ratu Mara"—a towering figure physically and politically, known throughout the South Pacific. As prime minister of the new nation his place was beside Prince Charles in the grandstand; but as a Fijian, he was required by local etiquette to sit below the representative of his sovereign, Queen Elizabeth II. Altogether, I reflected, the scene properly befitted the departure of empire and the birth of a mini-super-power, or super-minipower, on one of the most enchanting islands in the South Seas.

Two years and four months later Ratu George, knighted by the queen and thenceforth to be known in Fiji as Ratu *Sir* George, became the governor-general and nominal head of the government. Said the venerable *Fiji Times,* "Once more a Cakobau heads the nation." The name is pronounced "THAK-om-bau," a peculiarity of the Roman spelling devised for the Fijian language by missionary scholars who, abhorring diphthongs, insisted that each sound be represented by a single letter. So "c" in the Fijian alphabet is pronounced "th," "b" is preceded by an invisible "m," "d" is "nd" (Nadi, a town, rhymes with "dandy"), "g" is "ng" as in "sing," "q" is "ng-g" as in "finger" (or the way a New Yorker pronounces Long Island—"Long Guyland"—which in Fijian would be "Loq Islad"). "Cub," therefore, spells "thumb." International airlines spell Nadi with the "n"—Nandi—for simplicity, but the highly traditionalist Fijians have resisted a trend toward phoneticizing their language.

It was because of the European characteristic of wanting things nice and tidy that Ratu Sir George's ancestor is identified in many histories as "king" of Fiji. As paramount chief of Bau ("Mbau"), a twenty-acre island off the coast of Viti Levu a few miles northeast of Suva, Cakobau obtained guns from friendly whites and established military superiority over the other chiefs in bloody interclan warfare. He later became a Christian, and the large stone on which his executioners used to smash the heads of captured enemies was converted to a baptismal font. The first Cakobau acquired his name, which means "destroyer of Bau," after he led a bloody uprising at the age of eighteen to restore his father Tanoa to the chiefship of the island, from which he had been deposed. Then, with the aid of white advisers, muskets, and cannon, he extended his power over most of Viti Levu (Great Fiji), the largest of the 361 islands in the chain (of which about one hundred are permanently inhabited). The name Fiji, incidentally, is a corruption of Viti by some early white explorer who did not hear the word right.

Meanwhile, Polynesians from Tonga were mingling with the Melanesians of Fiji, particularly in the outlying Lau group, of which some islands are closer to Tonga than to Viti Levu. The original purpose of the Tongans was to purchase the superior Fijian canoes, which they sometimes paid for by serving as warriors for feuding chiefs. The contact has made Fiji the place where Polynesia and Melanesia meet; the strong Polynesian strain in many Fijian families is often visible in the softening of the Negroid features that distinguish most Melanesians among Pacific races. Sir Kamisese Mara, who was paramount chief of Lau besides being prime minister, looked pure Polynesian.

Unlike Cakobau, the contemporary first king of Tonga, who called himself George Tupou I after his conversion to Christianity by Wesleyan missionaries, was a true monarch in the Western sense of the term, ruling all the islands of the vast Tongan archipelago. At his urging Cakobau also embraced Christianity in 1854, whereupon the Tongan ruler sent him two thousand fighting men to help consolidate his power over all Fiji. Five years later, a rival whom Cakobau hanged was one Kamisese Mara of Lau, whose descendant and namesake in 1973 would give the principal speech at the investiture of George Cakobau as governor-general. In the rigidly stratified hierarchy of Fijian nobility, which counts for more than political office in personal relationships, the head of the Cakobau family takes precedence among the six paramount chiefs, while the prime minister, as leader of Lau, is only fourth. In fact, Sir Kamisese is two steps behind his own wife, a magnificent-looking woman almost as tall as her

six-feet-four-inch husband, who as Adi Lala (Adi, pronounced
"Andy," is a Fijian woman's title) is paramount chief of Rewa,
a district on Viti Levu near Suva, and ranks second only to Cakobau.

On becoming a Christian, the first Cakobau prohibited cannibalism in his realm. Fijians are not sensitive about their cannibal
ancestry, least of all the regal Cakobaus whom I met in Suva. One
of these, the late Ratu Sir Edward, a highly urbane Oxford product who commanded a Fiji battalion with distinction against the
Communist insurrectionists in Malaya, liked to boast that he was
"part Scottish" because his great-grandfather "had eaten a Scottish missionary." A common item on souvenir counters in Suva
is a four-pronged wooden instrument called a "cannibal fork."
There is a display of real ones in the Fiji museum. "Did cannibals
really use forks?" I asked a young Fijian woman attendant at the
museum. "Certainly," she replied with a mischievous smile, adding: "We weren't savages, you know."

His conversion to Christianity earned Cakobau valuable support by missionaries, but chiefly squabbles and other disorders
continued. A growing stream of white men came to Fiji as planters, traders, sandalwood buyers, and adventurers hoping to make
their fortunes advising the chiefs (a shipwrecked Swedish seaman
named Charles Savage gained great power and a harem on Bau).
The arrival of British and American consuls in the old capital of
Levuka, a quaint port town on the small island of Ovalau east of
Viti Levu, was followed by the entry of even more foreigners.

The American Civil War exerted a critical influence on the
history of Fiji. Cotton planting boomed in the islands when a
world shortage of that commodity developed following the dev-
astation of the American South. As the self-sufficient Fijians saw
no reason to engage in hard, dull plantation labor for whites
when they owned lands of their own that they did not care to
work, the planters turned to the notorious "blackbirders" for
field hands from other islands, especially the Solomons and the
New Hebrides. Thus began the system of importing indentured
labor, which soon led to wholesale recruitment in India and eventually made the Fijians a minority in their own country.

The appearance of the British consul prompted speculation
that London had designs on Fiji, which caused an influx of whites
hoping to get in early on the expected colonial loot. Britain had
no such intentions at the time, but meanwhile the American
consul speeded up history by letting his house catch fire during

a convivial celebration of the Fourth of July. Blaming the conflagration on Fijians, he lodged a claim for nine thousand British pounds—a staggering sum at the time—against Cakobau and got the United States government to back his demand.

Cakobau, all-powerful in his domain but lacking in cash, and apparently fearing that American warships would soon be on the way if the claim were not paid, longed for the protection of a more powerful state. Accordingly, he offered the islands to the British crown if Britain would pay the Americans. The British, involved in bloody conflict with the Maoris of New Zealand and unanxious for more South Pacific entanglements, declined. Next, Cakobau asked the United States to take over, forget the debt, and protect him from his eager enemies, the rival chiefs. Washington, occupied with the Civil War, did not even reply. Cakobau tried Germany, which at that time was cool to colonial adventures, and was ignored again.

Meanwhile, conditions in the islands were becoming increasingly disorderly. Blackbirding was rife, some forty wrangling chiefs were at each other's throats, and the lives of white men, mostly British, were constantly in danger. London found such a situation intolerable. A commission sent by the British government to assess the situation in Fiji reported back that conditions had deteriorated to a point that made it imperative for some outside power to step in. Under strong pressure from British colonists in nearby Australia and New Zealand, London opened negotiations with Cakobau. On 10 October 1874, Cakobau and the other principal chiefs signed a "Deed of Cession" that made the islands a Crown Colony of Britain, and Cakobau sent his war club—the symbol of power—to Queen Victoria. A later British ruler would send the club back to Suva, where it became the mace of the sovereign Fiji Parliament.

Britain set about restoring order. The authority of the chiefs was confirmed in tribal and village affairs, and the titles to land held by foreigners were carefully examined, a program that resulted in the affirmation of Fijian communal ownership of 83 percent of the land in the islands. These two acts of the British shaped the social pattern that endured when Fiji became independent, and became a source of both stability and trouble for the new nation.

Blackbirding was abolished, but in 1879 another event occurred whose effects over the long term were to change Fiji from a reasonably homogeneous community into the racially volatile society that exists today. This event was the arrival of the first indentured laborers from India to work on the foreign-owned cotton and coconut plantations. There were 481 in that first group of Indian migrants, after a shipboard outbreak of cholera and smallpox had taken its toll on the long voyage under sail. When the indenture system ended in 1916, as the result of public revulsion against abuses, 64,000 Indians had landed in Fiji, and 40,000 of these chose the option of staying on after their work contracts expired. Other Indian settlers came as moneylenders, merchants, marriage brokers, and priests. These were the progenitors of most of the Fiji Indians who constituted 52 percent of the population of 520,000 at the time of independence. The indigenous Fijians had declined to 43 percent, the remainder being whites, Chinese, and people from other Pacific islands.

The Indians of Fiji became a special kind of Indian. Caste distinctions of the homeland were left behind when they boarded the ships. Some disguised their lowly origins by assuming high-caste names. Many were dark-skinned Tamils from southern India and most were Hindus, but there was a fair representation from other parts of India. There also grew up an Indian Moslem community, one prominent member of it being Siddiq Moiuddin Koya, the leader of the opposition in the first Parliament of independent Fiji. Through successive generations (by 1970 more than 90 percent of the Indian residents in Fiji had been born in the islands) they retained their ancestral religion, dress, customs, and languages, including the lilting accents of Indian English.

With the demise of the Fiji cotton industry, which could not survive the competition of the rejuvenated American South, the Indian work force was shifted from picking cotton to cutting sugar cane. The end of the indenture system was followed by a structural change in what had become Fiji's principal industry, with the big sugar estates being broken up into small plots which were leased to individual Indian growers, who thus became independent tillers. Gradually, the Fiji sugar industry became almost completely dependent upon the Indian output of cane.

Driven by the same ambition to better themselves that had brought the Indians to Fiji in the first place, they saved their money by frugal living and educated their children. The rising generation of young Indian men tended to forsake the cane farms to go into trades, business, and the professions, and soon the Indians dominated those fields as well.

The bulk of the Fijians possessed neither the aptitude nor the incentive to rival the Indians. The South Pacific custom of communal sharing, called *kere kere* in the Fijian language, was inimical to the work ethic. At the time of independence, nearly three Fijians out of every four lived in classic village surroundings, sleeping in a *bure*—the traditional thatched hut with basketwork walls—and obeying the orders of their hereditary chief. Evenings were passed drinking *yaqona*, the Fijian name for *kava*, a spicy, slightly narcotic drink made from the beaten root of the pepper tree. (A polished wooden bowl kept filled with *yaqona*, an essential ingredient of ceremonies and hospitality, and a coconut drinking cup are included in Suva office furnishings for the refreshment of visitors.)

Fijians clung tenaciously to tradition. Men usually wore the knee-length *sulu,* women the ankle-length *sulu* and long blouse fitted at the waist. (When the chiefs banned miniskirts, fashion-conscious Fijian girls adopted a transparent *sulu.*) The brawny, broad-shouldered Fijian women invariably wore their black, kinky hair in a bouffant style resembling the Afro cut, stiffened with a solution of lime and clay and teased with a long-toothed wooden comb (men dropped the style during World War II, when Fijians in the armed forces found it difficult to cram a helmet over bushy hair).

Most Fijians in the towns were employed in lower-level jobs. A tourist boom in the early 1970s provided jobs as attendants and entertainers in the new hotels. The breezy, amiable Fijians turned out to be very popular in these occupations. The visitor influx brought relative prosperity to the grass-skirted dancers and drummers, makers of the distinctively patterned Fijian *tapa* (bark cloth) called *masi,* and the tribe on tiny Beqa (or Mbengga) island, whose members have developed an unexplained ability to walk barefoot on white-hot stones without being burned. Numerous villages have derived a handsome revenue from leasing land to tourist enterprisers for hotel and resort sites. Less happily, as has happened on other South Pacific islands, tourism has encouraged prostitution by both sexes. Moreover, officials estimated that at least half the revenue from tourism left the islands for tourist-oriented merchandise or in profits to foreign entrepreneurs.

Another Fijian problem common among other Pacific islanders was the sketchy education obtained by significant numbers of children, which left more and more young adults maladjusted to village life, but unequipped to take advantage of urban opportunities. Hardly any Fijians were found in the professions. In business enterprises, Fijian executives were as rare as icicles. "Any Fijians who could qualify for one of the professions is likely to be in the government," a well-informed young Fijian official told me. "Absenteeism is high, because a Fijian who decides not to come to work today knows that he isn't going to be hungry tomorrow because of it. Even with myself, the time ethic was something I had to learn."

In a typical pre-independence year, I discovered, only 29 Fijians had taken university entrance examinations, of whom 13 passed, whereas 376 Indians took the tests and 246 passed. The average Fijian wage-earner made less than half as much as the average Caucasian employe, 40 percent less than a Chinese, and 16 percent less than an Indian, according to tax statistics. Some two thousand Fijians were employed as skilled laborers in the Viti Levu gold mines, which for a time following the discovery of the ore on the main island in commercial quantities in 1932 constituted Fiji's second largest source of revenue after sugar. But the Fiji mining industry, which included silver, copper, manganese, and bauxite besides gold, had become uncertain by the time of independence.

The Indian outlook on life was dramatically different. Chiragh Ali Shah, a senior Indian member of the legislature, gave me a simple explanation for the economic success of the Indian community in general, despite the meager earnings at which many of them began. "It isn't how much money you earn but how much you save that counts," he said. So, in Suva and other towns, the names on the signs above shops and outside the offices of doctors, dentists, lawyers, accountants, and so on were mostly Indian, never Fijian. In 1972, two years after independence, a Fijian tour guide named Meli Loki became an instant national celebrity when he opened a store purveying Swiss watches, Japanese electronic items, and other imported luxury goods in the heart of Suva's teeming duty-free shopping area; he was the first Fijian to own a downtown shop.

"Indian and Chinese family enterprises should open their doors," a Fijian complained. "They give Fijians menial jobs and keep them there; they should train them to move up." This sentiment came from an educated, urban Fijian. The masses, content with the serene rural life, were uninterested in commerce or office work.

The built-in Fijian sense of guaranteed personal security, a product of the communal system, was buttressed by their attachment to the land. In virtually all South Pacific societies, including that of the Australian aborigines, association with the land or a specific portion of it is the basis of individual and clan identity; in short, it is by identification with land that a man knows who he is. Loss of the land, as in Hawaii, has been followed by social decline. The affirmation of Fijian land rights by the former British government had assured the continued health of Fijian native institutions.

Land claims by foreigners that survived the strict British scrutiny immediately after the cession resulted in alienation of less than 10 percent of the land area of Fiji. Vacant land for which no Fijian owners could be found, amounting to about 7 percent of the total, reverted to the crown. The rest—83 percent —remained with the Fijian people, under the traditional system of communal ownership by landholding units, or clans, called *mataqali*. The *mataqali* land was immobilized from 1875 to 1905, when a few transfers were permitted. The last sale of Fijian land was in 1909. In 1940 the control of all Fijian holdings was placed under a government organization called the Native Land Trust Board, which acted for the *mataqali* owners in granting leases, limited to ten years at a time, and collecting rents.

The ten-year limit on leasing distressed the Indian sugar growers, who produced most of the cane but owned very little of the land on which it grew. There was a wholesale resumption of cultivated areas by the *mataqali* owners upon the expiration of leases, as Fijians prepared to take over the government. This caused great disruption in the Indian community, of whom at least 70 percent were on the farms. Indians at that time already slightly outnumbered the Fijian population.

Ramchand Sharma, a cane farmer on Viti Levu for forty years, showed me around a 5,000-acre location in the rural Koronobu district that had been resumed by the government when the leases held by an Australian milling firm expired. The government, he said, had subdivided the area and parceled out 182 separate small plots to Fijians, while the Indians who had been there for generations were relocated on vacant, hilly land that had never been cultivated before. Glum but undaunted, the hardworking Indians set about the expensive and painstaking task of clearing and draining the new site, preparing to start over. "The Fijians just sold off the farm animals and tools, rented their plots to others for 50 percent of the crop, and went back to the village," said my Indian guide. "Indians had been settled there for ninety years and had a moral right to buy," said Raojibhai Dahyabhai Patel, a leading lawyer and Speaker of the House of Representatives in the Fiji Parliament. He lived in Lautoka, a milling town and the principal port for sugar, from which Fiji derived 68 percent of its export income.

The industrious Indians were infuriated by the tendency of the easygoing Fijians to neglect plantations that had been efficient producers in Indian hands, in many cases letting fertile acreage revert to jungle. Patel cited instances in which plots that had produced 100 to 150 tons of cane in each crop had declined in output to as little as 20 tons under Fijian management. "The result is, while the Indians have lost the land, the country is losing the production," he said. "The Fijians," said another Indian politician, Karam Chand Ramrakha, "must take a more responsible attitude in developing their land as a national asset." Ramrakha, also a lawyer and deputy leader of the opposition in the Parliament, defended the overwhelmingly Fijian ownership of land. "I would even strengthen the law, for if anyone tried to disturb the Fijian land rights, there would be bloodshed," he declared.

The specter of racial violence haunted Fiji. Comparisons have been made with the racial division in such places as Mauritius, Guyana, and African countries, where there has been conflict between the large, commercially successful Indian community and the less prosperous blacks. Intermarriage between Indians and Fijians, though increasing, has been uncommon; when it occurs, usually an Indian man is marrying a Fijian woman, rarely the opposite. Indians consider Fijians their cultural inferiors, while the rank-conscious Fijians hold themselves socially above the immigrant Indians. I noticed that those on both sides who professed indifference to racial attitudes still referred to "us" and "them."

Sublimated racial tension often surfaced in politics. The Fijians, seeing their proportion of the population slipping behind, feared that the more prosperous and better-educated Indian community was on the way to taking political control if not curbed by a voting system rigged to favor the Fijians. The Indians, led by a militant, charismatic Gujarati lawyer named Ambalal Dahyabhai Patel, Raojibhai Patel's older brother, were demanding independence on a basis of "one man, one vote," a slogan that became the rallying cry of the Fiji Indian movement.

As late as September 1969 the protagonists agreed only that full internal self-government, within the Commonwealth, was desirable. This they already had, in effect. "We receive no instructions from London," Ratu Mara, then called chief minister and not yet knighted, said in a long conversation in his office. "We just tell London what we are doing." "The political problem is complicated by race, unfortunately," Ratu Mara explained, adding that the Fijians resisted very strongly "the danger of being dominated by another race in a part of the world they call their own." He continued: "I and others feel that the Indians have made a contribution . . . if only they were satisfied with participation, not domination. . . ."

Ratu Mara, who had been a star athlete at Oxford, was strongly for racial equality. He still had bitter memories of mistreatment by an Australian customs officer because of his skin, and of having been paid less, as a young Fiji civil servant, than Britons doing the same work. In the view of Ratu Mara and other ranking Fijians, it was the Indians who stood aloof, with their racial exclusiveness and apparent eagerness to seize power, as exemplified by Patel and his Indian political organization, the National Federation party. "Fijians don't want independence," Ratu George Cakobau, who was then the native lands commissioner, said bluntly. "The main reason is fear of domination by the Indian majority, [who] don't adapt themselves easily enough to the country they've come to adopt as home. Time will probably find a solution, but I see no indication of it at present."

In an attempt to defuse the racial division in politics, the government had devised a complex electoral system called "cross-voting," in which Indians elected Indians, Fijians elected Fijians, the third community—whites, Chinese, and others—elected its representatives, then everybody voted across racial lines for a specified number of Indian, Fijian, and "general" seats. "Cross-voting tends to elect moderates, as the candidates have to please all races," Sir Robert Foster, the last British governor, said in an interview in his spacious office in an old wooden, colonial-style building that was tied down with steel cables when a typhoon threatened.

Both the National Federation party, representing the Indians, and Ratu Mara's Alliance party, which advanced Fijian interests, attempted to deracialize politics by recruiting members of all communities. The effort was only partially successful. Racial animosity came to a dangerous boil following an election in 1968, in which Indian candidates of the National Federation party defeated the Indians backed by the Alliance party, which had expected to win two or three of the nine seats at stake. The outcome suggested to the Fijians that the Indians were using block voting to gather power. After some ugly incidents, Ratu George intervened and, through the chiefs, succeeded in cooling the violence. With the racial outbreaks in Malaysia fresh in memory, the episode suggested all too chillingly what might occur in Fiji as well, if feelings were unchecked.

When I left Fiji on 29 September 1969, independence seemed remote after all I had been told. At the airport I heard that the ailing Patel had died. When I returned a few weeks later, the entire outlook had changed. Patel's successor at the head of the National Federation party, Siddiq M. Koya, a moderate man, dropped the Indian demand for "one man, one vote" in return for an assurance by the Alliance party that "one man, one vote" would remain a national goal. "We decided to end the confrontation and talk with, not at, the other side," Koya, a big, good-natured man, said when I found him in genial conversation with Ratu Mara at a large cocktail party given in Suva by my friend Ramrakha on some family occasion.

Negotiations with the British on the conditions of independence proceeded smoothly. The entire Fiji Parliament was airlifted to London to approve the final agreement. This agreement was a compromise. The Indians dropped their demand that the new state be a republic, with a president, and consented to go along with the Fijian preference for remaining in the Commonwealth, with the British queen as the formal head of state. The communal voting for members of the House of Representatives—the lower chamber of the new parliament—was retained for the time being; Fijian dominance was virtually assured in the appointed Senate, in which eight of the twenty-two members would be named by the Fijian Great Council of Chiefs.

A Royal Commission of three distinguished British lawyers, appointed with the Fiji government's concurrence to make recommendations on improvements to the electoral system, reported after nearly six years of study with a proposal that a number of the seats decided on a racial basis should be transferred to the common roll. The Indian party accepted the suggestion, with reservations, as at least a start toward the ideal of "one man, one vote." The Fijians rejected the modification flatly, with Prime Minister Mara declaring in the parliament that the country was not ready for "any change in the method of election which is suitable to our multiracial society." An outburst of antiwhite racism, with both Fijians and Indians participating, enlivened the Suva city council's election of Leonard G. Usher, the New Zealand–born retired editor of the *Fiji Times,* as mayor of the capital. The ensuing uproar culminated in another vote, which came out a tie; thereupon, names were drawn from a hat and Usher, who had served several terms in the job before, won again.

Many politicians, including Prime Minister Mara, hoped gradually to achieve racial integration in the two major political parties. On successive visits over five years to six of the main islands, I kept getting more assurances of social adjustment between the Fijians and Indians, but I noticed that both sides still spoke of "us" and "them."

A question left for the future was what citizens of Fiji should call themselves. The term "Fijian" applied only to members of the indigenous race, but the Indians objected to a racial designation for themselves that associated them with India, a country from which most of them had been separated for generations. *The Fiji Times,* owned by an Australian company, suggested "Fiji Islander."

Meanwhile, the enthusiastic participation by Indian women in the government-sponsored family planning program—a month's supply of contraceptive pills cost ten cents, intra-uterine devices were supplied and fitted free—brought a dramatic downturn in the birth rate for Indians. The Fijian birth rate dropped much less slowly, more from apathy than from any negative attitude toward contraception. There was a decided prospect that the indigenous race might regain numerical equality with the Indians, or better.

The best chance for achieving racial harmony to the fullest, however, appeared to lie in the education of Fijians to fit them for participation in business and the professions. Meli Loki's duty-free shop was an encouraging sign, as was the appearance of the first all-Fijian investment company. The idea of pooling money, Ratu George explained to me, was "in accord with the communal tradition." "If we can convert the social structure to modern methods, Fijians will be a force," he said.

Although Fiji was not the first Pacific colony to become independent (Western Samoa, tiny Nauru, and Tonga were ahead), sovereignty made sultry, rainy Suva, a polyglot port town with about sixty thousand population and streets shaded by huge banyan trees, the premier capital of the South Seas. The ambassador from Suva would be the only voice from the South Pacific community in the United Nations General Assembly for the next five years, until Papua New Guinea joined the world body.

In many respects, Suva was my favorite South Seas town. Telephone communication with the principal countries of the world was virtually instantaneous, and the great British communications firm of Cable and Wireless provided superb telex service to practically anywhere abroad, although telegrams to outer islands had to be read over the government radio broadcasting system. The University of the South Pacific, with an international student body, and medical and vocational institutes made Suva a center of education for the entire South Pacific.

Facilities available in Suva influenced the improvement of family life throughout the South Seas. The Community Education Training Center, a project of the South Pacific Commission, taught girls from a dozen island territories how to achieve a balanced diet with the limited variety of food available in most tropical villages, and how to utilize materials, such as empty containers, that would have been thrown away to defile the landscape and become mosquito breeders.

The sleepy old town, which the British had chosen as the new capital in 1877 because of the fine natural harbor, retained numerous buildings redolent of the by-gone colonial period. The Cable and Wireless headquarters, with its pillared front porch, lent a touch of the Victorian era to the main street, appropriately named Victoria Parade. Another landmark, evocative of descriptions by Somerset Maugham, was the stately old frame-construction Grand Pacific Hotel, also on Victoria Parade across from Albert Park, with its second-floor veranda and old-fashioned ceiling fans that once stirred the muggy air around Maugham himself.

A less welcome anachronism was the rutted, bumpy main road around Viti Levu, called Queen's Road when it ran between Suva and Nadi along one side of the island, and King's Road on the other side. To the regret of independent Fiji, the bone-rattling highway is a monument to British chauvinism. During World II, when Nadi was a major United States logistics base, traffic between there and the main seaport at Suva was heavy. The Americans therefore wished to build, at their own expense, a first-class highway connecting Nadi and Suva through the center of the island. The British, feeling that an American contribution of such magnitude would reflect on the colonial administration, refused the offer. This British sensitivity would cost independent Fiji millions of dollars.

As in many other developing countries of the former colonial world, where material wants outstripped the average pocket-book, corruption became a common feature of life in Fiji. Paying bribes for licenses, and other petty graft, became so prevalent that the Fijians coined a word for it in the local language: *ghoose.* A cabinet minister in a position to do favors for businessmen was dismissed for questionable activities. Labor unrest flourished, as did prostitution and violence.

But the lovely countryside, the spectacular marine vistas, the dazzling sunsets, the gentle climate, and the tolerant good nature of the island people, both Fijian and Indian, remained unchanged. With all its problems, the emergence of Fiji as an independent state with full membership in the United Nations carried the political development of the South Pacific to a new level in its time.

EIGHT

Graustark South

ONTACT with the quarrelsome chiefs of Fiji, from whom they learned more of the art of war than they had known before, honed the bellicose tendencies of their Polynesian neighbors in Tonga. The Tongans were the brown imperialists of the South Pacific, at times extending their power into Samoa, as well as Fiji's Lau islands. Their historic background of having ruled much of the surrounding area, and the survival of an ancient aristocracy headed by the only reigning king in the South Pacific, have imparted to present-day Tongans a pride and exclusiveness that sometimes grate on other islanders, who are far from lacking in status consciousness of their own.

Tongans insist that their country alone among the South Pacific territories had never been a colony, only a "protected state" of Great Britain. When the powers ceded to Britain were taken back on 4 June 1970, in ceremonies mixing Polynesian pomp with that of the fictional toy kingdom of Graustark, Tonga referred to the occasion not as the attainment of independence but as the "Re-entry into the Comity of Nations," a phrase that appeared on huge signs all over Nuku'alofa ("abode of love"), the rickety capital.

The feisty little state refused to join the South Pacific Commission because of the convention that gave the member states with Pacific territories an extra vote for each dependency. "One country, one vote," the Tongans insisted, and stayed out. (Eventually they got their way in an overdue restructuring of the former colonial organization.)

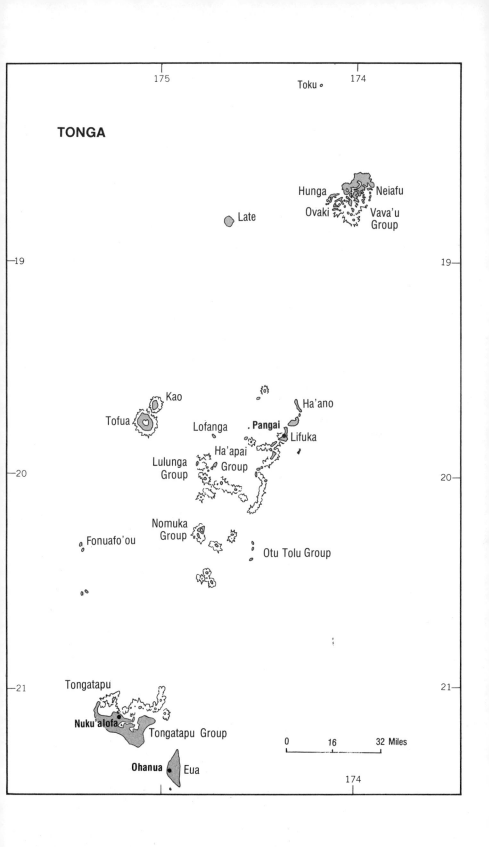

Yet the Tongans are an ingratiating people. When Captain Cook spent three months in Tonga in 1777, he was so entranced with the hospitality of the high chiefs that he called the group the Friendly Islands, a name that still appears on maps and the kingdom's postage stamps, and supplies the Tonga Visitors Bureau with an appealing image. Cook was unaware, however, that the same chiefs were plotting to murder him and his men and seize their two ships. The plot fell through when the chiefs were unable to agree on the timing of the deed, and Cook sailed on to Hawaii to be murdered there.

Cook's only complaint about the Tongans was their tendency to appropriate, in good, communal Polynesian fashion, whatever appealed to them in the expedition's equipment. American Peace Corps volunteers in Tonga also found this proclivity an annoying feature of the initial "culture clash" when they went to work in Tongan villages. " 'Sharing' has turned out to be what we used to call 'stealing,' " one volunteer remarked.

The image-makers in the Visitors Bureau contend that Tonga is "The Land Where Time Begins," since this is the first inhabited place in the world where the new day dawns. The international date line was bent eastward around Tonga to keep the islands on the same calendar date as New Zealand—though Samoa, due north, is a day behind. To some, however, Tonga was the land where time ended.

There are various theories as to the origin of the Tongan nation. For the "correct" version I consulted Chief Ve'ehala, a recognized authority on Tongan history, language, and customs. He was also a member of the king's privy council, a cabinet minister, and governor of the Ha'apai islands, a subgroup. Ve'ehala said he believed the Polynesian race to be the culmination of a protracted migration that began in the Euphrates Valley, moved through India and Malaysia, and continued in canoes to various Pacific islands. The Tongans, he said, were descendants of the group that settled in Western Samoa on the island of Savai'i. This is one of several islands (Raiatea, in the Society Islands, is another) identified in different accounts as the original of the legendary island of Hawaiki, where the settlement of Polynesia began. From Savai'i, the story goes, the forebears of the Tongan nation set out in huge canoes, with sails of woven pandanus, for their present home.

The name Tonga, according to Chief Ve'ehala, means "garden" in Samoa, where the Tongans came from, although in some

Polynesian dialects it means "south." Tongatapu, the island on
which the capital was placed, means "sacred garden." It was
indeed a gardenlike setting in which the voyagers from Savai'i
settled, among 150 islands in a ragged line extending about four
hundred miles from north to south, just east of Fiji. Only thirty-
six of the islands are inhabited. Their existence was unknown to
Europeans till two Dutch navigators sighted part of the northern
group in 1616.

About a thousand years ago, so the story goes, a mating between a Tongan woman of rank and the Polynesian deity Tangaroa produced a son, Ahoeitu, who became the first *tui tonga,*
or sacred king, a semidivine spiritual as well as temporal ruler.
The *tui tonga* line ruled for five centuries, during which customs
evolved that survive to the present. All land is the property of
the crown. The royal family is held in almost religious reverence.
Authority descends patrilineally, but sisters outrank brothers in
ceremonial affairs.

Eventually the *tui tonga* handed over secular duties to a collat-
eral line of chiefs, and Tonga then had two kings. As time went
on, chiefly rivalries divided the islands into warring groups. This
was the disturbed situation when the mutineers of H.M.S. *Bounty*
put Captain Bligh and loyal members of his crew into an open
boat in 1789 between the Tongan islands of Nomuka and Tofua,
in the Ha'apai group.

A significant turn was foreshadowed when a party from the
London Missionary Society arrived in 1797. The first group was
driven out (three of the missionaries were murdered), but the
Wesleyans who followed them succeeded in converting many
Tongans to Christianity. One of these was a chief named Taufa'a-
hau, a towering figure in Tongan history whose achievements
resembled those of Kamehameha I, the king who united Hawaii
under one rule.

Coming to prominence around 1830 in the Ha'apai group,
Taufa'ahau first united those islands, then the Vava'u group, and
finally Tongatapu. By 1845 he was the undisputed temporal ruler
of all Tonga, and in 1865, on the death of the thirty-ninth *tui
tonga,* the two royal lines were merged with the consent of the
chiefs. Thus the present dynasty was founded.

Meanwhile, the ruler, having been converted to Christianity by
a Tongan of Wesleyan persuasion, changed his name to King
George Tupou I, after the king of England. Soon all Tonga was
Christianized, and a controversial missionary named Shirley

Baker became premier. The Free Wesleyan Church of Tonga, a
breakaway from the mother organization, was made the official
state church of the kingdom, with the sovereign at its head. King
George Tupou I laid the foundation of present-day Tonga by
abolishing the ancient feudal serfdom. He established a constitutional monarchy in 1875; seven years later, education was made
compulsory.

Allegations of religious persecution by the dominant Wesleyan
church, involving the energetic Reverend Mr. Baker, led to a
series of British interventions. A treaty in 1900 placed the kingdom under British protection and gave Britain the responsibility
for defense, foreign affairs, and economic matters affecting British interests, such as shipping. The British stepped in again, in
1904–5, to overhaul a disorderly Tongan administration, which
resulted in the exile of a premier and treasurer. After that, the
Tongans were left in charge of the kingdom's domestic affairs,
though a British agent maintained a close watch from his bungalow near the palace.

The government consisted of a privy council, headed by the
king, whose other members were his appointed cabinet ministers.
The parliament was made up of the cabinet, whose head in recent
years has been a prime minister who happened to be the king's
younger brother; seven representatives elected by the thirty-
three hereditary nobles from among their own number, and
seven commoners elected by all male taxpayers over twenty-one
years of age.

Tonga has a distinctive personality in the Polynesian world.
The people of the kingdom seem more like the dour Marquesans,
at the eastern extremity of far-off French Polynesia, than their
ebullient nearer neighbors and ethnic kin in Samoa and Tahiti.
Arriving for the first time in August, at the height of the southern
hemisphere's winter, I found the air slightly chilly by tropical
standards. I suspected that climate had less to do with the prevailing sober demeanor than generations of heavy puritan influence
and the stifling social immobility built into a class system that has
largely disappeared elsewhere in Polynesia.

The deadening hand of the missionary ethic was visible in the
flat, uninspiring landscape of Tongatapu and the profusion of
dull frame cottages that might have been transported to the
serene palm groves from some dying village in New England. In
the architecture, at least, there was no indication anywhere of a
South Pacific heritage.

Yet the Tongans, despite the complete Westernization of their surroundings, exhibited an extraordinary affinity for tradition in other ways. An example was the virtually universal adherence, by both sexes, to the uniquely Tongan garment called a *ta'ovala,* a woven mat tied around the waist with a cord of coconut fiber. The story of the custom as told to me by Chief Ve'ehala gave an insight into the background of certain enduring Tongan attitudes, such as the extreme veneration of the nobility.

"*Ta'o* means to press down, and *vala* means skirt," he said. In common parlance, the *vala* is the skirt alone, adapted from the Samoan *lavalava,* while the *ta'ovala* is the mat worn above the skirt. The mat also covers the lower part of the *kofu,* the blouse worn by Tongan women. "The custom of wearing mats began when the first settlers traveled here from Samoa about a thousand years ago," Ve'ehala said. "On the voyage, the people wore clothes made of leaves. It was the custom never to appear unclothed before a chief, so when the leaves began to wither the people cut up some of the sails, which were made of woven pandanus, and covered themselves with these. On arrival at Tonga, they found pandanus to be abundant, so they continued to weave mats for clothing. When the *vala* was adopted, the people continued to wear the mats to show that they had arrived here respectfully clothed."

There were traditional variations in the *ta'ovala.* Working people commonly wore lightweight mats, more comfortable when moving about, especially in hot weather. "Chiefs and officials, who spend most of their time sitting, wear the heavy ones," said Chief Ve'ehala, who wore a heavy one. The king, I discovered, wore a finely woven mat as part of his daily attire. I asked Ve'ehala why. "The king wears a mat to show his respect for the past, for the chiefs and for his people," he said. Mats worn at weddings are the most finely woven, and may be decorated with feathers. At funerals, close relatives of the deceased wear their oldest mats, closely woven and often tattered. "Each family has traditional mats, especially the nobles," Ve'ehala explained. "The oldest is believed to have come from Samoa eight hundred years ago." And the older and more frayed a mat, the more respected it is. Many of these have names, by which they are well known.

The pretty Tongan girls on the unpaved streets of Nuku'alofa displayed a wide variety of *ta'ovala* around their still-slender waists. I saw strings of decorative seashells, streamers of bark cloth, nets embroidered with glass beads, and endless combinations of decorative basketwork dangling from belts. "These are new styles that have appeared only in the last few years," said Mrs. Mary Tongilava, a retired schoolteacher working in the Women's Handicraft Center in an ancient frame building on the main street of the town, where I went looking for a *ta'ovala* that I could buy for a souvenir. The shop had hundreds of the new variety on sale for a dollar or so. "The main thing is to have something around the waist as a sign of respect in case the king's car, or a chief, passes by on the road," she said. I gathered that a Tongan girl who appeared in public without at least a token *ta'ovala* would draw disapproving stares. "It isn't necessary to wear them at home, though," said Mrs. Tongilava.

Nuku'alofa, which has been described by other visitors as looking more like Cape Cod than the South Seas, dribbles along the waterfront in a succession of low frame buildings, with the modern, three-story International Dateline Hotel as the principal landmark visible when approaching the island from the sea. The harbor faces a vista of palm-clad coral islets marching along the reef. Between the hotel and the main part of the town, Tongan women gather in an open field to empty tons of green tomatoes and peppers from huge baskets of woven palm fronds. The vegetables are wrapped and crated in the shade of a row of ironwood trees for shipment to the markets of New Zealand by freighters tied up at the nearby wharf.

Beyond, in a seaside glade among tall Norfolk pines, stand the most photographed buildings in the kingdom, the monarch's palace and, beside it, the royal chapel. The gleaming white clapboard palace, built in 1867 by the founder of the Tupou dynasty, is a wonderfully nostalgic Victorian structure, with a veranda running the length of the second story, a central cupola, and roofs painted dull red.

His Majesty King Taufa'ahau Tupou IV, great-great-great-grandson of King George Tupou I, nearly filled the settee on which he sat as we talked in a reception room of the palace one afternoon. Standing six feet two inches tall and weighing more than 350 pounds, the ruler of Tonga is the biggest king in the world, though his country of 269 square miles of land and about ninety thousand people—half of them on Tongatapu—is one of the world's smallest. Bigness is a badge of nobility throughout Polynesia, where people of rank traditionally get the pick of the food. It also suggests a gross overabundance of carbohydrates in the Polynesian diet.

A story is told how the king, traveling in the United States, visited a distinguished doctor for a medical checkup and was urged to go on a reducing diet. His Majesty, the story goes, mentioned his fondness for yam, a giant tuber that commonly grows to forty-pound size in Tonga. "What's a yam?" the doctor asked. "Like a potato," said the king. "Well, don't eat more than one a day," the doctor ordered. The king solemnly promised.

The king's late mother Queen Salote (Tongan for Charlotte), who had ruled for forty-seven years at her death in 1965, captivated London and television viewers around the world when she attended the coronation of Queen Elizabeth II. A statuesque, handsome woman more than six feet tall and appropriately proportioned, she rode in an open carriage without an umbrella or head covering through the rain that drenched the spectacle, smiling and waving graciously to the cheering crowd. This, I learned in Tonga, was just good breeding; no Tongan, I was told, would cover the head in the presence of a person of higher rank.

Queen Salote educated her two sons for the future good of the kingdom. Her heir, as Crown Prince Tungi, was sent to the University of Sydney, Australia, to study law and government, and took a degree in jurisprudence with honors. His younger brother, Prince Sione, studied agriculture in Australia and later became his brother's prime minister, with the title of Prince Tu'ipelehake.

The future king traveled widely and was especially impressed by Japan, a country he visited several times as crown prince and king. After one such trip he promoted the use of battery-operated transistor radios in primitive villages throughout the kingdom, thus bringing isolated fishermen and coconut growers into contact with the outside world for the first time. He introduced the soroban, a Japanese version of the abacus, into Tongan schools as an aid in the teaching of arithmetic. He also encouraged the Japanese to enter into commercial connections with the kingdom.

The king was fascinated with the Japanese sport of sumo, a specialized and highly popular form of wrestling in which the professional competitors are men of extraordinary size for any race, let alone the ordinarily short and slender Japanese. The husky Tongans are fond of combative sports; a number have gone abroad as professional boxers, and one of these, a light-heavyweight named Johnny Halafihi, once fought in London for the championship of the British Commonwealth (he lost). The

Tongans were ideally proportioned for sumo, a sport requiring massive strength and skillful application of leverage, for which weight and outsize dimensions help.

The king decided to make sumo the national sport of Tonga, engaged instructors from Japan, and eventually sent four strapping Tongan youths to Tokyo to try for the long climb through the six stages of sumo ratings. One of the Tongan boys won the championship of his novice class in his first season. Tonga may be responsible for the internationalization of sumo.

The king's conversation revealed a range of knowledge. Discussing pending exploration for suspected offshore oil, he knew the geology involved and was aware of precedents for awarding a possible drilling contract to an international consortium, as was done a few months later. The American Peace Corps group working in the kingdom had been "well screened." The airport needed to be upgraded so that the Pan American and Air New Zealand jets that droned overhead, flying between Honolulu and Auckland, could stop at Tongatapu. The king complained that Britain was uninterested in developing a jet airport in Tonga that might compete with Fiji, then a British colony. In his development plans, however, he gave the airport and a tourist industry only second priority over a shipbuilding and marine repair facility at Nuku'alofa for vessels of up to five thousand tons.

It was in this interview that the king disclosed his intention to resume the governing powers that had been ceded to Britain at the turn of the century, retaining only a treaty of "friendship" with the former protecting power. "The old treaty was useful early in the century to bridle imperialism, and it did protect Tonga among the rival powers in the Pacific," he said. "But I think that it has served its purpose. We can now look after ourselves much better in foreign affairs, to our own advantage. The relationship was a purely voluntary one."

I recalled a remark by the finance minister, whom I had seen earlier, that Tonga was "almost entirely an agricultural society," largely on the subsistence level. The budget at that time was on the order of $6,500,000 a year, including about $540,000 in aid funds provided by Britain. When I asked what the gross national product was, the minister had smiled and said, "I must confess that such sophisticated economic indicators have not been worked out yet." The principal exports were coconut products and bananas. Fancy postage stamps—one was shaped like a banana, another like a coconut—for sale to collectors were an important source of revenue. "What has been holding up Tonga's development?" I asked the king. "Well," said the hefty monarch, "I've only been king of Tonga for two years."

Rehearsing for his coronation ceremony on 4 July 1967, his forty-ninth birthday, the king had complained that his velvet and ermine robe was too hot, adding: "Oh well, it happens only once in a lifetime." The king's everyday dress, which he wore at the interview, consisted of a lightweight *vala* and buttoned-up tunic with closed upright collar, and a finely woven mat of extra size to encircle his impressive girth.

Over a glass of orange juice, His Majesty talked of the kingdom's most famous archeological curiosity, a gatelike structure of three enormous coral blocks, described as a trilithon. The creation, believed to date to around A.D. 1200, consists of two thick, forty-ton uprights sixteen feet high, with a thin nineteen-foot block connecting them across the top, like a lintel. The weathered, partly moss-covered object, sometimes called "the Stonehenge of the Pacific," is known to Tongans as the Ha'amonga-a-Maui—literally, "burden of Maui," a Polynesian demigod. It had been generally accepted that the structure had been built by the *tui tonga* of the time as an archway over the entrance to a long-gone royal compound. The king disagreed.

"A beautiful entrance could have been made by carving wood—why stone?" he said. "Obviously it was meant to commit a vital message to future generations, which only stone could do, and the builder wanted it to be earthquake-proof. I felt that it must have been an observation platform for obtaining astronomical information. How would they have known the beginning of the year unless there was some system of marking the seasons and the passage of time?"

Carefully examining the monument, the king found grooved markings on the top of the crosspiece. Further observation by His Majesty revealed that the clefts were lined up exactly with the sun's rays at dawn on the longest and shortest days of the year, marking the beginning of the summer and winter solstices. To the king's mind, the discovery confirmed his theory. He declared the area a national park. The weathered trilithon is one of the main points of interest for tourists, along with the ancient terraced tombs of the *tui tonga* rulers, the grove where thousands of "flying foxes" (a type of bat) hang head downward from the trees all day, and the magnificent line of saltwater spouts, or "blow holes," where white columns of sea spray, forced through holes in the coral rocks by wave action, shoot sixty feet into the air.

Tourists have the island's beautiful beaches to themselves on Sunday, when the law of the kingdom forbids virtually all activity for Tongans except church-going. As far as I know, Tonga is the only country in the world where the sanctity of the Sabbath is protected by the constitution, which says in part: "The Sabbath Day shall be sacred in Tonga forever and it shall not be lawful to do work or play games on the Sabbath, and any agreement made or document witnessed on this day shall be counted void and shall not be recognized by the government." The bar of the International Dateline Hotel, a popular rendezvous, is off limits on Sunday except to residents of the house. The only commercial vehicle permitted to run on the Sabbath is one specially licensed bus for tourists only.

I returned to Nuku'alofa the following June for the ceremonies attending the resumption of independence and found the tatty little town dressed up with arches of woven palm fronds and countless hand-painted signs hailing the great event. The accompanying celebration was a three-day extravaganza in which Tonga showed its most colorful side for an international collection of notables, including a few ambassadors and the heads of government of the surrounding South Pacific island states.

The young Prince William of Gloucester, representing Queen Elizabeth II at the dissolution of yet another remnant of empire in the South Seas, was the most glamorous figure at the event as far as the royalty-conscious Tongans were concerned. To others, a highlight of every day was the appearance at breakfast, in the International Dateline Hotel dining room, of His Excellency Tupua Tamasese Lealofi IV, the blue-blooded prime minister of Western Samoa, always preceded by a middle-aged royal orator or "talking chief." This impressive personage, bare-chested and bearing the symbolic fly whisk of his office, would chant a lengthy eulogy as the prime minister sat down to his bacon and eggs.

A notable Tongan recalled from abroad for the occasion was Crown Prince Tupouto'a. Schooled in England and Switzerland, he was an exceptionally engaging young man, handsome in a continental way with his thin black moustache and not yet endowed with the royal *embonpoint* that his ample frame would no doubt acquire in later years.

At the hour-long changeover ceremony on the sunny greensward beside the wooden palace, the official guests in the central pavilion covered with woven pandanus mats were a Graustarkian spectacle in their top hats and morning coats, which the representatives of the Pacific island governments wore over their traditional skirtlike nether garments. The crown prince and Prince William wore dark uniforms with braid. The king was the most impressive of all in a black uniform trimmed with gold, the left breast covered with glittering decorations, a sword at his side and on his head a tall, plumed hat.

With stately tread in the beating sun, His Majesty reviewed the kingdom's entire armed force of 300 men, including the palace guard, the Tongatapu police department, and a mechanized contingent consisting of two motorcycles and a truck, the men in dazzling white uniforms of *vala* and tunic, with military caps. After the formal exchange of documents between the king and the British representative, the royal battery boomed twenty-one times to salute the world's newest independent state. Each shot was followed by a high-pitched yell from the thousands of Tongans seated on the grass.

Later, 800 guests partook of a typical Tongan royal feast, sitting cross-legged on mats before long tables covered with broad banana leaves in a series of tentlike enclosures. Seventy golden-skinned Tongan girls cut and served the food, fetched beer and soft drinks, and chased flies from the tables with leafy switches.

An official provided me with an inventory of the food, which he said would be standard fare for an occasion in the presence of the king. Provided by villages throughout the island, he said, were 1,050 suckling pigs, 1,500 to 1,600 chickens, 1,020 servings of *lupulu* (corn beef, coconut cream, and onions, wrapped in taro leaves and baked in an *umu*, or underground oven), 3,000 crayfish, 2,500 yams, 4,000 plantains, 1,300 servings of *ota* (raw fish with coconut cream, onions, and herbs, marinated in lime juice), 300 watermelons, and 1,700 drinking coconuts.

The staggering munificence of the feast was dictated by Tongan etiquette, which requires that a guest be offered an entire pig, chicken, crayfish, and so on, to select the part he prefers. For ordinary week-end entertaining, I learned, between two thousand and three thousand suckling pigs are slaughtered every Sunday on Tongatapu. "It is not wasteful," the official said, anticipating an objection. "After the feast, all the food left over will be returned to the villages and be eaten to the last morsel."

Sated, we watched sinuous Tongan dances by hundreds of grass-skirted girls from all the major islands, accompanied by a single instrument, the nose flute. Girl jugglers, demonstrating an art practiced only in Tonga among the Pacific islands, kept half a dozen candlenuts or oranges in the air, with hand movements synchronized to the rhythm of a song.

Later, at the royal ball in the garden of the International Dateline Hotel, portly Tongan dowagers tucked paper money into the dancers' clothes in the middle of the performance to show admiration. Sometimes a bill was just slapped onto the dancer's oiled skin, and a particular favorite would finish a number festooned with currency; if a bill fell to the floor, she picked it up when the dance was finished.

One of the tens of thousands of American servicemen who had been stationed on Tongatapu during World War II, when the island was a supporting base for operations in the Southwest Pacific, came back for the celebration. Ernest G. Johnson, of Corvallis, Oregon, a former chief warrant officer with the navy Construction Battalion—the famous Seabees—was the lone representative of a brief but exciting era in the island's past. "The first Seabee battalion created came here," he related. "They built the airfield and the main wharf. There were 10,000 army men on the island, and a Marine division stopped here on the way to Guadalcanal. One day I counted sixty-five ships out there," he said, indicating the harbor where only a British frigate, in port for the independence festivities, and a couple of scruffy island vessels were tied up beyond the soft light of the festive torches that outlined the shore.

As the war moved north, Tonga became one of many more or less forgotten rear bases manned by a few homesick Americans who spent their time longing to be somewhere else. By July 1944, when Johnson finally received his departure orders after two years and five months on Tongatapu, there were only thirty-one Americans left on the island. Presently, back came the expatriate legion of comely young Tongan women whom the pious Queen Salote had sent to the inaccessible islands of the Ha'apai and Vava'u groups to preserve the racially pure Polynesian population of Tongatapu from unsanctified dilution.

Unlike a certain island in the Solomons where men were in short supply and the chiefs encouraged American troops to mate with the local girls—provided that the temporary spouses and any children were left behind when the visitors left—Tonga needed no help in increasing the population, which was swelled daily by an annual birth rate of 3.76 percent, one of the highest in the world. At the same time, with free medical care provided by the Tongan government through mobile clinics and three general hospitals, one in each of the three groups, manned by capable graduates of the Fiji School of Medicine in Suva (they were called "medical practitioners," not doctors), the death rate fell to a record low of 2.9 per thousand population.

Tongatapu thus became one of the most overcrowded major islands in the South Pacific, with nearly five hundred persons to the square mile. Too few people had too much of the limited land, and too many educated young Tongans—60 percent of the population was under twenty-one years old, with an average age of sixteen—were determined to realize their capabilities in the attractive urban milieu of Nuku'alofa instead of returning to the soil on the roomy and verdant, but isolated, outlying islands of the sprawling archipelago.

Inevitably, social pressures were changing Tonga from the idyllic South Seas kingdom that Queen Salote had ruled for nearly half a century with tender, if autocratic, motherliness. The land system instituted by the first Taufa'ahau ruler, King George Tupou I, had insured stability in a simpler era. All land is owned by the crown, but large estates have been placed in the care of members of the hereditary nobility. Every male Tongan, on reaching the age of sixteen, is entitled to an allotment, called 'api, of eight and one-quarter acres of rural land and a town site of two-fifths of an acre, in consideration of an annual poll tax of between three and four dollars. The intention of the law, which is embodied in the constitution, was to maintain a universal interest in agriculture, the base of the kingdom's economy, once mainly for subsistence but increasingly for cash in recent years.

New landholders under the distribution law are required to plant 200 coconut trees—the number deemed scientifically right for eight and one-quarter acres—in the first year, and to keep the property free of weeds. Selling the land is forbidden. Among the coconuts, a prime source of cash, properly indoctrinated Tongans would plant such food crops as bananas, plantains, taro, sweet potatoes, and yams. Pigs were a menace to the gardens when left to wander freely and forage for food in the traditional way, so the government has been endeavoring to introduce more orderly pig-raising methods, and also to encourage cattle-raising.

The South Pacific ethic of sharing makes it improbable that an unemployed Tongan will be in danger of going hungry. With the population explosion, however, the government has run short of available land in the areas where young Tongans with education and ambition are willing to settle. Consequently, I was informed, only a third of the Tongan youths eligible for *'api* plots had received their allocations. "Our biggest problem is to find work for the growing population of young people," said Mahe Tupouniua, the deputy premier and minister of finance. A commoner who had been educated in New Zealand and the London School of Economics, he was one of the kingdom's most capable officials, and was eventually drafted to head a regional economic cooperation organization. "Our human resources simply go unutilized," said Mahe as he was called in governmental circles throughout the South Pacific. "Between four hundred and five hundred young people come out of the schools every year, reasonably trained, and the job market is able to absorb perhaps a quarter of them. The rest return to the villages, or hang around town—another problem."

Mahe's concern was well founded. Gangs of unemployed youths were blamed for an outbreak of house burglaries in Nuku'alofa, once known as a town where nobody thought of locking doors. Aware young Tongans returning from schooling in the egalitarian atmosphere of New Zealand, where most South Pacific islanders go for higher education, began to question political and social institutions that had gone unchallenged for generations in the kingdom. The complainers were a minority, but the dissatisfaction was infectious.

There was a stir in the Tongan Parliament when a fifteen-year-old high school girl, giving the prize-winning speech in an English oratorical competition, attacked the system of giving the thirty-three hereditary nobles equal representation in the legislature with the entire remainder of the electorate. The distribution of seats, she declared, was "unbalanced, unfair, and simply undemocratic." Some blue-blooded members of the Parliament demanded action against the kingdom's one newspaper, the weekly *Tonga Chronicle,* for publishing the speech. The Speaker, himself a noble, ended the debate by reminding the assembly that the constitution guaranteed freedom of expression.

A few Tongans dared to sign their names to letters and articles criticizing the nobility and even the throne that appeared in *Pacific Islands Monthly,* the popular news magazine of the South Seas, published in Sydney and circulated to every island and atoll. Such statements were radical indeed for a strongly traditionalist island country where many older people still dropped to their

Robert Trumbull/*New York Times*

Ha'amonga-a-Maui, "the Stonehenge of the Pacific," on Tongatapu

Albert Henry, premier of the
k Islands, on the beach of his
ttonga home in 1973

Robert Trumbull/*New York Times*

Beach Road, the main street of Apia, Western Samoa, after one of the frequent rains. All distances on Upolu are measured from this clock tower

The waterfront at Apia

knees by the roadside when the king's car was seen approaching.

In spite of the new temper of the times, however, veneration of royalty remained strong even among articulate youth. There was no noticeable outcry on the score of human rights when King Taufa'ahau abruptly invoked royal powers to annul the marriage of a nubile twenty-one-year-old niece, Princess Mele, the daughter of Prince Tu'ipelehake. At school in Auckland, New Zealand, the girl fell in love with a fellow Tongan student and they were married. The boy happened to belong to the lowest class in the three-tiered Tongan social gradation. When I spoke of the affair to contemporaries of the young man in Nuku'alofa, they agreed that he had been wrong in aspiring to marry into the royal family and that the king had acted rightly. Shortly afterward, the princess was married to an official of noble lineage.

As the last functioning kingdom in the South Pacific, Tonga was an exotic addition to the roster of sovereign states. Its political evolution continued, after independence, at the unhurried pace traditionally associated with Polynesia. Five years after the royal government had assumed full sovereignty, the parliament cautiously proposed an amendment to the century-old constitution that would give the greatly swollen population more representatives in the legislature, along with more seats for the nobles, too.

The Western image of Tonga as a museum-piece kingdom, interesting only to anthropologists and missionaries, abruptly changed after the Soviet ambassador to New Zealand, Oleg Selyanninov, appeared in Nuku'alofa in April 1976 to present his credentials to the king as the first Soviet ambassador to Tonga. The envoy conveyed an offer by Moscow to improve the international airport, extend port facilities, and set up an oceanic research station, among other assistance. All Moscow asked in return was a base in Tonga for the Soviet fishing fleet. King Taufa'ahau was interested. The repercussions of this news, with its implications for Big Power relations in the Pacific, shook Washington and Peking. Australia and New Zealand reacted with dismayed shudders. Crown Prince Tupouto'a, who was reported to have initiated the Soviet contact while he was Tonga's high commissioner in London, responded blandly to the general concern at a news conference during a visit to Sydney, Australia. "Tonga has many friends, and all we ask of them is that they don't choose our enemies for us," he said. Suddenly, the Kingdom of Tonga became more than a tropical Graustark.

NINE

Too Many Cooks

---

*H*APPY with a lesser political status juridically than neighboring Fiji, Tonga, and Western Samoa, but none the less proudly self-governing within the British Commonwealth, are the lonely, jewellike Cook Islands. The Polynesian inhabitants have run their own affairs for the most part since the beginning of their history. In emerging from colonialism, they avoided the common error of equating freedoms with sovereignty. In practice, the status of the Cooks as an autonomous state in free and voluntary association with New Zealand, which controls foreign relations and defense and influences economic affairs through assistance allotments, has been envied and to some degree copied by other emerging Pacific island states.

The beauty and hospitality of the Cook Islands and their comely, brown-skinned people are legendary in the South Seas. The sweep of the serrated green hills of Rarotonga, the main island of the group, is one of the unforgettable sights of the Pacific. Wartime American pilots in the South Pacific made excuses to stop overnight—longer, if possible—on Aitutaki, where the United States had an air base. (Aitutaki's shapely girls are renowned as grass-skirted dancers in a stirring genre resembling the Tahitian style, and regularly outdo the Tahitians themselves for the top prizes in Pacific-wide competitions.) One American who had served on the island, named John Harrington, liked it so well that he returned after the war to stay.

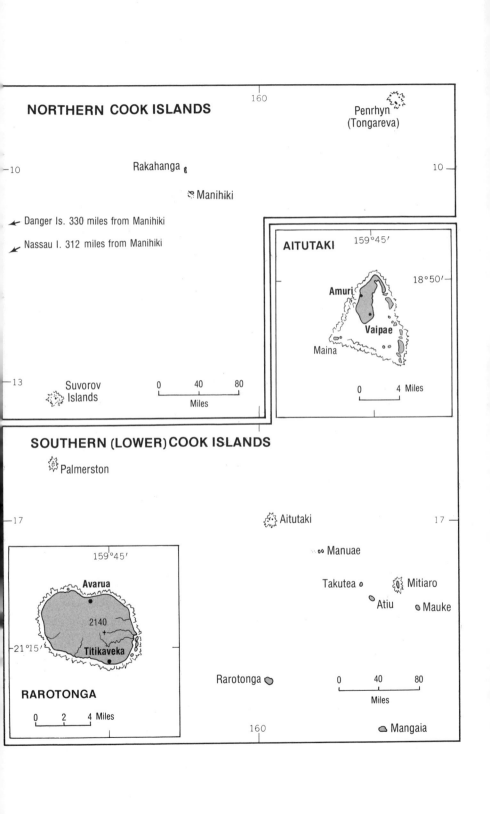

NORTHERN COOK ISLANDS

160

Penrhyn
(Tongareva)

−10   Rakahanga   10

Manihiki

Danger Is. 330 miles from Manihiki

Nassau I. 312 miles from Manihiki

AITUTAKI   159°45′

18°50′

Amuri

Vaipae

Maina

−13   Suvorov
Islands

0   40   80

Miles

0   4 Miles

SOUTHERN (LOWER) COOK ISLANDS

Palmerston

−17   Aitutaki   17

oo Manuae

Takutea o   Mitiaro

Atiu   Mauke

159°45′

Avarua

2140

−21°15′   Titikaveka

Rarotonga

0   40   80

Miles

RAROTONGA

0 2 4 Miles

160

Mangaia

The relative inaccessibility of the Cooks burnished the legend. Till recently, air and ship passage have been difficult to obtain. Most cruise passengers saw Rarotonga only from the ship's rail. Until World War II brushed the Cooks lightly, bringing contingents of American servicemen to Aitutaki and the northernmost atoll of Penrhyn (also called Tongareva), few outsiders were seen in the islands other than the ubiquitous missionaries, venturesome yachtsmen (who sometimes left their boats behind, impaled on a coral reef), and unobtrusive administrators and traders from New Zealand. Under the benevolent guardianship of New Zealand, the unhurried islanders became the healthiest and best-educated native people in the South Seas.

The fifteen tiny islands and atolls of the Cook chain, of which twelve are considered to be permanently inhabited, march down the middle of the vast sweep of Polynesia in a wavy line straddling thirteen degrees of southern latitude. The archipelago encloses 750,000 square miles of sea, but the total land area of the islands —all so small that they are measured in acres—is only 93 square miles. Most are accessible only by small trading vessels, and some go unvisited for months.

So small, remote, and widely scattered are the Cooks that the discovery of all fifteen by western navigators took 240 years. The Spanish explorer Alvaro de Mendaña de Neyra is believed by some authorities to have sighted the outlying atoll of Pukapuka first, in 1595. The last was said to have been an American, Captain John D. Sampson, who came upon a previously uncharted 300-acre patch of sand and palm trees and called it Nassau, after his ship, in 1835.

Cook himself discovered five obscure islands: Manuae, which he called Hervey, after a British naval figure, in 1773; Palmerston in 1774; and Mangaia, Atiu, and Takutea in 1777. He missed all the others in the chain that bears his name. Captain Bligh is credited with having discovered Aitutaki in the *Bounty* before the famous mutiny; and the mutineers themselves are believed to have been the first Europeans to call at Rarotonga, where they are said to have left the orange seeds that began a now-thriving citrus industry on that island.

Local tradition had it that the Polynesians of the Cook Islands were descended from two legendary warriors, Karika, of Samoa, and Tangiia, of Tahiti. On separate expeditions of discovery, they met at sea and came to the Cooks together after deciding not to fight because there was no one to watch. Legend places this meeting around A.D. 1200, but archeological evidence suggests that the Cooks have been inhabited for fifteen hundred years. It is thought that the progenitors of the Maori race of New Zealand jumped off from Rarotonga in giant sailing canoes in A.D. 1350.

Much of the present character of the Cook Islands was foreordained with the arrival of the famous proselytizer of the London Missionary Society, the Reverend John Williams, in the 1820s. All the Cook Islanders were converted in relatively short order. Soon the stern British clerics acquired such influence with the ruling Polynesian chiefs that they virtually controlled the government on every island. As the missionaries did everywhere, they persuaded the islanders to envelop themselves in unsuitable western clothes. Through their sway over the chiefs, they got their own Puritan code incorporated into the law of the land. One of the most notorious of these "blue laws," as they were called throughout the easygoing South Seas, prohibited "cohabitation" outside wedlock. It stayed on the books in Rarotonga until 1966, when it was repealed, but the law remains on other islands where the governing local councils are run by strait-laced church-goers. The islands are dotted with impressive churches of coral stone, painted dead white and invariably adjacent to a graveyard crowded with eroded headstones.

Along with their deadening influence on the vivid Polynesian personality, however, the missionaries imparted a zeal for education and a sense of hygiene. Less constructive visitors were the labor recruiters for the mines of Peru, more slavers than blackbirders, who almost depopulated Penrhyn in the 1860s. At one time, I was told, thirteen islets in this huge atoll were inhabited; today there are people on only two (Americans built an airstrip on the main island during World War II, but it is seldom used).

Because of their isolation and comparative poverty of resources, the Cooks suffered less than other Pacific island groups from the corrosive attention of predatory whites, barring the limited depredations of the Peruvian slavers. Minerals and timber attractive to exploiters were lacking. No fine harbors drew the interest of naval strategists. There were only missionaries and traders to impinge on the easy Polynesian way of life.

Inevitably, the flag followed the cross. With France and Germany expanding in the Pacific, the existence of the Cooks in a power vacuum bothered the British. Britain therefore moved to annex the chain, and finally did so in 1888 with the agreement of the hereditary chiefs, called *ariki*. The British government handed the administration of the islands to New Zealand in 1901. There was little interest among the New Zealanders for wholesale colonization, however, for there was still plenty of scope for developers at home.

The hand of empire fell lightly on the Cooks. The generally mild-mannered New Zealanders conducted Cook Islands affairs in characteristic low key. A council of *ariki* from all the islands— later subordinated to a representative elected body—made the governmental decisions, subject to the approval of a New Zealand administrator in Rarotonga and his agents on other islands, the latter often Polynesians.

Under the relaxed supervision of New Zealand, the widely scattered islands and atolls developed along lines suited to their separate traditions and needs. Thus the individual islands maintained a recognizable identity that still endures under the umbrella of a general Polynesian ambience. The seven hundred or so people of the outlying atoll of Pukapuka even speak a different dialect of Polynesian from the rest, more like Samoan than Rarotongan. The eighty-odd people of tiny Palmerston atoll, with one square mile of land, speak a mixture of nineteenth-century Gloucestershire English and Polynesian as it is spoken on isolated Penrhyn atoll. They are all descendants of a British seafarer named Marsters, who settled on the uninhabited islet in 1862 with two sisters from Penrhyn as wives, built a home from the wreckage of ships deposited on the beach, and was joined by a third Penrhyn woman. All three women bore children, who grew up and intermarried, begetting more children, and so on for several generations.

Pukapuka atoll, also known as the Danger Islands, would have been known around the world, at least briefly, but for U.S. Navy censorship in World War II. Three American airmen, whose plane crashed in the empty Pacific when the crew lost the way back to their aircraft carrier and ran out of fuel, washed up on the main islet—also called Pukapuka—after thirty-four harrowing days in a tiny rubber life raft. Because of security considerations, navy censors excised the name of the atoll from news stories on the remarkable survival experience, an international sensation at the time, and from my subsequent book on the episode, called *The Raft.* On a visit to Rarotonga thirty years later, I came upon an official guide published by the Cook Islands government that mentioned the book as one of several giving "good descriptions" of Pukapuka—though I had never seen the place. The tribute belongs to Harold Dixon, one of the men in the raft, who had described the island to me.

"The Cook Islands are islands of contrast," the premier, Sir Albert Henry, once said in that loving tone that all South Pacific people use when they talk of their islands. "There is Rarotonga, the island of flowers, with its bold skyline and thriving agricultural industry . . . and there are lovely coral atolls with still lagoons and sweeping white sand beaches." Rarotonga, the largest island and administrative center, is shaped like a slightly flattened profile of one of the juicy oranges for which "Raro" is known throughout the South Seas. Avarua, the villagelike capital, lies along the sparkling sea in the indent where the stem of the orange would be. The whole island is ringed with creaming surf and white sand beach; it is only a twenty-mile drive all the way around on a paved highway, one of the best in the South Seas, called Ara Tapu, meaning "sacred road." Back from the seaside is a second belt road hacked from the jungle centuries ago and paved with coral rocks, called Ara Metua, or "old road"; it is still in use, though broken in several places by jungle growth and sometimes made impassable in spots by flooding.

Inland, the green hills of Rarotonga rise in sharp folds to the matched central spires of 2,140-foot Mount Te Manga and the slightly lower peak of Te Atukura. Most of the island's ten thousand people, half the population of the group, live on the shelf between the mountains and the beaches; their palm-shaded villages of neat, Western-style cottages with metal roofs and clipped lawns look more like a suburb of Auckland than a South Seas settlement as a result of the extensive interchange of peoples with New Zealand over the decades.

Avarua is the prototype of the South Seas port, brought up to date with a couple of one-story department stores and motor scooters ridden by dusky girls with garlands of frangipani crowning their black, flowing hair. Most buildings are of wood, with the usual red corrugated iron roof, among the palms and ironwoods. "Traditional houses disappeared fifteen years ago," a resident said. "Not only did people acquire New Zealand tastes, but replacing the thatched roofs every five years or so became too expensive. Unfortunately, the New Zealand–style houses with their tiny windows are badly ventilated for the tropical climate." At one end of the village, which is six streets long and four streets wide, is the enormous Protestant church of weathered stone, with a forest of battered headstones in the adjacent cemetery; at the other end is the wooden wharf, where cargo and passengers are deposited from ships anchored beyond the coral reef a few hundred yards offshore. The town's trademark has long been the tattered hulk of the American yacht *Yankee*, blown onto the wicked coral heads by a gale in 1964 and still there a decade later. While I was on the island, *Yankee* was joined on the reef one stormy Sunday night by a second, smaller American yacht, *Wind Waggon II*, owned by a retired California lawyer.

For many Cook Islanders from outlying islands and atolls, Rarotonga was a way station en route to New Zealand, where they hoped to find jobs and integrate with the modern world depicted so attractively in magazines and films. The twin results were depopulation of the smaller islands, and overcrowding on Rarotonga. According to officials on Rarotonga, there were at least half as many Cook Islanders living in New Zealand as in the home islands. The metropolitan magnet for ambitious Polynesian youth was Auckland, the industrial center. The city of half a million contained a population of native-born Maoris and immigrants from the Cooks and other Pacific islands numbering about one hundred thousand, making it the biggest Polynesian city in the world.

As full citizens of New Zealand, the Cook Islanders and the Polynesians of the other New Zealand dependencies of Niue and the Tokelau Islands were free to come and go in the Dominion. This was a privilege greatly envied by restless Fijians, Tongans, and others who longed to escape the confinement of their islands, but encountered immigration bars everywhere.

For the islanders, the adjustment to big-city life was frequently an unhappy experience. Although the Cook Islanders called themselves Maoris, like their racial kin in New Zealand, relations between the two groups of Polynesians were often abrasive. Fights between Cook Islanders and New Zealand Maoris, and even between Polynesians of different islands, were said to be a bigger police problem in Auckland than interracial friction involving whites.

Like the annexation by Britain, self-government had come to the Cook Islands almost casually, partly as a result of indirect influence. The New Zealanders, who regard themselves as one of the most egalitarian peoples in the world, quietly chafed under pressure from the decolonization committee of the United Nations—a notably unpragmatic bunch when it comes to dealing with questions of dependent peoples—to demonstrate political advancement in the islands. To the surprise of many Cook Islanders, New Zealand announced in 1962 that the group would become self-governing three years later.

The changeover was formally effected on 4 August 1965, after a series of necessary constitutional and legislative steps, including the election of a new parliamentary organ called the Legislative Assembly. The juridical connection with New Zealand was maintained, at the wish of the islanders, through the retention of Queen Elizabeth II of Britain as queen of the Cook Islands. Sensibilities in Buckingham Palace were jarred, it is said, when the Cook Islands honored the queen by minting—in Australia—a one-dollar commemorative coin pairing Elizabeth's likeness with a representation of the Polynesian god Tangaroa, in which the deity's male attributes were, so to speak, outstanding; specimens were selling for thirty-five times the face value when I was last in Rarotonga. (A later distribution brought the price back down to face value, I have been told.)

The Cook Islanders have four levels of the social order, with the twenty-four *ariki* of the various islands constituting the thin top layer. Just below these are the *mataiapo*, then the *rangatira*, both subchiefs. Last are the *unga*, or commoners. For an *ariki* to be a woman is not uncommon; Polynesian societies in general accept the equality of the sexes. An *ariki* from Atiu, with the exotic local title of *rongomatane*, a lovely twenty-one-year-old who worked in the post office in Avarua, was a shipmate of mine on a trip to Atiu in the old government vessel *Moana Roa*. She played the ukulele in the nightly songfest in the ship's bar, and the Atiu boys aboard seemed to regard her as almost a goddess. The titles, I learned, generally were passed down through a complicated selection process, not always in the same family. Through the influence of the missionaries, who seemed to have found it difficult to think in Polynesian terms and liked to fit all royalty into the British pattern, the *ariki* titles became hereditary in some areas.

The British—and later the New Zealanders—had governed the islands through a council of the *ariki*, with the Makea Nui of Avarua as head chief, or queen, until the system of elected representation evolved. With the coming of self-government in 1965, a permanent body called the House of Ariki was established as a kind of nonlegislative senate, with thirteen members appointed from among the twenty-four chiefs to advise on matters involving customs and traditions, including land tenure (under the Cook Islands system of communal possession of land, a single acre may have dozens of owners, and disputes are frequent).

I managed, after much telephoning, to obtain an audience with the current Makea Nui, who had been elected that year's president of the House of Ariki (the speaker of the Legislative Assembly was also a woman, Premier Henry's sister, Marguerite Story). This distinguished matriarch presumably would have been the Polynesian queen of the Cook Islands had not her grand-aunt handed over power at the turn of the century, although I encountered some question of her paramount status in conversation with several other *ariki* on Rarotonga, Atiu, and Aitutaki. She received me in her rambling stucco residence, where Queen Elizabeth had been her house guest not long before.

Makea Nui Teremoana Ariki (all *ariki* use the title at the end of a string of names or lesser titles, like a surname) assured me that she was indeed the paramount chief of the Cook Islands, but preferred to put the subject aside. "I don't talk about it, so as not to bother the other *ariki,*" she said. The matriarch, who said her friends called her "Tere," was an aristocratic figure at the age of sixty-seven years, with alert black eyes and an aureole of plumeria blossoms in gray hair pulled severely back. A portrait of the earlier Makea Nui who had signed the islands over to colonialism hung above a door.

Behind the classic colonial house stood the hurricane-damaged remains of the 170-year-old former palace of the Makea Nui line, on the site of a revered *marae* (temple ground) called Taputapua-tea (approximately, "most sacred place"), after the original on Raiatea, in the Society Islands. It was on this spot that the British flag was raised over Rarotonga for the first time and the annexation ceremony took place. The last queen was permitted to fly her own flag over the property till her death, said the *makea nui.*

The Makea Nui Teremoana Ariki represented the twenty-ninth generation to hold the title, which, she said, was "about as old as the British crown." Like most Cook Islands aristocrats—and commoners, too, I surmised—she was opposed to immediate independence for the islands. "We are not ready," she said. She had, in fact, opposed self-government insofar as it loosened the tie with New Zealand, and had resigned from the Legislative Assembly in protest just before the event took place. The *ariki,* she added, were "disappointed with the government," which was "making laws over the heads of the *ariki,*"ignoring the consultative status conferred upon the chiefs in the constitution.

Power in the Cook Islands was held firmly by Premier Henry, who was said to have acquired progressive political ideas from contact with American servicemen on his home island of Aitutaki during the war, and from later association with radical unionists in Auckland, where he held a variety of obscure jobs ranging from labor in the fruit markets to teaching school.

Sir Albert Royle Henry (he was knighted by Queen Elizabeth in 1975) was one of the notable men among the new political leaders of the South Seas. He became a frequent and effective spokesman for the emerging people of Pacific territories at international meetings, although he was not the head of a sovereign government. His surname came from a British ancestor, and his middle name honored a famous Cook Islands missionary. To those who came to know him well at numerous South Pacific gatherings he was "Uncle Albert," a title of respect and affection. He was a gracious host at his comfortable cottage on a Rarotonga beach, and a congenial companion after working hours at various official conferences in the region. I once saw him bound onto a stage on Wellington when a group of Cook Island girls were demonstrating their spirited dances and join in the frenzied gyrations. "I just had to back up those little girls," he explained later.

Back home in the islands, Premier Henry was unbeatable at the polls. There was no shortage of critics of his forthright style of running the government, however. Opposition was manifested, for example, just before self-government when, having just returned from New Zealand with the expectation of taking over the reins, Henry was prevented from running for the assembly by a three-year residence requirement. As soon as the islands became politically autonomous, the law was repealed by the new legislature. Henry's sister thereupon resigned her seat in that body, Albert was victorious in the subsequent by-election, and was promptly named premier.

A favorite theme of the opposition to the premier was the number of people named Henry on the government payroll—"thirty by count," one critic told me. At the cabinet level, these included the minister of financial services and the minister of social services, besides the premier, who also held the portfolios of external affairs, finance, economic development, works, and communications. As mentioned before, his sister was speaker of the Legislative Assembly.

Sir Albert was a staunch defender of the tie with New Zealand, except during periods of annoyance when Wellington chose to show muscle. One such occasion arose when the premier, with a new-found enthusiasm for tourism, considered letting Pan American World Airways into the islands, breaking the Air New Zealand monopoly of this potentially lucrative tour market. He was reminded that New Zealand controlled foreign relations and that, furthermore, if a foreign airline came in, New Zealand economic aid might depart. The New Zealand subsidy at that time, about three-quarters in grants and the rest on loan at reasonable interest, covered more than half the islands' budget. This gave Wellington a powerful voice in Cook Islands affairs.

In travels around Rarotonga, Atiu, and Aitutaki—three of the four islands with more than 750 people on them—I found no one in favor of full independence, or at least not immediately. On the other hand, according to a member of the legislature from Atiu, at least six representatives of islands other than Rarotonga, including himself, formed a parliamentary bloc in favor of complete integration with New Zealand. "What we want is water and electricity," said the man from Atiu, indicating that these amenities would be developed faster if the Cooks became a county of New Zealand.

"The Cook Islanders prize New Zealand citizenship beyond rhyme or reason," said George Brocklehurst, the bespectacled New Zealand high commissioner, who occupied a unique position as the head of state of the Cook Islands, representing Queen Elizabeth, while serving as the diplomatic representative of New Zealand at the same time. "In one capacity I represent the Cook Islands in dealing with New Zealand, in the other I represent New Zealand in dealing with the Cook Islands," he said. "I often get papers submitted to me in one capacity that I'm not supposed to see in the other."

It was as head of state on one of his island tours that he was carried in procession from the rocks that served as a dock for Atiu in a wooden palanquin, decorated with leaves and flowers. The parade ended in the central square of the main village, where the party was greeted by the resident agent, holding a microphone. After a short speech of welcome, he said, "And now there will be a short service by the Reverend Mr. Tui. Over to you, Reverend Tui."

Religion and wild dancing were the incongruous accompaniments to a lavish *umukai*—the Cook Islands version of the Hawaiian *luau,* cooked in an *umu,* or underground oven, with heated rocks—with which the high commissioner was feted wherever he went on his tours. "It's a way of preserving our culture," a Polynesian official commented.

Atiu, a flattened volcanic outcropping encircled by a natural rampart of coral rock (a formation known in the South Pacific as a *makatea*), was an example of an island in a promising early stage of economic development. Besides the ubiquitous oranges and bananas, its fertile red soil grew pineapples, coffee, and cocoa. The ample possibilities for agricultural expansion on the eleven-square-mile island suffered, however, from a lag in long-standing plans to upgrade the meager harbor facilities. The venerable *Moana Roa,* Atiu's only regular link with the outside world, called there only once a month—but the bananas had to be picked every fortnight. Fruit was damaged in the transfer from lighter to ship by cargo slings. Children played in the shade of a large, open shed whose only purpose was to provide a slanted roof of corrugated metal for catching rain water.

"His Excellency," the high commissioner, was welcomed to Aitutaki, the second most populous island in the group with nearly three thousand inhabitants, by a dance on stilts to the beat of a slit drum, performed by young men in white shirts and black trousers, with grass skirts around their waists. A tablet marked the sacred spot where the first Christian missionary arrived to spread the Gospel throughout the group.

"Aitutaki has everything," said Edson Raff, a retired American paratroop colonel from New York, who had lived on the island for thirteen years while running a one-plane air charter service out of American Samoa. "My plane is based in Pago Pago, but I prefer to make my home here, where life is still unspoiled, with a beautiful lagoon, lots of fish, beaches, perfect climate, hospitable people . . . everything!" Raff and John Harrington, the returned wartime veteran, gave Aitutaki an American population of two. Thousands of American servicemen passed through Aitutaki during World War II, when the place was an air base. Raff was not one of them, however; he had spent the war in Europe, and wrote a book about his paratroop experience called *We Jumped for Victory.*

Like many Pacific islands, Aitutaki is a volcanic remnant surrounded by a coral reef dotted with small, sandy islets—in short, a combination of volcanic island and atoll, with a large lagoon. The people are self-sufficient, providing their own food from the lagoon, which is said to be the best for fishing in the whole group, and their vegetable gardens. Oranges and bananas were grown as cash crops. The climate, natural beauty, and superb swimming and fishing, especially off the dazzling white beaches of the reef islands, provided a still-unexploited tourist potential. "After the war, when the Americans left, this was the dirtiest and most depressed island in the South Pacific," said Doctor Joe Williams, the Cook Islands minister of social services, who was my guide on part of the tour of Aitutaki. "The departure of the Americans abruptly ended a lush period of cash economy, and the people couldn't readjust."

With aid from New Zealand, Aitutaki had just acquired a new forty-bed hospital of cement-block construction, with wards and rooms commanding a spectacular view of the lagoon and its necklace of palm-clad islets. With its junior high school (the Cooks were the only territory in the South Seas with free compulsory education) and the finest banana plantations in the group, the island appeared to be on the way to becoming the economic as well as the scenic jewel of the Cooks.

Appearances are deceptive, however, in the South Seas. Visual delights and the sunny nature of the attractive people often mask an underlying economic malaise. This was decidedly the case in the Cooks. "Because the islands are so small, the agricultural production can't be increased more than 25 to 30 percent, and that's not enough for a growing population," said Doctor Tom Davis, the leader of the opposition party in the Legislative Assembly. "Wages, averaging fifteen dollars a week, are far too low. Opportunity is practically nonexistent outside government service. And Albert Henry gives development grants only to the islands that support him, with just token grants to the others."

The meager wage pattern, combined with the prevalence of large families and a traditional diet overemphasizing starchy foods, produced widespread malnutrition, although nobody went hungry. "With a low level of wages and large families generally, the balance between sufficient food and malnutrition is a fairly precarious one," the Cook Islands Department of Internal Affairs stated in an official report. "Ignorance, laziness, and neglect of child care" add to the problem, said David Hosking, the president of the government workers' association, in a public statement.

The solution proposed by Doctor Davis, known to everybody on Rarotonga as "Doctor Tom," was to develop light industry. "We can do it, because wages will always be lower than in New Zealand," he said. Doctor Tom was doing his share to promote industry, having started a small factory producing souvenir carvings of miniature Polynesian canoes and the like for the curio trade in New Zealand.

Doctor Tom, born on Rarotonga in 1917 of mixed Welsh and royal Polynesian ancestry (he was a cousin of the Makea Nui), was one of the remarkable personalities of the South Pacific. As a young man he had been sent to New Zealand for training in medicine, then took degrees in tropical medicine and public health in Australia, and studied public health at Harvard. He began a distinguished career in medicine as a health officer in his native Cook Islands, then went back to the United States in 1953 and taught nutrition at Harvard for several years. As a specialist in environmental research in the American space program, he had been in charge of putting the first monkeys in space. After working on the Mercury space project, he joined the well-known scientific consultant firm of Arthur D. Little of Cambridge, Massachusetts. When he returned to Rarotonga to go into politics, it was in his own yacht.

Disturbing political news from the Cooks brought Doctor Tom back. He looked around, did not like what he saw, wound up his affairs in the United States, and returned to the Cooks again to form the Democratic party in opposition to Premier Henry's Cook Islands party. Henry's amendment to the constitution, annulling the three-year residence requirement so that he could run for office and become premier, now worked for his opponent. Davis and his Democrats won seven seats to the Henry party's fifteen in the twenty-two member parliament, and Doctor Tom became the official leader of the opposition. In the next election, three years later, Doctor Tom's party won eight seats, depriving Henry of the two-thirds majority needed to change the constitution again, which was what Doctor Tom feared. Sir Albert, furious over the setback, threatened to fire all Davis supporters from the civil service.

Sir Albert apparently had second thoughts on his threats of retaliation after a trip to New Zealand, which had meanwhile upgraded the political status of the Cooks by transferring the responsibility for relations with the islands from the Department of Island Affairs to the Department of Foreign Affairs, a move connoting greater independence for the former colony. There were reports of a roundabout hint from Wellington that if the Cooks wished to retain the cherished ties with New Zealand, it would be advisable for the government in Avarua to conform to the standards of democracy in effect for other citizens of the dominion.

Doctor Tom, chatting on the airy veranda of his spacious cottage on a green hill overlooking Avarua, explained that his disagreements with the widely respected premier mainly concerned matters of style, or "methodology," as the scientist put it. "Actually, we're good friends, and we respect each other," he said, "but I disagree with his socialistic approach to the control of production, which comes from his background in radical New Zealand unionism." These kind words were uttered before Henry accused the Davis party of corruption in the 1975 election, in which Sir Albert was elected with only thirty-six more votes than Doctor Tom got in retaining his assembly seat. It had been a bitterly fought contest, with some islanders feeling strongly enough to fly home from New Zealand to vote. It was widely accepted that Doctor Tom, a beloved figure because of his earlier medical work in the islands, would become premier after "Uncle Albert" left the political scene.

With the democratic example of New Zealand kept before them through the constant interchange of people, the Cook Islands remained committed to British parliamentary forms in their semi-independent government. The rending racial factor that underlay politics in Fiji was absent in the homogeneous Cooks. Nor did the Cooks suffer the dissatisfactions flowing from an authoritarian role for the hereditary chiefs, as in Tonga. At the same time, New Zealand citizenship was a safety valve for the stresses of overpopulation.

But free emigration to New Zealand, a cherished privilege, also had a price. (Every favorable development in the Cooks seemed to have a dark side, even the eradication of the disfiguring disease of yaws. This once prevalent malady, a spirochete infection, was believed to immunize its victim against syphilis. When yaws ceased to be endemic, according to island doctors, the incidence of syphilis increased.) Cost of New Zealand citizenship was an inevitable leakage of needed talent from the islands. "The brighter lads go to New Zealand for jobs," said the head of the treasury department, Jim Ditchburn, one of a number of New Zealand civil servants who had been "seconded" to the Cook

Islands government for specialized jobs. "The treasury has lost four or five men to New Zealand in the year I've been here," he added.

Most of the Cook Islanders going to New Zealand are untrained laborers, but their children grow up learning skills in their new homeland, said Phillip A. Amos, then the New Zealand minister of island affairs, at a social gathering in Avarua. "Only 1 percent, at most, return to the islands," he declared. "There's nothing to lure them back when they can earn as much in a week in New Zealand as they could make in six weeks here."

One balmy afternoon I had an unnerving peek behind the curtain of the future in store for Rarotonga. With some Polynesian friends, I had been watching the horse races staged by the local jockey club on the beach opposite Muri village on the eastern side of the island. The horses were ridden bareback by shoeless boys in jeans or shorts. The steeds would thunder down the beach, kicking up white sand, wheel at a marker, and gallop back to the starting line with waves licking at their hoofs. Afterward, we went to a seaside glade where the Cook Islands Women's Federation was to hold a dance exhibition for a group of tourists from a cruise ship.

A tremendous feast of Polynesian fare had been laid out on a long table covered with banana leaves. There was taro, the basic tuber, cooked underground with *kumara* (sweet potatoes), pumpkin, and *kuru* (breadfruit); pork and chicken wrapped in taro leaves with coconut cream and chopped onions, cooked underground on hot rocks; fish marinated with lemon in coconut milk; various combinations of banana, papaya, and coconut with a variety of shellfish collected from the reef. The food had been provided by the women, each supplying a portion and cooking it together. ("If you want anything done, you have to go to the women. They are the driving force behind the men," Tom Davis said.)

The tourists arrived like one of the typhoons that periodically rake the islands, bringing bedlam. Mostly middle-aged or older, all shapes and sizes, in a wild variety of shorts, slacks, flowered shirts, and nondescript protective headgear, they poured out of the chartered buses, chattering and exclaiming, cameras ready for action. Advancing purposefully in a formless line, they instantly surrounded the waiting dancers and the smiling hostesses from the women's federation. Piercing voices remarked hilariously on the dancers' pseudo-traditional attire of bleached grass skirts, with tops fashioned of pandanus leaves molded over New Zealand-made brassieres, and leis of sea shells arranged to look like flowers. Then the horde was everywhere, taking pictures, asking questions in the slow-paced basic English that tourists use with "natives," cautiously sampling the food, taking more pictures. In an hour precisely they were gone, herded back into the buses by businesslike guides, leaving behind a detritus of used flash bulbs, crumpled yellow film boxes, and a thick sprinkling of cigarette ends made indestructible by filter tips.

Returning to my charmingly rudimentary motel, The Little Polynesian, where I stayed in one of a cluster of thatched cottages on a surf-swept beach near Titikaveka village, on the opposite side of the island from Avarua, I reflected sadly on the fate of a serene tropical isle about to enter the jet age. Soon there would be an outcropping of hotels with lobbies in mock-Polynesian decor, and notice boards summoning one tour group for early-morning departure, "bags outside the room at 6 sharp," another for sightseeing with the inevitable "authentic dancing show," and so on. Inexorably, Rarotonga was being edged out of classic Polynesia.

TEN

The People-Losers

ESIDES the involvement with the self-governing Cook Islands, New Zealand maintains a characteristically low-posture political role in two other former British outposts in the South Seas: lonely Niue, and the tiny Tokelau Islands. The existence of a New Zealand sphere of influence in these remote waters escapes the attention of most of the world, barring the fussy watchdogs of the United Nations decolonization committee. These obscure and minuscule territories are of interest, however, as examples of small South Pacific islands where the most viable response to isolation and a constricting economic base is the wholesale removal of people.

Like their racial kin in the more fortunate Cool Islands, the Polynesians inhabiting these lorn outposts are citizens of New Zealand. Even more than the Cook Islanders, they tend to regard New Zealand as a promised land. On Niue (pronounced NEW-way), the name for New Zealand in the local Polynesian dialect is Palataiso, meaning "paradise."

The exodus of young people from Niue to New Zealand has resulted in a shortage of needed talents and skills on the island. In the Tokelaus, a cluster of coral atolls whose meager cash income depends almost wholly upon copra, handicrafts, and postage stamps sold to collectors, the drain of capable youth has left the islands largely to the elderly and the conservative.

For New Zealand, the possession of a modest empire in the

169

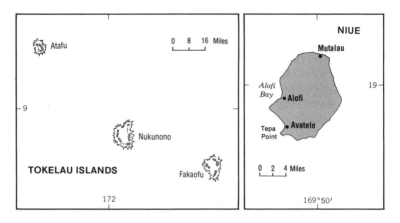

South Pacific is a burden, rather than a benefit, whose weight is
borne uncomplainingly. Besides opening the country's doors to
settlers from Niue and the Tokelaus, New Zealand pours out
money and talent to further the welfare of these distant island
appendages, without hope of return. As the zealots in the United
Nations decolonization committee view Pacific affairs, granting
independence to these minuscule territories would be to set their
people free; but the islanders themselves would see the move as
cutting them adrift in dangerous seas. "To us," a leading Niuean
told me, "the word 'independence' has no meaning."

According to my Niuean friend Young Vivian, who became the
minister of education, agriculture and development in the island's first elected autonomous government, the name Niue
means, literally, "here is a coconut." Traditions hold that the
island was populated a millennium ago by separate migrations
from Samoa and Tonga, each bringing coconuts. The name of
the island conveys an image of friendliness, the coconut being
the symbol of hospitality throughout the South Seas; when a
visitor shows up, he is immediately handed a freshly opened
coconut. The legend of Niuean origins is supported by linguistic
similarities to both the Samoan and Tongan dialects, and the
division of the 100-square-mile island's population—about four
thousand—into distinct northern and southern groups.

Niuean hospitality must have been selective in early times.
When Captain Cook landed on the island on 20 June 1774, the
first European to do so, he and his men were greeted not with
coconuts but with a shower of coral rocks hurled by near-naked,
black-painted Polynesians who charged the visitors, Cook

related, "with the ferocity of wild Boars." Cook and his party hastily returned to their ship and sailed away. Because of the hostile demeanor of the inhabitants, Cook called the place Savage Island, a name that is still sometimes used and is greatly resented by the Niueans of the present generation. The fierce Niueans of Cook's day were tamed under the influence of the London Missionary Society, especially a Samoan missionary named Paulo, who arrived in 1849. But the first London missioner, the well-traveled Reverend John Williams, was given the same reception as Cook when he attempted to land in 1830 with two Polynesian aides.

The social system on Niue, encouraging self-expression, has made the Niueans a notably independent branch of the Polynesian family. Unlike other Polynesians, the Niueans have no authoritarian tradition of hereditary tribal or clan chiefs. Family heads and elders are powerful in community affairs and matters concerning land, but each young man gains the right to speak in village meetings when he marries. Since 1967, under New Zealand influence, the fourteen villages have been administered by elected councils.

The oyster-shaped island sits alone in a vast expanse of empty sea, with no neighbors nearer than the Vava'u group of the Tonga archipelago, some 300 miles to the west; Aitutaki in the Cooks lies about 600 miles eastward, American Samoa is 350 miles north, and to the south there is only open sea all the way to Antarctica. Niue, in spite of its evocative name, is far from the ideal South Sea island. A raised coral ledge, believed to be the result of repeated subterranean upheavals, it is bordered by high, steep cliffs that are constantly pounded by heavy waves. The rocky soil is dry and poor. Alofi, the seedy main village and capital, extends in a thin line of drab buildings along the grim shore of Alofi Bay, the island's only sheltered anchorage.

Missionary influence apparently turned the thoughts of the Niueans to the outside world, and in 1887 they petitioned Queen Victoria to be taken under British protection. They approached the reluctant British again in the following year, and the year after that. Finally, on 20 April 1900, the Union Jack was formally raised on the island and Niue was declared a British protectorate. Administration was handed over to New Zealand, which annexed the island on 11 June 1901. Self-government in association with New Zealand, along the lines of New Zealand's arrangement with the Cooks, was discussed for years and finally came to pass on

19 October 1974. New Zealand's gift to the island for the occasion was a building for the Legislative Assembly.

Meetings of the South Pacific Conference were regaled every year by Robert R. Rex, who always led the Niue delegation and would become the first premier, with a recital of the island's woes. Rex, the island's leading merchant and politician, a kindly, urbane man in his sixties, was deeply troubled by the continual exodus to Auckland. It was common for whole families to pack up and go, and a survey by a youth expert for the South Pacific Commission reported in 1971 that 83 percent of the island's young people could be expected to show an inclination to emigrate. "The cold reality of the situation is that Niue could almost depopulate in 10 years," said *Pacific Islands Monthly*. "The biggest political decision is whether to deliberately accelerate the departure rate, or improve conditions so that those who choose to stay can maintain a high standard of living."

From Premier Rex's point of view as a patriotic Niuean, if not as a businessman, the Westernization of the island was proving to be counterproductive. "Niueans have learned to accept the Western concept of material prosperity," he said at a South Pacific Conference meeting when his turn came to air the problems of his island. "And the more education and development we have, the easier it is for people to leave."

Premier Rex, a part-Polynesian with an intense commitment to the island side of his ancestry, was determined to upgrade life on Niue to the point where the outward movement of population would be reversed. When he took office as the elected head of the first fully autonomous government, there were at least three thousand Niueans—three-quarters of the number on the home island—in New Zealand. The task he set himself, with New Zealand's help, was formidable.

The coconut for which Niue was named was the principal crop produced by the island's shallow soil. Families had small subsistence gardens, and there was some commercial growing of bananas, passion fruit, and limes, with a little cattle-raising and bee-keeping. The main source of protein in the local diet was fish. All males fished, laboriously lugging their heavy dugout canoes fitted with outriggers up and down steep paths in the cliffs, sometimes having to resort to ladders on the most precipitous slopes. There was no attraction for the young in grubbing a meager living from the island by the sparse means available, while the bright lights of Auckland beckoned.

Yet Niue had been blessed with a benign climate, barring the occasional hurricane. Health conditions were among the best in the South Pacific; venereal disease was nonexistent—an enviable distinction in the South Seas. Everyone was well housed (not in grass shacks, but Western-style cottages). Schooling was compulsory and good under New Zealand direction (and, of course, contributed to the yearning for wider horizons).

For the educated, questing young, life on Niue was quiet, pleasant, and dull. The Saturday cricket match, played in a style peculiar to Niue with thirty on a side instead of eleven, was the recreational highlight of the week. The Sunday rules of the missionaries were strictly observed. Most of the islanders belonged to the church of Ekalesia Niue, the independent successor to the London Missionary Society. Serious crime was rare: when an amnesty was declared to celebrate self-government, there were only three prisoners in the island jail to benefit from it.

Such amenities as electricity, sewage, and running water, however, were lacking in many of the villages. Premier Rex, with advice from New Zealand, laid out a program of material improvement to make life more attractive, in the hope of luring back some of the expatriates. Priorities were given to electrification of the entire island and diversification of industry. A forty-bed hotel was begun and the airport was enlarged to receive jet planes, in anticipation of a modest tourist business.

In a step believed to be unique in constitutional history, the act of the New Zealand parliament granting self-government to Niue contained a clause guaranteeing continued economic assistance. "As far as I know, this is probably the first time a country has undertaken . . . to give legal guarantees of this nature," said Young Vivian, the Niuean representative sent to New York to explain the new status to the United Nations.

While the Niueans yearned for their expatriate sons to return and help build the miniature nation, removal of population remained an official policy for the three small, isolated atolls of the Tokelau group.

Emigration has a tradition in the Tokelaus. Hurricanes have periodically stripped the palm trees from the islets, whereupon the population migrated en masse from one atoll to another, or to Samoa, by outrigger canoe. German and British planters recruited in the Tokelaus for plantations in Samoa and Fiji, and Peruvian slavers made raids.

The three atolls of Atafu, Nukunonu, and Fakaofu have had

a meandering political history. Britain declared the group a protectorate in 1877, at the request of the chiefs, but took till 1889
to get around to a formal flag-raising by the captain of a passing
naval vessel. The British annexed the islands in 1916, again at
the wish of the chiefs, and added them to the crown colony of
the Gilbert and Ellice Islands. At that time the group included
Swain's Island, an atoll in the classic doughnut shape with a
completely enclosed lagoon, owned by the mixed-blood Ameri-
can-Polynesian Jennings family of coconut planters. When Britain transferred the Tokelaus to New Zealand administration in
1925, Swain's was turned over to the United States for incorpora-
tion into American Samoa—the last American territorial acquisition before World War II. New Zealand governed the islands as
a colony, without colonists, until 1948, when they were made
New Zealand territory effective 1 January 1949.

Lying in a northeast-southwest line north of Samoa, with some
fifty miles of tossing sea between each low, sandy atoll and the
next, the Tokelaus were off the sea lanes used by early Western
navigators in the South Pacific. It was once believed that they had
been sighted by de Quiros in 1606, but authorities now think the
Spanish explorer was really looking at Rakahanga atoll in the
northern Cooks. One of the early firsthand accounts of the Tokelaus is contained in the writings of the Australian traveler Louis
Becke, who aptly dubbed them the "almost-forgotten islands."

The New Zealand administrator is an official on the staff of
Wellington's high commissioner in Apia, the capital of Western
Samoa. The administrator has his permanent station in Apia but
visits the atolls frequently by chartered ship, from which he must
transfer, upon arrival off an atoll, to a small boat for the precarious ride ashore through tumbling surf. The few foreign temporary residents, aside from the New Zealand schoolteachers (they
are usually recruited as husband-and-wife teams), have included
the crew of a United States Coast Guard air navigation station
on Atafu during World War II, which was the Tokelauans' only
brush with history.

Tokelau epitomizes the common problem of many South
Pacific atolls: too many people on too little land. The three atolls
contain more than a hundred islets, with a total land area of 2,500
acres; but the people prefer to live on one or two main islands
of each atoll and use the others as gardens. The population of
Nukunonu are all Roman Catholics, Atafu is all Protestant, and
the two religions mix on Fakaofu.

The New Zealand administrators found some two thousand Tokelauans crowded into a few villages of thatched huts, arranged attractively along coral paths lined with flowers and sea shells. The principal occupations were copra production, subsistence gardening, and the weaving of pandanus ware for sale in Apia. The restricted space prevented much increase in the production of anything but babies. The improved medical care under New Zealand, a country famous in the South Pacific for its fine medical schools, reduced infant mortality and disease, causing the population to soar. The villages became more overcrowded than ever.

Officials tried to persuade the villagers to spread themselves around on the unoccupied islands, but tradition interfered. In one instance, the administration built a new village, with houses and a water system, on an empty island only a few hundred yards from the main village of Fakaofu atoll, only to find that none of the Tokelauans would live in the place because the island was believed to be the abode of ancient Polynesian ghosts.

The solicitous New Zealand government devised a program called, officially, the Tokelau Islands Resettlement Scheme, under which islanders willing to move to New Zealand would be given subsidized passage and guaranteed employment. Not wishing to obliterate the Polynesian culture of the Tokelauans, the immigrants were installed in one area around Rotorua, a town on New Zealand's North Island that has a large Maori population. The first group of 152 left the Tokelaus in 1966, and of these only one man returned to the islands.

Under the New Zealand program of removing a maximum of fifteen families a year, the population of the islands swiftly fell below fifteen hundred. Again, as in the migration from Niue, it was the young and ambitious islanders who were anxious to emigrate, leaving the middle-aged and elderly behind. "A Tokelauan arriving in New Zealand is like an Eskimo moving to New York," an official said. "They've never seen a bicycle, a shop, a kitchen range, or a flush toilet. But Polynesians are adaptable."

Rotorua and Taupo, also on the North Island, were chosen partly for the Polynesian ambience of the Maori settlements, in which the Tokelauans might feel more at home, but mostly because in these areas there was work available for the unskilled in forestry, and housing was available in a Maori settlement project. "We would like the world to know how much New Zealand has done for us," a Tokelauan said. "But we don't want to be a burden—we want to develop our own territory as much as possible," he added.

A "fact-finding" delegation from the United Nations decolonization committee, visiting the Tokelaus in 1976, reported that the islanders were strongly and unanimously in favor of remaining a New Zealand dependency—the last non–self-governing territory linked with Wellington. The report put the population of the islands at 1,520, while the number of Tokelauans living in New Zealand had risen to 2,200.

There seems little prospect, however, that these obscure specks in the middle of the vast South Pacific will be drawn into the modern world. With tourism out of the question on any significant scale, for atolls generally lack a sufficient water supply to support a hotel industry, they shall probably remain unspoiled outposts of the past.

ELEVEN

Two Samoas

---

*L*ANDING at Faleolo, the international airport of Western Samoa on the main island of Upolu, and driving the twenty-three miles to Apia, the capital, must be the most glamorous introduction to any South Pacific country. The brief trip is a journey through the pure Polynesia of the past—which, in the independent and conservative monarchic state of Western Samoa, is part of the present as well. Except for the cars, mostly Japanese models, what the arriving newcomer sees along the twisting road has changed little since the English poet Rupert Brooke wrote in an ecstatic letter home, "It's all true about the South Seas!"

On one side of the roughly paved highway, the sea twinkles in myriad shades of blue; on the other side, green palm groves curve upward on the island's spinal range. Following a winding shore that alternates between dark coral and bright beaches, the road passes through a succession of villages that have looked essentially the same for centuries.

Tourists on Upolu inhabit air-conditioned hotel rooms, but the average Samoan prefers the traditional open-sided hut, called a *fale,* of plain poles arranged in an oval and supporting a conical thatched roof, on a platform of white coral reinforced with black stones. Between the poles, roll-up curtains of woven pandanus are let down for protection against rain and wind. Privacy is an insignificant factor; some American Peace Corps workers living

177

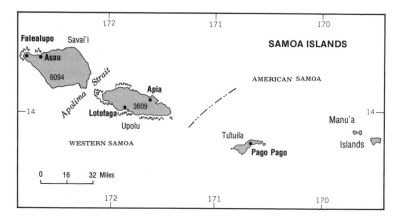

in Samoan villages suffered psychic disturbances attributed to an unaccustomed feeling of never being alone.

The Christian heritage dating from the arrival of the peripatetic Reverend John Williams in 1830 is evident in the profusion of imposing churches, many of them large enough to be cathedrals. I counted thirty-six religious edifices on the twenty-three-mile ride from Faleolo to Apia, and was told that I had missed a few that were set back from the road.

In the government tourist literature, Western Samoa is called "The Heart of Polynesia." It is not too grandiose a boast. The place exercises a spell on visiting writers. "It is pure beauty," wrote Rupert Brooke, "so pure it is difficult to breathe in it." Said Henry Adams: "For once, the reality has surpassed all expectation." Robert Louis Stevenson spent the last four years of his life on Upolu, "a simple and sunny heaven," and lies buried on a hill near Apia as he said he wanted to be, "under the wide and starry sky."

Here the old communal society under the rule of clan chiefs, called *matai,* survives in competition with modern social currents. The respect for rank is immense. To satisfy traditional protocol, when Western Samoa became the first South Sea island nation to regain complete independence on 1 January 1962, the two pre-eminent chiefs were both named to the office of head of state, to serve jointly until one died.

The co-existence of new and old is even more pronounced in nearby American Samoa, the only United States territory south of the equator, which is said to be "neither American nor Samoan." American Samoa is more western than Western Samoa, however: most of the islanders live in houses with walls, and the chief with a ceremonial fly whisk in one hand may be holding a ten-inch cigar in the other.

The two Samoas were split apart in 1899 in a struggle of contending powers, like Korea, Germany, and Vietnam in a later era. The ensuing decades under divergent influences have widened the division, and the movement for a reunion is small and inconsequential at the present time.

Samoan aristocrats, of whom there are many, project an aura of nobility in some indefinable way by their mere presence. Two white-haired grandmothers, heiresses of ancient rank, whom I noticed at a function given by the head of state for delegates to the South Pacific Conference, were the most regal-looking women I have ever seen anywhere. Although the written history of the Samoan race goes back only to 1834, when the language was first put into writing by missionaries, the genealogies handed down by word of mouth extend to around A.D. 1250, and archeological findings indicate that the island may have been populated a thousand years before Christ. It is widely believed that Savai'i, the larger of the two principal islands, is the original for the legendary Hawaiki where the migrants from Southeast Asia settled, thence to colonize the great Polynesian Triangle of today.

Whatever the anthropologists may believe about the origin of the Polynesians, the Samoan villager feels certain that his people have always been right where they are today, and it is difficult to argue, from the evidence of nature, that these islands were not the original Garden of Eden. This makes the Samoans feel superior to other Polynesians, all of whom sprang from Savai'i—or so the Samoans believe.

In fact, the Samoans have their own version of the Adam and Eve story. In the legend, the first man was named Ao, which means "day," and the woman was called Po, or "night." According to some students of the Pacific, the theory that Polynesia was settled by navigators from Samoa is supported by the presence of recognizable Samoan words in all the other Polynesian tongues. (Another view ascribes the similarities in words to a common linguistic core running through all Polynesia, rather than to any primacy of the Samoan language). The language as spoken by Samoans is intricate and allusive, with the same word often having many meanings. There are numerous everyday expressions whose meanings have changed with time. Some of these originated from customs that are no longer practiced. An example of such usage is the common admonition, "ia seu le manu, ae silasila i le galu," meaning "proceed with caution." The phrase translates literally, however, as "catch the bird, but watch the waves," a reference to the ancient pastime, long abandoned, of hunting sea birds from outrigger canoes.

Subtle and flowery use of language is the specialty of the skilled orators known as "talking chiefs," who function as spokesmen for a clan or village and are the experts on Samoan history and customs. There is a superior order called "high talking chiefs," who conduct discourse on important matters on behalf of clan, village, or district authorities. Samoan nobles are ranked as royal chiefs, paramount chiefs, high chiefs, and ordinary chiefs, the last-named heading the traditional extended family, or *aiga* (pronounced ah-ING-ah), which may have scores of members.

If the order of rank in Samoa appears complicated when recounted in English, it is far more so in Samoan, with each title having a specific meaning. At the top are the holders of the four royal titles of Malietoa, Tupua, Mata'afa, and Tuimalealiifano, known as the *tama'aiga,* or "four royal sons." All are in Western Samoa, a factor that contributes to keeping the two Samoas apart. "If I moved over there," a high chief in American Samoa told me, nodding westward, "I'd become an instant hick cousin." Originally there was a fifth royal title of Tuimanu'a in American Samoa, but the rank was abolished by law shortly after the eastern islands came under United States Navy rule.

Traditionally, titles mean everything in Samoa—both Western and American. The holders, known collectively as *matai,* constitute a ruling class from the family level outward. In fact, however, the system is a kind of limited democracy; it is democratic, in a sense, because the *matai* is elected, but limited because he (or she, for there is equality of the sexes in the Samoan social order) is normally chosen from the close kin of the preceding holder and retains the title and its attendant authority for life, unless deposed for failing in the demanding responsibilities of the office.

Under the system in effect in all the villages of the Samoan islands, including the American side, the *matai* is responsible for the well-being of every individual under his authority. He allots the farmland for tilling, assigns community work, and administers the common funds. It was customary for members of an extended family who held paying jobs to hand over all their earnings to the *matai* on payday. This practice even extended to the American Peace Corps volunteers who lived with Samoan families.

There are 1,635 *matai* titles in American Samoa and more than 8,500 on the Western side. Rival claims to vacant titles busy the courts. Many prominent Samoans hold more than one title, and since titles customarily serve the purpose of surnames, the practice presents foreigners with confusing identification problems. Ideally, the decisions of the *matai* are the outcome of consultation and consensus. The system is basic to *fa'a Samoa,* "the Samoan way," a phrase one hears every day in the islands. How long this will withstand the new influences brought in by progressive young people returning from higher education abroad in increasing numbers troubles the older, more conservative generation. The subject came up many times in my conversations with Samoans and resident *papalagi,* as Caucasians are called.

Papalagi—sometimes written as *palagi* and pronounced pah-LONG-ee—means "sky burster," supposedly from the white sails of the first European vessels seen in the archipelago, looming white against the blue firmament. Presumably these were the ships of the Dutch navigator Jacob Roggeveen, who sailed past the islands in 1722 but did not land. A later visitor, the French explorer Bougainville, called the group the Navigator Islands because of the great number of canoes observed in the lagoons. By that time, however, the once far-ranging Samoans had abandoned their great seventy-foot double canoes, with housing on platforms between, and had become homebodies who had to fight off recurrent raids by Fijians and Tongans.

In the more or less united free Samoa of the nineteenth century, internecine warfare brought frequent interventions by Britain, Germany, and the United States in the interests of their nationals. Beleaguered chiefs occasionally pleaded with one power or another to take over the islands, but were ignored for the time being. Annexation would come later.

A notable, if brief, period of peace and unity that foreshadowed developments in Western Samoa nearly a century later occurred between 1873 and 1875 through the picturesque agency of a remarkable American, Colonel Albert B. Steinberger. The career of this romantic figure paralleled those of two other extraordinary white men who became premiers of Polynesian kingdoms at different times in the same colorful era of Pacific island history, the Reverend Shirley Baker, the missionary prime minister of Tonga, and Walter Murray Gibson, an American adventurer of more dubious antecedents who became premier of Hawaii under King Kalakaua.

Steinberger arrived on the troubled Samoa scene with impressive credentials as special agent of President Ulysses S. Grant. The hopeful Samoans interpreted his appearance as a promise of United States protection. This was a historic example of wishful thinking that Steinberger encouraged by permitting an exaggerated idea of the nature of his commission, which was merely that of an observer. With his considerable personal charm and undoubted political acumen (his understanding of Samoan attitudes was extraordinary for a white man) he helped install the foremost *tama'aiga* of the time, Malietoa Laupepa, as king of a pacified, independent Samoa, with an advanced constitution that in some important respects anticipated the constitution of 1962. Steinberger, who was liked initially by everybody—consuls, missionaries, white settlers, and, especially, the Samoans—became premier and virtual dictator.

Inevitably, Steinberger's power fostered jealousy among the foreign consuls, with the exception of the German representative. The British and Americans were puzzled by the German's attitude at first, but not for long. The white premier's downfall followed the disclosure that he had secretly undertaken to advance German commercial interests in Samoa, while being involved with American business associates at the same time. Although Steinberger's honesty was never questioned officially in Washington, the two unfriendly consuls persuaded King Malietoa Laupepa to sign an order for his deportation—an illegal act under the constitution, by the way—and he was forcibly taken aboard a British warship and removed to Fiji, never to see Samoa again.

Back in the United States, Steinberger won a measure of vindication. The consuls responsible for his deportation were recalled, and the captain of the British warship that had taken him to Fiji was reprimanded. Steinberger filed a suit for damages against the British government, which chose to settle the claim out of court. The government that Steinberger had set up in Samoa is remembered by the Samoans as the best in many decades. It did not long survive Steinberger's forced departure, however.

Warships of Germany, Britain, and the United States lay in Apia harbor to protect the interests of their respective countries in the succeeding disorders, which immediately toppled King

ypical Samoan village of Falealupo, on the island of Savai'i, in 1973, one of many in Western
a that remain unchanged

'ono (Parliament) Building of Western Samoa in 1973. The building in the foreground was the
before the bigger structure behind it, which simulates a *fale*—only with air-conditioning—was
ned by a U.S. Peace Corps architect

The late Prime Minister Mata'afa and his wife, the Masiofo Fetaui, in front of their hybrid Samoan-Western home near Apia, in 1968

Masiofo Fetaui in front of the Women's Center, Apia; she is wearing a typical example of the *puletasi,* the feminine garment of Samoa, in the popular tapa design

Malietoa Laupepa. The three consuls took over the government of Apia as a foreign-run enclave, while Samoan factions struggled for supremacy in the royal capital of Mulinu'u, a village of sacred significance on a small peninsula west of the town.

The tension was broken by an event that the Samoans regarded as a divine intervention. This was the great hurricane of 16 March 1889, the most famous storm in South Pacific history, later to be commemorated on postage stamps of independent Western Samoa. Ninety-two Germans and fifty-four Americans, and three naval ships of each nation, were lost in the disaster. The one British warship present managed to make her way out to sea, with American sailors, lining the rail of the doomed U.S.S. *Trenton,* cheering her on. The hulk of the wrecked German ship *Adler* remained a feature of Apia harbor up until a few years ago.

Recalling the historic catastrophe, Samoans apply an apt proverb: It's an ill wind that blows no good. The hurricane blew the three contending foreign powers right out of the Samoan scene for a decade. Discouraged from further adventures in such a risky place, the three governments signed a treaty in Berlin three months later, formally recognizing the independent Kingdom of Samoa, once more under Malietoa Laupepa.

Peace in Samoa was again short-lived, however, and ten years later the same three powers met again in Berlin. They annulled the 1889 treaty and drew up a new agreement giving Germany possession of Upolu, Savai'i, and their satellite islands, while the United States took over the six smaller eastern islands, thenceforth to be called American Samoa. As was mentioned earlier, Britain dropped out in return for Germany's withdrawal from Tonga, Niue, and the Solomons, except for Bougainville.

A significant German commercial presence had already taken shape in Apia long before, with the arrival of the famous South Pacific trading firm of J. C. Godeffroy and Son, of Hamburg. The company went bankrupt in the German economic upheaval following the Franco-Prussian War of 1870 and was replaced by the equally celebrated firm with what may have been the most formidable name in the world, Deutsche Handels und Plantagen Gesellschaft de Sudsee Inseln zu Hamburg, better known throughout the South Seas as "D. H. and P. G." or "the Long-Handle Firm."

The original home of Godeffroy's, later occupied by D. H. and P. G., was still in use on my latest visit to Apia. The white-painted frame structure, built in 1857 in typical South Seas colonial style with a second-story veranda running the width of the two-story building and a peaked roof of shakes, is one of several nineteenth-century landmarks along Beach Road, the main street overlooking the seashore. Its latest occupant was the Western Samoan Trust Estates Corporation, or "Westec," the government-owned company whose predecessor in the days of New Zealand's rule had taken over the huge German plantation interests as war reparations. A plaque presented to D. H. and P. G. in 1913, commemorating the one-hundredth anniversary of the birth of the original Johann Cesar Godeffroy, the architect of Germany's prosperous but short-lived South Pacific empire, caught the visitor's eye on the wall halfway up the main staircase.

There were two other old white frame buildings on Beach Road that I always lingered by for a moment, savoring their evocative associations with the colorful past of this meandering waterfront town. Over the plain front door of one of these, tucked into the tacky little commercial complex near the clock tower from which all distances on Upolu are measured, was the simple signboard of O. F. Nelson and Company, Limited. With its old-fashioned lettering, it looked as if it might have been put up by the original Olaf Frederick Nelson, an eminent name in Samoan history. The son of a Swedish trader and the daughter of a chief of Savai'i, Nelson became the leader of the Apia business community and the father of the independence movement as head of a powerful nationalist organization called the Mau. Thus the drab little boxlike building was intimately connected with the birth of free Western Samoa.

Farther along the same bow-shaped street stood a similar building whose historical association I discovered by accident when I went there to talk to Eugene Paul, an elderly half-German, half-American businessman who had held high positions in the local administration before his retirement from active politics in 1961. The austere second-story office in which we sat, he told me, had been part of the suite occupied by Robert Louis Stevenson when the writer first came to Apia in 1890—a fact apparently unknown to the majority, if not all, of the people who came into the building every day on business with the numerous Paul enterprises. Stevenson, I was told, had stayed in the apartment as the guest of a prominent American-born businessman of Apia, Harry J. Moors, whose half-Samoan son of noble lineage on the Polynesian side became the renowned Afioga Afoafouvale Misimoa, the first Pacific islander to head the South Pacific Commission as secretary-general. (Afioga is a Samoan honorific and Afoafouvale is a *matai* title, he explained to me, while Misimoa is the Samoan rendering of "Mr. Moors"; but everyone referred to this beloved man, now dead, as "Uncle Harry.")

The German period in Western Samoa was one of material advancement, mostly to the benefit of D. H. and P. G., and tight political control through the reduction of the kingship to a nominal position of adviser, or *fautua*. This post was shared by two *tama'aiga*, Malietoa Tanumafili and Tupua Tamasese Lealofi. The institution of *fautua* was to evolve into the dual monarchy that followed independence, with the title of head of state assumed jointly by the current holders of the Malietoa Tanumafili and Tupua Tamasese titles.

A New Zealand expeditionary force seized the undefended islands of German Samoa shortly after the outbreak of World War I. The military administration of New Zealand was marred by an epidemic of influenza in 1918 that killed off more than 20 percent of the population in a few months. The victims included twenty-four of the thirty-one members of the Fono, an advisory council of district leaders. The epidemic was traced to the failure of the white authorities to quarantine a New Zealand ship that arrived at Apia with infectious cases aboard. The omission was the first of a series of errors that kept the New Zealand administration in ill repute with the Samoans for many years.

The days of colonialism by outright annexation of territory in the South Pacific were over, however—although dependencies would still be acquired, by means that just sounded more respectable. None of the victorious powers in the war wished to assume formal sovereignty over the German colonies they had occupied, so the responsibility for their disposition was handed over to the new League of Nations, which set up a system of "mandated territories" to parcel out the scraps of empire. The process, in essence, consisted of formalizing what had already taken place under military occupation.

To the intense humiliation and resentment of the Samoans, they were placed under New Zealand as a Class C Mandate, the category for primitive populations considered incapable of governing themselves. The reaction to the insult by the Fono, representing the Samoan people, was to petition King George V of Great Britain for self-government under a governor appointed by the British crown. The request was ignored. Agitation for political advancement continued through an organization of Samoans and whites called the Citizens' Committee, headed by Olaf Nelson, who seemed an ideal choice. Half-white and half-Samoan, he was a respected figure in white society as the pre-eminent businessman of the islands, and at the same time stood high among the Polynesians as the holder, by that time, of a revered Samoan title that linked him to the *tama'aiga*. The response of the New Zealand administration, which had become a civilian one although the earlier administrators were all retired military men, was to impose restrictions on freedom of speech and movement. Repression, as usual, proved to be counterproductive.

Petty New Zealand officials were unthinking at best, and haughty at worst, in their attitude toward Samoans and their customs. Individuals inexperienced in their authority not only alienated powerful Samoans but antagonized the white community as well. The inevitable dislocations accompanying the introduction of a money economy against the background of a communal society, which was nowhere stronger than in Samoa, were treated so clumsily that the tendency of conservative Samoans was to reject anything new out of hand.

Under these unpromising circumstances, the mildly activist Citizens' Committee developed into the militant organization known as the Mau (the word means "testimony," in the sense of representing political opinion) with the slogan of "Samoa mo Samoa"—literally, "Samoa for the Samoans." There was no racial implication in the phrase, for "Samoans" in the sense used included whites like Nelson.

The Mau, headed by Nelson, launched a broad program of noncooperation with the New Zealand authorities. Children were removed from government schools, all Samoan organizations involved in local administration ceased to function, traveling New Zealand officials were ignored, taxes went unpaid, births and deaths were not registered, the banana plantations were left untended, and coconuts meant to be converted into valuable copra rotted on the ground. New Zealand countered by deporting Nelson and the editor of a sympathetic newspaper for five years, another supporter for two years. Immediately the Mau became more militant, appearing on the streets of Apia in uniforms featuring purple *lavalava* and matching turban, with white shirt.

"The natives have the minds of children," wrote the New Zea-

land administrator at the time, who seems to have been a singu-
larly insensitive specimen of colonial officialdom. Such a statement would be unthinkable in the South Pacific of today. New
Zealand's troubles, of her own making, compounded. The Mau,
under the leadership of the *tama'aiga* Tupua Tamasese Lealofi,
drew up a petition to the League of Nations setting forth Samoan
grievances against the administering power. The document was
signed by—or for—85 percent of the adult males. Still nothing
happened.

Then, on 28 December 1929, a day still known as "Black Saturday" in Western Samoa, police tried to arrest the leaders of a
Mau procession to the wharf to greet a returning deportee whose
banishment had expired. A scuffle ensued and the police opened
fire. Eleven Samoans died as a result; they were all *matai,* and
included Tupua Tamasese Lealofi. The incident caused the previously peaceful agitation to take a violent turn, and sporadic
fighting went on for years. "Had the League of Nations been
anything but a thing of cardboard, it would at this stage have
taken the Samoa Mandate away from New Zealand," wrote R. W.
Robson, the New Zealand-born founder of that forthright organ,
Pacific Islands Monthly. Reading over the record of the period, so
uncharacteristic of the thoughtful New Zealanders one meets all
over the South Pacific today, it seems incredible that little ill
feeling, if any, against the former ruling power is discernible in
the new independent state of Western Samoa—testimony, perhaps, to the essentially warm Polynesian nature of the Samoans.

A remarkable turnaround in the posture of the New Zealand
administration occurred with the installation of a new, reform-
minded government in Wellington in 1936. World War II, bringing a massive influx of Americans, lucrative jobs, and high prices
for copra and cocoa, the principal products of the islands, and
its aftermath were accompanied by significant changes. Politics
were more or less in recess during the war, and afterward a more
sophisticated generation of Samoan leaders appeared.

Most importantly, the transfer of dependent territories from
the old League of Nations Mandate system to the more enlightened United Nations Trusteeship concept completely changed
the political objectives. No longer were native populations regarded as incapable of self-government. Now the administering
powers were put under formal obligation to bring all dependent
peoples along the road to self-determination. And New Zealand

became the first country to achieve that ultimate goal in the South Pacific, with the establishment of Western Samoa as a sovereign state in 1962.

The constitution of independent Western Samoa, compiled with the assistance of a salty New Zealand political scientist of vast Pacific experience named Jim Davidson, proclaimed that the new state was "based on Christian principles and Samoan custom and tradition," the two streams that run strongly through the life of both Samoas. The method of government worked out by the framers of the constitution was a blend of British parliamentary forms and the time-honored functioning of the Fono, or council of *matai.* It was decided that the new national Fono—called the Legislative Assembly in English—would be elected every three years. Western Samoan citizens of more than half non-Polynesian blood, belonging to the islands but living outside the traditional society and listed on the so-called European roll for voting purposes, would be represented by two of their number elected by universal suffrage in their community of about fourteen hundred adults. The other members would be elected by the *matai.*

A minority in the constitutional committee wanted suffrage for all, but the majority held that such a derogation of the supreme role of the *matai* in Samoan decision-making would be too drastic a departure from custom, leading to a breakdown of a social system that had served the people satisfactorily from the beginning of Samoan history. Later, however, in interviews with many *matai,* I found a widespread conviction that a change would come eventually, though not soon.

The question of how to choose the head of state was debated for two weeks before a consensus was reached, in Polynesian fashion, that the office should be given jointly to the two current *fautua,* Tupua Tamasese Mea'ole and Malietoa Tanumafili II, both *tama'aiga.* On the death of one, the survivor would reign alone. When the second died, a new head of state would be elected by the Legislative Assembly every five years—like the Yang di Pertuan Agong (king) of Malaysia, an office rotated among the reigning sultans of the former Malay States.

Preserving proper respect for the historic status of the four royal lines was considered basic to the security of the new state, for rivalries among the *tama'aiga* and their respective followers had been the weakness of the Samoan political structure in the past. Thus the question of whether the office of head of state should be confined to the holders of *tama'aiga* titles was important. A minority faction wanted to broaden the eligibility for the office. The dissidents were mollified by the possibility for change inherent in the compromise under which the limitation was left out of the constitution but was recommended for a resolution by the Legislative Assembly. The conservatives were confident that such a fundamental deviation from tradition would never occur, and the progressives felt equally certain that it would.

To make it possible for all four *tama'aiga* to occupy a position of dignity in the government, the constitution created a body to be known as the Council of Deputies, which would perform the functions of the head of state in his incapacity or absence. There were to be no more than three members, and the qualifications were such that only the *tama'aiga* were eligible for the honor, since membership was limited to persons qualified to be head of state. As affairs turned out, there was to be only one deputy to the head of state, for the *tama'aiga* Mata'afa Faumuina Fiame Mulinu'u II elected to go into politics, leaving only Suilauvi Tuimaleali'ifano, the fourth royal chief, eligible for the council. As independent Western Samoa adjusted to the modern world, politics became more important than royal status to the ranking chiefs.

The intricacies of Western Samoan politics were operative aspects in the personality of the emerging South Pacific community of self-governing nations. The inexorable passage of time simplified some of the complexities in Apia. One of the joint heads of state, Tupua Tamasese Mea'ole, died on 3 April 1963, leaving the courtly Malietoa Tanumafili II as the sole occupant of the office for life. Like Mata'afa, the successor to the deceased *tama'aiga*, Tupua Tamasese Lealofi IV, chose a political career in preference to membership in the Council of Deputies.

Before going into politics, however, Mata'afa had made waves that rocked the ship of state. A descendant of kings, he held a title that was older than that of Malietoa. (The title of Malietoa, which means "brave warrior," originated with the Samoan victor in a battle with the Tongans around A.D. 1600, according to tradition.) A young man of strong mind and deep consciousness of his status, Mata'afa was incensed at being passed over in the selection of the joint heads of state and threatened to remove his powerful family from association with the government. The other chiefs, fearful that such a split would renew old rivalries that had kept Samoa in turmoil before, prevailed upon him to put the unity of the new state before personal and family considerations.

The incident was a warning of the perils in the imposition of new forms on a strongly traditionalist and conservative South Pacific society.

Mata'afa perceived, however, that the path to power in the new Samoa lay through politics. A huge, nearly bald man of such retiring outward demeanor that he seemed almost inarticulate in English, he was actually a forceful and eloquent speaker in his own language. His goal was to become the first prime minister of the new state. Cannily, he ran for a seat in the new Legislative Assembly not as Mata'afa but as Fiame, thus keeping his royal title disassociated from politics. But since Fiame was also a title of overpowering prestige, he was easily elected from the district of Lotofaga. Prior to independence he was chosen by vote of his colleagues, in a contest with two others, to be prime minister upon the formal handover of power by New Zealand.

When I first met Mata'afa in Tokyo, at the home of the New Zealand ambassador to Japan, it was anything but easy to make conversation with this deceptively quiet man. Our next meeting years later, after I had been reassigned to the South Pacific by *The New York Times,* was in the less constraining ambience of his own home in the stunningly picturesque village of Lepea, near Apia, and he was almost voluble. His family mansion in Lepea was an extraordinary blend of Samoan *fale,* with a conical roof of corrugated metal instead of thatch, and old-time plantation bungalow. Smaller homes of traditional *fale* construction formed a semi-circle on either side of the larger structure, like chicks trooping after a fat mother hen.

A large black-and-white television set stood in the center of the room. The programs came from the video station in American Samoa. Mata'afa remarked that he "didn't like the American accent"—a feeling heartily reciprocated by the American Samoans, who joked about the "British accent" that their western kin had acquired from the New Zealand contact.

Lepea was a magnet for tourists who passed by on the road between Apia and the airport. Mata'afa became so annoyed one Sunday when a bus load of Germans invaded the tidy little village, peering into houses and taking pictures in every direction, that he punched the bus driver and a guide. Hotel bulletin boards displayed a notice the next day, signed by the chief of police, putting Lepea off limits to visitors except when personally invited.

By arrangement with the former ruling power, Western Samoa

conducted most contacts with other countries through the New Zealand diplomatic service. Foreign promoters planning to exploit the inexperience of the Western Samoans to make a fast *tala* (the Samoan equivalent of the dollar) found themselves being coolly screened by capable New Zealand consular officers.

Mata'afa, in his conversation with me, dismissed the question of Western Samoa's joining the United Nations as "too expensive" for a small country with an economy based on coconuts, bananas, and cocoa, and an annual budget of less than ten million dollars. The country was, however, the grateful recipient of various services of the United Nations specialized agencies, such as the World Health Organization, and Apia was the site of the Western Pacific regional headquarters of the United Nations Development Program for some years. A call on that organization's offices in the old Casino Hotel, a ramshackle white frame structure whose musty rooms and ceiling fans inevitably reminded visitors of the South Sea tales of W. Somerset Maugham, was like a step into the past. The government-owned establishment, now replaced by a glossy tourist hotel of pseudo-Polynesian design, had been the temporary home of many a high-ranking Allied officer during World War II.

In those years the Casino was managed by a handsome part-Samoan woman whose first name, being Mary, naturally caused her to be identified later as a probable inspiration for the James Michener character, Bloody Mary. The same distinction is also claimed for her well-known hotel-keeping sister, Aggie Grey. Aggie is noncommittal on the question, but Mary, when I asked her, replied that "there's no Bloody Aggie in the book." Mary Croudace (her married name) returned to Apia after years of running apartment houses in the United States and opened a new hotel that she whimsically named Apian Way. Aggie became an enduring celebrity throughout the islands as the proprietress of the best-known hotel in the South Seas, called Aggie Grey's in her brochures but just Aggie's Hotel on the sign in front. Aggie is the only innkeeper in the world, I believe, who has been honored with a picture of herself and her hotel on a postage stamp, one of a Western Samoan series with a tourism theme.

Aggie's hotel, on Beach Road where the slow-moving Vaisigano River flows into the sea, is legendary among seasoned Pacific travelers. The spacious grounds between a quadrangle of newer wings and the venerable main building, which has broad verandas in the style of the mansions built by wealthy planters early in the century, boast two swimming pools and an enormous *fale*, for parties, described in hotel brochures as "the biggest Samoan-style building in the South Pacific" and, as if that were not enough, as "the biggest nail-less wooden structure in the Southern Hemisphere." The plain rooms, cooled by groaning window-mounted air-conditioning machines, contain refrigerators and ironing boards that let down from the wall. A small table outside each door is decorated each morning with a spray of freshly picked hibiscus, placed beside a pot of hot "morning tea" and a banana. The decor is a melange of simulated South Pacific art, not readily identified with any island, but the wooden Samoan drum whose staccato beat calls guests to meals is genuine. The basement bar, open to the soft trade wind on three sides, is the evening rendezvous of all Apia; the cheery Samoan girls who both mix and serve the drinks call guests by their nicknames, personifying a breezy ambience unknown in the stereotyped tourist hotels that have followed the big jets to the South Seas.

Aggie ran a respectable hotel, but virtue underwent relentless assault nightly by the prostitutes of both sexes who lounged by the seawall across the street and lined the railings of the bridge over the nearby river. On all the islands, vice seemed to proliferate with the growth of tourism.

As an ancient way of life having nothing to do with tourists, homosexuality is so widespread in South Pacific societies that male homosexuals are known in many Polynesian groups by the same term, *mahu.* The corresponding word in Papua New Guinea is an indelicate expression in Pidgin explicitly describing a form of the practice. In Samoa, male transvestitism is institutionalized in a community known as *fa'a fafine,* or "women's way." A *fa'a fafine* may be welcome, I was told, in a family with sons but no daughters to help with the household chores customarily left to women and girls.

Some Polynesian male homosexuals are accomplished professional performers of the women's dances. One of the stars of a *sivasiva* troupe appearing regularly at the periodic *fiafia,* a Samoan feast, for guests at Aggie Grey's was a talented *fa'a fafine* who, when he turned away from the audience in the movements of the dance, could be told apart from the real girls only by the absence of a bra strap across his tanned back.

The lusty, generously proportioned real women of Western Samoa played a strong role in the home, village, and nation. "As in some Eastern countries, the apparent submissiveness of women in Samoan society is put on for public consumption," said Doctor Fana'afi Larkin. Married to an American physician, she earned her doctor of philosophy degree—the only doctorate held by a Samoan at the time—at the University of London, and, as director of education, was the first woman to head a department in the independent government of Western Samoa.

"We really have equality of the sexes here," said Doctor Larkin. "Women become *matai*. Female adulthood doesn't depend upon chronological age. If a girl is only fifteen years old when she is married, she simply becomes a fifteen-year-old woman and takes on the duties and functions of that state. There's no psychoanalyzing about whether a person is mature enough." Samoan women, she added, are not popular at international gatherings like the periodic meetings of the Pan-Pacific and Southeast Asian Women's Association. "Because of our independence at home, we tend to be more self-assertive," she said. "So we Samoan women tend to stand out in international groups, and this makes us disliked."

One who would stand out in any group was the energetic and articulate Masiofo Fetaui, the handsome wife of Prime Minister Mata'afa. One of only four women entitled to be addressed by the Samoan honorific Masiofo ("equivalent to "lady," she explained), she was also authorized to put the initials O.B.E. after her name, having been inducted into the Order of the British Empire by Queen Elizabeth II for service to women and education.

When leading women of Western Samoa decided that they needed a suitable headquarters in Apia, Fetaui marshaled an Amazonic crew of blue-blooded volunteers to put up a building on a vacant lot on Beach Road, across from the clock tower. A Swedish woman architect drew the plans. They raised money by running regular lotteries, and got funds from the New Zealand government and the Foundation for the Peoples of the South Pacific, Inc., a private philanthropic organization in New York.

Women volunteers mixed cement, carried bricks, painted, pounded nails, unloaded trucks. Men who wished to help were given food and tobacco, but no money. Finally, the women had a building estimated to be worth one hundred thousand dollars, the finest in Apia. The formal opening was accompanied by a parade through the town by the women sponsors, resplendent in multicolored *puletasi,* the flowing Samoan national costume of long blouse worn over an ankle-length wrap-around skirt.

The main purpose of the building was to serve and promote projects to improve the health of mothers and babies. "District nurses and dispensaries aren't enough," said Masiofo Fetaui. "Besides," she added, "having a good building affects initiative and morale." Although principally concerned with maternal and child health, the building was also to be the focus of civic activities in Apia. It contained the town's only auditorium suitable for public functions, with a stage and projection room, done in appropriate Polynesian decor with shells, mats, and murals of island scenes. There were a cafeteria, four guest bedrooms (paid for with donations by the Australian community), a handicraft shop to be used in the promotion of village industry, and a clinic staffed by aides furnished by the World Health Organization and the American Peace Corps.

"We built more than half of this building with our own hands," Masiofo Fetaui said as she showed me around the place one morning. The villages would take turns furnishing teams of women to maintain the building, each being responsible for a fortnight. The name inscribed on the apex of the structure, in big letters carved into the masonry, was Maota O Le Alofa, which means "house of love" in Samoan. "In English," said Masiofo Fetaui, "we prefer to call it the Women's Center."

Traditionally, the women of Samoa are highly organization-minded. Girls join a village club, Aualuma, for communal activities (the boys have a counterpart, Aumaga). One girl, usually a chief's daughter, who must be a virgin, is chosen for the office of village *taupo,* the ceremonial princess, whose duties include preparing the *kava* for meetings of *matai.* Under the aegis of the New Zealand administration, the so-called village health committees—"a modern label on an old village organization that still functions," according to Doctor Larkin—were formed to improve the appalling state of community hygiene and sanitation, which was taking a dreadful toll among children.

When the program started in 1925, the annual rate of infant mortality was 200 deaths for every 1,000 live births. The principal cause of infant fatalities was diarrhea, a result of ignorance of hygiene and bad feeding habits at the weaning stage. Many mothers were so debilitated by hookworm that they were unable to give their babies sufficient sustenance. Nearly every child suffered from yaws. Tuberculosis was common.

The aroused New Zealanders, to attack these conditions at the root cause, first formed committees consisting of the wives of government officials and pastors. These would appoint as their president the wife of a chief, who would be able to influence village affairs. The committees were equipped with medicines and trained to give talks on health and hygiene to others.

Soon the whole village was involved. Each morning, and again at the end of the day, a bell summoned mothers to bring any children needing medical attention to the house of the committee president, who would hand out medicines. Committee members were assigned to supervise the daily bathing of all children in the fresh-water pool that adjoins each village. They policed the water supply and saw to the provision of fly-proofing of latrines, commonly the *fale lailiti* (the "little house") on a platform somewhere just off the beach, where the tide provided flushing. They supervised the children's play areas, made sure that the roaming pigs were kept out of the village, and inspected all houses, cooking huts, and latrines at least once a week. Attention was given to all sick children and expectant mothers, and any disease was reported immediately to the nearest dispensary. Nearly every village committee had its special *fale* that served as a treatment center for minor ailments and was the site of the monthly clinic set up in each village by traveling government nurses.

Mainly through the work of these committees, infant mortality declined from 200 to 35 deaths for every 1,000 live births. Yaws was wiped out, and tuberculosis declined. Mothers began to place greater importance on schooling for their children. "The schooling ratio is remarkably good," said the director of health, Doctor Johann Thieme, an Apia-born physician of German stock who had served in the medical corps of the German army in World War II and wore a dueling scar on the right cheek. He estimated that more than 90 percent of the children of elementary school age were in school, and that illiteracy among children more than ten years old was "almost nil."

Independent Western Samoa is indebted to a New Zealand woman, Lady Eileen Powles, the wife of Sir Guy Powles, a former New Zealand high commissioner, for the constructive mobilization of the country's womanpower. It was she who maneuvered the amalgamation of the village health committees into the Western Samoan National Council of Women, an association with the potential of organizing the entire adult feminine population of the country behind projects it favored. The national president was none other than the determined Masiofo Fetaui. Through a vice-president, Masiofo Tiresa Malietoa, the New Zealand–

educated wife of Malietoa Tanumafili II, the organization bore the imprimatur of the head of state.

Led by Masiofo Fetaui, the strong-willed women of Western Samoa attacked an insidious malady that was eating away at the basic well-being of the state. This was the paradoxical problem of widespread, severe malnutrition among children in a land rich with food from the fertile soil and teeming sea. "Malnutrition in Western Samoa is not due to any lack of food, but rather to the traditional customs in feeding children," Doctor Sang Tae Han, the South Korean head of the World Health Organization team in Apia, explained to me. In the normal Samoan family, where precedence in everything is governed by status and age, the children eat last and are likely to find that the adults before them have consumed all the tasty protein-rich items such as meat and fish, which tend to be relatively scarce in the average Samoan larder. The result, said Doctor Han, is a severe deficiency of animal protein in the children's diet, a condition often leading to irreparable brain damage in the young. "A low intake of animal protein retards brain growth in children, which results in a lowering of the general intelligence level," Doctor Han said, adding that a survey of health in schools had shown that 5 percent of the pupils were being affected by protein deficiency, although "their stomachs were full."

Masiofo Fetaui was highly aware of the protein problem. "The main source of protein used to be fish," she said. "There is still plenty of fish, but not enough people fishing. Also there's a lack of consistency in the diet; there may be a bit of meat or fish at one meal, and all the other meals will be starchy foods like *palusami*" (the national dish of Samoans, a delicious creation consisting of thick coconut cream wrapped in a tender taro leaf, baked underground and served with slices of baked taro). Protein deficiency would be even more acute, no doubt, but for the national predilection for *pisupo,* originally the Samoan word for pea soup but now applied to imported corned beef because it also comes in a tin can.

"Improving dietary habits involves a basic change in the social system that must be accomplished by education at the village level," said Masiofo Fetaui. In the extremely conservative society of Western Samoa, the women were undertaking a forbidding task. In coming to grips with the problem, the dauntless women of Western Samoa demonstrated an encouraging capacity for progressive action.

Masiofo Fetaui and her cohorts were carrying on simultaneously a campaign to force the government of New Zealand to
stop requiring unmarried Samoan women of child-bearing age,
seeking to emigrate to that country, to undergo a pregnancy test
before admittance. The debate that ensued was taken up by the
New Zealand newspapers with delight. According to immigration
authorities in Wellington, nearly five hundred Samoan women
emigrated to New Zealand every year. Of those who were unmarried, said Immigration Minister John Marshall, between 10 and
15 percent turned out to have been pregnant on arrival. The
leader of the opposition party replied that there was a regular
two-way traffic between New Zealand and Australia of girls going
to the other country to bear illegitimate babies. The Western
Samoan National Council of Women denounced the singling out
of Western Samoan women for pregnancy tests as a "social stig-
matization, personal humiliation, and invasion of individual dignity and privacy." The New Zealand Women's Liberation Front
called the practice "humiliating," "racialistic," and "an affront
to womanhood." Eventually this piquant international incident
dropped out of the news.

Western Samoa soon underwent a test that any democratic
state must survive if it is to remain a democracy: a peaceful
transfer of power from one political group to another. And it
passed. There were no political parties as such, but factions
formed and dissolved in the legislature, which met in a building
constructed in simulation of a giant *fale* next to the royal burial
grounds at Mulinu'u, to a design drawn by a Peace Corps architect. The Legislative Assembly voted Mata'afa out of the prime
ministership in a political dispute, and elected Tupua Tamasese
Lealofi IV, a *tama'aiga* who had been a government medical officer. Later Mata'afa again became prime minister, and on his
death in 1975 the job went back to Tupua Tamasese. A visiting
African statesmen remarked that such a shuffle in his country
would have been accompanied by shooting.

The monarchial form of government adopted by Western
Samoa was supposed to provide continuing stability unaffected
by politics. Under the constitution, the head of state was also the
chief executive officer of the government and presided over the
Executive Council, to which the prime minister and other members of the cabinet belonged.

Malietoa Tanumafili II, handsome and silver-haired, frequently called informally on old friends around Apia. When Mary

Croudace was building her Apian Way Hotel, he would stop by to inquire how the work was progressing. His official residence on a breezy hill four miles from Apia was visited by every tourist, not because it was Western Samoa's White House but because Robert Louis Stevenson had lived there the last four years of his life and was buried on nearby Mount Vaea, where his tomb is an object of pilgrimage for visitors hardy enough to make the arduous 500-foot climb. The name of the Stevenson home, Vailima, means "water in the hand" and comes from the legend of a princess who used her hand to drink from a stream on the estate.

Upolu had long been accustomed to foreign contact and accepted the impact of the twentieth century with aplomb. In contrast, the appearance of a big American lumber company on the sister island of Savai'i clashed with the languor of that slumberous milieu, with social effects to be felt ever after. Potlatch Forests, Inc., with headquarters in San Francisco and its main mill in Lewiston, Idaho, operated on Savai'i through a subsidiary, Potlatch-Samoa, Inc., under a contract with the Western Samoan government to remove timber from the island's heavily forested hills, reduce the logs to boards in a new sawmill, and ship the product to markets abroad.

The company paid a royalty on the felled trees, of which two-thirds went to the village that owned the land and one-third to the government for reforestation. When I visited Savai'i to see the program in action, the government was being severely criticized for the slow pace of reforestation. Meanwhile the villagers tended to convert the cleared land to cash crops, such as cocoa, instead of turning it back to regrowth of timber. There was doubt that the reforestation would ever catch up with the cutting, as originally planned.

Asau, an ancient thatched village whose three thousand residents made it by far the largest settlement on the island, had been a sleepy place until Potlatch arrived on the tranquil scene. Swiftly, much changed. To facilitate the Potlatch shipments, the government constructed a harbor and an airport with funds advanced by the company against future royalties. Potlatch also lent money to Samoan private companies, without interest, for the purchase of a small ship and an eight-passenger plane that would make use of the harbor and airport. The upgrading of roads for the company's needs, including the first paving seen on the island, opened communications between villages (many people of Asau had never seen any other village than their own). Clearing and milling provided jobs for more than three hundred local people, with opportunities to learn skilled trades and qualify for higher-paid employment, and the twice-daily plane connection with Apia started a modest tourist business on the seldom-visited island. The new revenue enabled villages to improve their water supply, a problem on the island of black volcanic rock. Potlatch also sold surplus power to the government for extended village electrification.

An insulated American-style suburb appeared in a sequestered enclave on the beach near Asau, as well as the sawmill, with ranch-type houses equipped with air-conditioning, wall-to-wall carpeting, and the most modern of kitchens and bathrooms for the foreign supervisory personnel. (In time, most of the foreigners were replaced by qualified Samoans who, on moving into the houses of their predecessors, promptly adopted a thoroughly Western style of living.)

The Samoans, both on Savai'i and Upolu, were delighted with the economic spin-off from the Potlatch development. But the social effects on the isolated community of forty thousand Polynesians were the subject of a conference of forty-two concerned clergymen, teachers, and village leaders, who saw the new affluence undermining the old values, lessening the authority of the *matai,* and eroding the entire historic system of communal sharing.

More money—Potlatch paid better than the government—brought a surge of alcoholism. As young men became independent earners, they began refusing to share their wages with the *matai* for common purposes. Families turned away from the traditional fresh foods in favor of imported tinned goods. Some moved out of the *fale* into the confinement of hotter, boxlike houses. Perhaps worst of all, said the Reverend Tanielu Amosa, the Congregationalist pastor of Auola village, was the new tyranny of the clock in a society that had regulated the daily routine since time immemorial by the coming of light and dark, and the rise and fall of the tides. (Customs statistics showed that Western Samoa had imported only 839 watches and 581 clocks in 1968.) Now, he said, Savai'i lived by the stopping and starting whistle at the sawmill.

American interest in Samoa goes back to 1839, when a naval task force called The Great United States Exploring Expedition, commanded by the eccentric and talented Lieutenant Charles Wilkes, visited Tutuila. In 1872 Commander Richard Mead, in

U.S.S. *Narragansett,* and High Chief Mauga of Pago Pago signed a treaty granting commercial and naval rights on Tutuila to the United States. Though the treaty was never ratified by the Senate, the agreement had the effect of keeping other countries out. A second treaty, with all the chiefs of the Pago Pago area participating, was concluded in 1879 and ratified in the same year. All of Tutuila and the satellite islands were put under naval administration with the cession instruments of 1900 and 1904, the latter document adding the Manu'a (ma-NOO-ah) group to the American holdings and providing an irresistible temptation to punsters.

Under the terms of the cession, the United States guaranteed the integrity of Samoan customs and land rights. Thus the authority of the *matai* in village affairs remained unimpaired, and the extended family units, called *aiga,* kept perpetual title to all the land except a few government sites and some private plots held by individuals and churches, altogether amounting to less than 4 percent of the 76.2-square-mile area of the entire territory. The American takeover did affect customs in some ways, however, such as in the abolition of the succession to the title of Tuimanu'a, the fifth *tama'aiga.* This action deprived American Samoa of its only royal chief, although the title itself continued to exist, unoccupied.

Naval responsibility for the government of American Samoa continued till 1951, when the administration was transferred to the Department of the Interior and the naval base at Pago Pago was deactivated. Tiny Swain's Island, annexed in 1925, was run by the Samoan-American Jennings family of coconut planters as a fiefdom until the government put its first representative there in 1954.

Generations of Americans, if aware of Pago Pago at all, probably knew it best as the locale of a famous play and a subsequent series of movies called *Rain,* based on a short story by Maugham. In the story, a missionary of ferocious piety, the Reverend Mr. Davidson, encounters Sadie Thompson, a loud, overpainted tart, in a dingy Pago Pago boarding house. The incongruous pair are forced into proximity by the relentless rain that inhibits movement in Pago Pago for long, steamy hours at a time. The severe cleric sets out to convert the bedizened Sadie. With the rain as his ally, he seems to succeed. But sin and Sadie—also abetted by the rain—are triumphant in the end, and the remorseful missionary commits suicide.

The bitter little tale by Maugham is a devastating, if extreme, portrait of the old-time Bible-pounding South Seas missionary. "We had to make sins out of what they thought were natural actions," Davidson relates, exulting that he had forced men into trousers and women into the ugly Mother Hubbard, had made sex a furtive thing for the unmarried, and had exterminated dancing in his territory. Davidson's real-life counterparts in Samoa were less successful.

Maugham insisted till his death that Sadie was entirely a fictional character, but there is much evidence that she existed in Pago Pago when the writer visited there in a rainy December in 1916. The file of *The Honolulu Advertiser* for that month shows that the passenger list of the steamer *Sonoma,* outward bound on 4 December from Hawaii for Pago Pago, contained the names of Maugham and his secretary, Gerald Haxton, and a "Miss Thompson."

The prostitute's brief but lurid career in Pago Pago is remembered well in local lore. When I first visited Pago Pago in 1968, an American businessman named Keith Landrigan recalled that his father-in-law, the late Benjamin Franklin Kneubuhl, had defended Sadie in court against the charge of disorderly conduct that led to her later deportation. A respected high chief, since dead, was named as having been her lover as a young man. Residents pointed out a plain, white frame building with a big sign, "Max Haleck General Store No. 3," as the identical former combination store and boarding house described in the Maugham story, where Sadie and the Davidsons stayed. Keeping the legend alive, a new tourist hotel on a point jutting into Pago Pago Bay had a bar called the Sadie Thompson Lounge.

Although more than fifty years had passed since Sadie had packed her gramophone and departed at the insistence of the law, could she have come back, she would have recognized the place. The old-fashioned mansion where the naval governor lived was the same, as was the seedy wooden government office where she had pleaded in vain to be spared deportation. The rundown wooden structures housing the government offices and the court were unchanged since Sadie's time, as was the antique stone post office. Whatever commercial establishments had appeared in the years since Sadie left were quartered in untidy wooden structures of the same featureless architecture as the rest, all clustered around the central *malae,* or common, and meandering along the main street and its few winding tributaries.

Nor had the weather changed for the better. The rain that had depressed Maugham still came down in battering torrents, between bursts of sunshine that set the heated earth to steaming until the next blinding shower. Dark, moisture-laden clouds built up above the flat dome of a mountain, aptly named Rainmaker, across the harbor from the hotel. All this precipitation—more than two hundred inches a year, four to five times the average in most of the world's temperate zones—kept the islands lush. While the rainfall gave the drab town a natural setting unsurpassed for tropical loveliness, it was only the jungle growth that profited. The incessant flooding, according to government agriculturists, washed essential nutrients from the soil and thus impeded the cultivation of food crops.

Yet, in the few relatively dry months when it was winter south of the equator and summer in the north, the residents of Pago Pago were without water for hours every day, when the government was forced to ration the supply by cutting off the flow at intervals because of inadequate reservoirs installed by the navy administration, and the persistent leakage of pipes left in disrepair.

Pago Pago (the name is pronounced PONG-oh PONG-oh and means "fine harbor") is really a collection of villages around the boot-shaped bay of the same name. Most of the government buildings are concentrated in one central village, Fagatogo. Looking down on the scene from the tip of a bluff, in traditional colonial fashion, was Government House, the residence of the American governor. Critical local residents often remarked that the white clapboard house had a revolving door, through which forty-nine governors had walked in, and out again shortly after, in seventy-five years of American administration. In the navy's half-century of control, Government House had been a comfortable and prestigious preretirement billet for a captain who was unlikely to become an admiral. As a rule, the governors in uniform concerned themselves with the small, widely forgotten naval station and paid minimal attention, if any, to the affairs of the brown-skinned Samoans.

The subsequent civilian governors were responsible to the Department of the Interior, on the theory that the branch of the government in charge of Indian affairs in the continental United States might as well take on the administration of a Polynesian community on the opposite side of the globe. Of the civilian governors who came and went in a quarter of a century or more, only a few have been remembered beyond their time in Pago Pago.

One who stood out owed the distinction to his name, Phelps Phelps. This genial former New York State politician and radio news commentator, later to be an ambassador, occupied Government House in 1951 and 1952. His repetitive name, so like the Samoan language, tickled the Polynesian sense of humor and produced the quip, "Phelps Phelps in a *lavalava* danced the *sivasiva* at a *fiafia* in Pago Pago"—which may or may not be apocryphal.

A successor, Peter T. Coleman, is remembered as the first governor of Polynesian blood. He was a half-Samoan of noble connections, with a stately sister, Mrs. Mabel Coleman Reid, who was well known in Samoan circles as the High Chieftess Tali. Coleman, who later became acting high commissioner of Micronesia (known officially as the Trust Territory of the Pacific Islands), was succeeded by another pure *palagi*, the energetic H. Rex Lee, a professional civil servant.

Lee's lasting fame in American Samoa rests upon his introduction of a widely publicized and controversial system of teaching by television in the public schools. Qualified teachers—always in short supply in American Samoa—recorded lessons in a central studio in Pago Pago, using all the tricks of the visual arts. The programs were then broadcast to the classrooms, on different channels for the various grades, from a transmitter on the 1,600-foot summit of Mount Alava, across the harbor from Fagatogo. The advantages, besides a uniformly high quality of instruction, included the use of familiar materials in the lessons; for instance, the children were given measurement problems for pandanus mats instead of carpeting, which they had never seen. Teachers, usually Samoan, monitored the lessons.

When I visited a number of television classes, the monitors interrupted the proceedings periodically to put the pupils through a few minutes of calisthenics. "The Samoan child's attention span is short," an American teacher explained, "so we give them exercises to keep them alert." The Samoan youngsters seemed in no way unusual to me, however, for I find television-watching soporific myself.

While educational television (universally shortened to ETV) had its enthusiastic proponents, there were also many detractors among educators and parents. In particular, the substitution of an image on the small screen for personal contact was deplored.

Eventually, the system was drastically modified and curtailed. Should ETV vanish from the scene without a trace, however, a by-product of the venture will remain a lasting monument to Rex Lee. This is the aerial tramway, originally built to carry television engineers from Solo Hill, on the town side of the harbor, to the Mount Alava transmitter site on the other side. The ride at 1,600 feet over the harbor, with a breath-taking view, became a prime tourist attraction.

Owen Stewart Aspinall, a lawyer, worked up to the governorship by serving as attorney general and secretary of the territory. He bore a familiar name in the South Pacific, his father being Congressman Wayne N. Aspinall, of Colorado. The elder Aspinall, then the chairman of the House Interior and Insular Affairs Committee, had a strong voice in American policy in the islands. A street was named after him in Agana, the capital of Guam. After becoming governor, Owen Aspinall married a beautiful Samoan woman of noble lineage, thus becoming a member of the community.

A dapper, slightly built, youthful man, Governor Aspinall was innovative and personally courageous. In a famous incident, he personally led a party of police in breaking up a riot between feuding Chinese and Korean fishermen, in which the quick-tempered Samoans had become peripherally involved. His permanent contribution was the construction of a Samoan-style village on the waterfront as a handicraft center where the traditional Samoan arts of weaving and tapa-making are practiced.

John M. Haydon probably accomplished more for American Samoa than any governor in the sixty-nine years of American rule preceding his arrival, but his practical contributions to the welfare of the territory were overshadowed by controversy. Like most of his predecessors, Haydon had no special preparation for the job. Being the publisher of *Marine Digest,* a maritime news magazine in Seattle, he may have been chosen for his knowledge of harbor problems. He had influential connections on President Nixon's White House staff and was outstandingly successful in obtaining funds for improvements to the neglected physical plant in American Samoa.

On his arrival in August 1969, Haydon made an inaugural speech pledging that, for the first time, there would be "a true involvement of Samoans" in the administration. High Chief Mauga, the top-ranking Samoan on Tutuila, declared in his reply that "every governor since civilian administration began in 1951" had made similar promises, and he hoped that the assurances would be carried out this time. Samoans had long desired more responsibility in the government. As an "unincorporated territory" of the United States, American Samoa enjoyed less autonomy than the French islands in the South Pacific. The constitution of 1960 established a bicameral legislature, with a Senate elected by the *matai* and a House of Representatives chosen by universal suffrage. Later, the territory began electing a delegate to Washington, but Samoa still had no vote in the Congress, unlike the French islands, which elect a senator and a member of the Chamber of Deputies.

Under the American system, the governor and his deputy, the lieutenant governor, were appointed by the Department of the Interior. Although all local laws had to come from the Samoan legislature, the governor had the power of veto. And the governor controlled the finances. Haydon decided, however, to involve the legislature in the preparation of the budget, "instead of just handing it to them."

Haydon was sympathetic to Samoan agitation for the right to elect the governor and lieutenant governor. "It is ridiculous and insulting to have an appointed governor," a legislative commission on the future status of the territory declared in its report. Haydon wanted the reform at once. "We will have to let the Samoans elect their own governor some day, so why not now?" he said to me in 1972. He let it be known publicly that he would like to go out of office with the distinction of having been the last appointed governor. But it was not to be. Three times during Haydon's five-year tenure, in November 1972, November 1973, and June 1974, the question was put to the electorate in a plebiscite, and each time it was turned down. The reasons for the rejection, I gathered from talks with many Samoans, included doubts of the administrative ability of the likely candidates for the office, and a belief that a well-connected American would do better in getting funds from Washington than one of their own. But the Department of the Interior, which wanted the reform, kept trying. A fourth plebiscite in November 1976 under a new governor, Earl B. Ruth, a North Carolina politician, brought the desired result. With two-thirds of the 6,693 registered electors turning out at the polls, 3,055 votes favored an elected governor against 1,368 who were opposed, thus passing the resolution with a majority of 70 percent. The Department of the Interior announced that it was "pleased."

The same legislative commission that had urged the election of the governor had opposed the alternatives of a reunion with Western Samoa—too little interest had been found, the report said—or independence, which the legislators considered a nonviable proposition. (Also, the report said in a revealing aside, it was feared that the United States might not agree to independence.)

"Without its close U.S. affiliation, American Samoa would be only another picturesque but impoverished archipelago in the South Seas," said a report on conditions in the territory by a New York consultative firm, Wolf Management Services, in 1969. A seeming majority of Samoans agreed with the Wolf assessment, but I found a lack of enthusiasm for making the link stronger by extending United States citizenship to the Samoans. The islanders have the legal status of "nationals," entitled to American protection and to the privilege of traveling freely to the United States, but are not bound by American laws and taxes in their home islands. One compelling objection to citizenship was a fear that application of the United States Constitution to the American Samoans would invalidate the treaty pledge to respect the traditional authority of chiefs in local affairs and the guarantee of Samoan land rights.

Haydon assumed office determined to gain the respect of the Samoans and to foster their interests, both politically and economically, to the utmost. Unfortunately, through bad luck and what must have been inadequate advice by subordinates, he was continually in trouble with the local people despite his good intentions.

An early stumble in the Haydon career in American Samoa, typical of the innocent misunderstandings that plagued his regime, concerned the affair of the fine mats. Government House had a spacious ground floor that served no purpose except as an entryway, with a stairway to the upper level. The governor's attractive and cultivated wife, a painter, sculptor, and linguist with a keen interest in people and her surroundings, decided to make this space a meeting place to which Samoans would be invited for adult education classes and discussions. There also she established the territory's first museum, with displays of tapa, fine mats, a canoe, and other Samoan artifacts. It was the fine mats that caused the trouble.

In Samoa, the term "fine mat" is applied generically to the sheets of finely woven pandanus, some of which are hundreds of years old, used on ceremonial occasions such as family weddings and funerals, and for formal presentation to notables on visits to villages. The recipient customarily passes on the fine mats in gifts to others, keeping them in circulation. The most prized examples are so finely woven that they look like linen and may have taken two to four years to make, sometimes at a cost of some damage to the weaver's eyesight. "The finest weaving isn't done now," Masiofo Fetaui told me, "because of the bad effect on the eyes. The newer mats look like sugar-bag material."

The fine mats routinely presented to Governor Haydon on his rounds of the villages went into Mrs. Haydon's museum, an unwitting breach of etiquette that the Samoans resented. The immobilized mats did, however, remain part of the communal wealth as exhibits in the new public museum established in the old stone post office.

Given a list of six persons recommended by Samoan leaders for appointment to a vacant district governorship, Haydon eliminated five names for reasons that seemed sound—for instance, one man had only recently moved to the territory from Western Samoa—and appointed the remaining nominee. Haydon then learned, to his astonishment, that he had selected the one person on the list who was totally unacceptable to the Samoans because of his low rank. "Why then did you nominate this man?" Haydon asked the Samoan leaders at a meeting. "They just looked at their feet," he said later. There was never a clear explanation.

Jean Haydon remarked that Samoans apparently expected the *palagi* to know the local etiquette and never hesitated to reprove the unwitting perpetrator of some breach. My wife and I were witnesses one night to the punctiliousness with which Governor Haydon strove to observe the niceties of Samoan protocol. We had just arrived at Government House, for a drink between planes while en route to Honolulu, when word came that a high-ranking chief had died unexpectedly. For the next hour the governor was on the telephone constantly, trying to verify the report and to determine what he should do if it were true. Should he telephone the chief's family, or call in person, and if so, when? Before all this was settled, we learned that the report was false, a case of mistaken identity through a confusion of names.

Haydon had the misfortune to be in office during a period of increasingly vocal reaction against the existing order. As governor, he was the natural target of the activists and of oppositionists in the press. The strangest episode involving Haydon, and the most serious, resulted in formal charges that he had violated a federal law forbidding civil servants to take part in politics. He was accused of having manipulated the government-controlled media to bring about the negative vote in the 1972 referendum on the question of an elected governor, an allegation oddly at variance with Haydon's frequent public advocacy of the very same reform. After a ten-day trial before a judge sent out to Pago Pago from Washington, he was exonerated. He resigned a year later, expressing disappointment that he would not achieve his ambition to be the last appointed governor of American Samoa, an honor that would go to a successor.

In his five years in Pago Pago, Haydon had made highly visible progress toward his goal, as he had described it to me, of erasing the effects of decades of neglect. The run-down government and port area underwent a large-scale face-lifting, with a new million-dollar complex housing the legislature, whose members were put on a full-time, salaried basis for the first time. The post office in the old stone naval structure, and numerous businesses that had been housed in ramshackle wooden buildings, were relocated in a multistory, air-conditioned office tower that would have looked at home in a prosperous Southern California town. Old buildings were spruced up with new roofs in pseudo-Samoan style replacing the rusting corrugated metal that had defaced the tropical scene for decades. Untidy waterfront areas were turned into neat parks. To relieve congestion in the capital, an eighty-six-acre industrial, commercial, and residential reserve was developed near the airport, on the opposite side of the island.

In dozens of trips to Washington, Haydon had succeeded in getting the annual budget for the territory nearly tripled from a stingy $13,100,000 in 1969, the year he arrived, to $36,700,000 in 1974, when he left. The results showed in new roads, improved water, sewerage, and telephone systems, among other accretions to the economic infrastructure.

Meanwhile, a publicity campaign in the United States had persuaded manufacturers to take advantage of the exemptions from American customs duties available in American Samoa. Fabricated articles with 51 percent domestic content—including the labor that goes into the making—are admitted to the mainland United States from American Samoa duty-free, a privilege also extended to goods made in the other American territories of Guam and the Virgin Islands. Soon hundreds of Samoans accustomed to using their hands to pick bananas and husk coconuts went to work for wages, assembling European watch movements, processing dairy products, and making clothing for sale in the United States.

Expanded operations by the two American tuna canneries across the harbor from Fagatogo provided new jobs for Samoans, besides bringing in more fishing vessels manned by South Koreans, Chinese from Taiwan, and Japanese from Okinawa. The fishermen imparted a cosmopolitan atmosphere to the dinky port, which formerly had been virtually empty between the one-day calls of big white cruise ships. At those times the wharf became a temporary bazaar of hefty Samoan women selling tapa, mats, carved wooden souvenirs, and shells to the passengers who arrive in the morning and depart in the afternoon, having "done" American Samoa. Expansion of the tuna fishing industry in American Samoa resulted in two exotic additions to the Pago Pago shoreline. These were the classic Korean pavilion, in the rococo traditional red and gold, built by South Korean fishing interests as a recreation center for their crews, and a similar establishment for the Chinese.

Reflecting all the increased commercial activity, banks in Honolulu and New York opened Pago Pago branches. And so, behind the consciously encouraged Samoan look of the new architecture in the capital, American Samoa was becoming more American.

Various changes under Haydon lifted Samoan morale. He abolished the dual wage system under which the government, which employed more than half of the Samoan work force, paid imported "Statesiders" higher wages than Samoans received for performing the same duties. Through Haydon's intervention, basic pay scales were equalized. It was in Haydon's time also that being a member of the legislature became a full-time, salaried occupation, and American Samoa elected its first delegate to Washington. He also worked out a scholarship program for Samoans in legal studies at the University of Southern California. Among the most far-reaching reforms accomplished under Haydon were the establishment of the Community College of American Samoa, the first post-secondary educational institution in the territory, with one thousand students, and the Tafuna Occupational Training Center, to turn out local craftsmen with needed skills that formerly had to be imported from Western Samoa and Tonga.

Observing the despoliation of the lush Samoan landscape by man-made pollution, such as careless disposal of garbage and the accumulation of solid waste in the form of abandoned hulks of old automobiles (short-lived in the corrosive tropical climate) and vast accumulations of discarded plastic packaging material, Haydon instituted a vigorous environmental protection program. He added a professional ecologist to his staff, formed an Environmental Quality Commission, organized a Pago Pago chapter of the pollution-fighting Sierra Club, and enforced strict clean-up regulations. Once he attempted to make a point about village cleanliness by dumping a collection of rubbish on a chief's desk; the action boomeranged because the Samoans interpreted the gesture not as the object lesson Haydon intended, but as a demonstration of his disrespect for chiefs. Undaunted, the governor ordered the abandonment of open garbage dumps in favor of using the waste in sanitary landfills.

Mrs. Haydon, who immediately began to add Samoan to her other language skills, took the lead in a new movement to preserve the traditional Samoan arts and crafts. Besides promoting the museum in the old naval post office, for which she obtained a grant from the National Endowment for the Arts and Humanities, she organized and headed an Arts Council and took a leading role in island beautification programs. "In American Samoa," the governor used to say, "we still have time to protect the beauty of nature against the impact of Western civilization." His various measures set up bulwarks against many environmental perils to come, as American Samoa modernized.

Haydon also inaugurated a new era of cooperative relations with Western Samoa. Till then, official contacts between the two Samoas had been desultory and irregular. (It had been out of consideration for American Samoan opinion that the Apia government rejected a proposal to appropriate the simple name "Samoa" for the new independent state, and adopted "Western Samoa" instead.) At Haydon's instance, legislators and officials of the two Samoas instituted a program of joint meetings, with the governor of American Samoa and the prime minister of Western Samoa alternating as chairman, to discuss mutual problems in various fields. Altogether, the record suggests that Haydon's tenure, though stormy and controversial, must have been the most productive five years in the history of the American administration. The old post office, now the Jean P. Haydon Museum, is a permanent memorial to the name.

One of the problems common to both Samoas was the lack of an operative work ethic. The ease with which life could be lived in complete security from cradle to grave in the subsistence economy of the villages left the young without incentive to enter regular employment for wages. The apathy toward work was a handicap to the development plans of progressive officials. "Hard work was never a Polynesian idea," Hans Kruse, the young part-Samoan, part-German director of economic development in Apia, remarked one day across a desk piled high with plans and reports.

"Samoans don't see any necessity to work while an abundance of coconuts can be taken for granted," said Pio Cardinal Taofinu'u, the Roman Catholic bishop of Apia and first Polynesian to wear the red cardinal's hat. In the sultry climate of Apia, the smooth-faced prelate discarded conventional ecclesiastical attire in favor of lightweight white slacks and a white sport shirt with a cross appliquéd to the breast pocket. He was engaged in an intensive farming program on church lands, giving young Samoans on-the-job training in scientific farming. "It's impossible to teach Samoans to develop their own lands scientifically except by example," said His Eminence, who remarked that young men were often embarrassed to see the cardinal wielding a hoe while a *matai* sat, watching. "Youths come to work with us as a contribution to the church," he went on. "We have more than a hundred boys in the program now, many of them school dropouts. We give them employment, teach them to save, and they learn good farming methods. Meanwhile, the income from the farms supports church schools."

Change was overtaking *fa'a Samoa*—the Samoan way—only slowly. I found many of the educated young, and older men who had come to like Western standards of living in long residence abroad, unanxious to alter traditional ways abruptly. "We have a better social security system than you do," said Palauni Tui'asasopo, a bright and articulate young leader. He was known in English-speaking circles as "Brownie," his nickname at a West Coast university. "You don't see either orphanages or old people's homes in Samoa," he declared. "Without the *matai* system," said Frank Galunao Brunt, the gray-haired private secretary to His Highness Malietoa Tanumafili II, "we'd need a police station in every district, but we have only two, one on each island. The village council reprimands and fines the fathers of erring sons, so it's the duty of the whole family to see that all obey the law."

Bill Hussey, the American director of the United Nations Development Program in the Western Pacific, knew Samoan attitudes intimately from his daily consultations with leaders on the spectrum of economic improvement plans falling within his responsibility. "Many Samoans aren't sure they want to be part of the twentieth century," he said one day in his office in the old Casino Hotel. "Those who do have to move slowly in order not to arouse the conservatives. Hence there's always a constant flux between eighteenth- and nineteenth-century and twentieth-century thinking. It makes U.N. decisions difficult."

Doctor Fana'afi Larkin, then the education director, highly educated and well past the student age, fell between the generations. She was observant of significant changes, such as the trend toward what she called the "biological unit" of husband, wife, and children, as opposed to the extended family. She believed that social change was in a gentle transitional stage. "A generation gap certainly exists," she said, "but the young people are still sufficiently respectful of the old values."

The election of 1970, which was followed by the unseating of Mata'afa and the installation of Tupua Tamasese Lealofi IV as prime minister, was considered indicative of a new progressive movement among the *matai*. The voting chiefs sent twenty-one new members to the forty-seven-man legislature, many younger than the men they replaced.

"There's a feeling among the young generation that the old, conservative element that has been in power and ruling village life should be supplanted by young, educated progressive men," said Lauofo Meti, the secretary to the government. He could have been describing himself, for Lauofo Meti, who represented Western Samoa at many South Pacific gatherings that I covered for *The New York Times,* was one of the outstanding younger men in the government. Originally known as Mike Meredith, he was one of a number of Europeans and part-Europeans who chose to use Samoan names in order to identify more closely with the indigenous community. "Youth is beginning to form itself into a force, but it has not yet expressed itself publicly," said Mike, as his friends called him. "There is always the fear that at some stage the *matai* will become incensed, and there are many ways he can kill business opportunities. But certainly there will be an acceleration of change."

For a man of royal title, Prime Minister Tupua Tamasese Lealofi IV had a liberal outlook on the question of youth and change. A middle-aged, light-skinned man whose specialty as a doctor before he went into politics had been psychiatry, he discussed the social outlook for Western Samoa at length in his simple corner office on the second floor of a creaky wooden building overlooking the crescent-shaped Apia waterfront. "We believe that change is inevitable, but we want it to be a slow-going, smooth transition, without sudden disruption," he said. He was referring to the opinion he shared with the majority of high-ranking chiefs. "For my part," he added, "I take a middle course in the need to adjust traditional values to new thought."

Political changes could be seen coming. Although the parliament overwhelmingly defeated a motion to introduce universal suffrage in place of election by the *matai* order, the youthful proposer of the motion, Tofa Siaosi, was taken into the next cabinet and became, at twenty-seven, probably the youngest finance minister in the world. Amoa Tausilia, who was forty-eight, told me that he had been one of the seven legislators who had supported votes for all adults. "If we fail to take progressive steps now," he said, "we may have greater difficulties in the future as our young people become better educated."

Many young in both parts of Samoa literally turned their backs on the *matai* system by emigrating, usually going from Western Samoa to New Zealand and from American Samoa to Hawaii and California. Not only was the pay much higher, but there was less need to share it with the *matai*.

Part way through the second decade of Western Samoa's independence, the dominance of the four *tama'aiga* in political life was increasingly questioned. It was clear that the future of the royal lines under a parliamentary system would depend upon the personal caliber of the holders of the titles. Dilution of the power of the aristocracy, according to some of the forward-looking Samoans, would enhance the prospects for a reunion of the two Samoas under one flag. "A sure indication of the tempo of change is the increasing number of contested elections," said Lauofo Meti. "Formerly, a single candidate was usually chosen by common consent. The traditional chiefs are not receiving the recognition they once had."

Western Samoa passed a bend on the road to democracy in March 1976 with the election of a prime minister outside the ranks of the *tama'aiga*, if not the *matai*. Following a national election in which Masiofo Fetaui, among other veteran members, lost her legislative seat, the *tama'aiga* Tupua Tamasese Lealofi was ousted from the prime ministership by the vigorously progressive Tupuola Efi, an experienced cabinet officer at the age of thirty-eight years, by the decisive vote of 31 to 16 in the 47-member parliament. The older man left politics to become deputy head of state. Tupuola Efi, a smooth-faced, serious-looking young man with rimless glasses who had impressed me with his performance at inter-island conferences, was no commoner, however; his father, Tupua Tamasese Meaole, had been a *tama'aiga* and, before his death, had been one of the two coholders of the title of head of state. Nevertheless, his election demolished a traditional barrier to political fulfillment for aspiring Western Samoan youth.

A new chapter in the political history of American Samoa opened in January 1978 with the inauguration of Peter Coleman as the first elected governor. Coleman, then 57 years old, had left United States Government service in Micronesia, where he had held the second highest post in the Trust Territory administration, to return to Pago Pago and campaign successfully for the office that he had held by appointment two decades before.

Former governor John M. Haydon of American Samoa with chiefs, one holding a fly whisk

Robert Trumbull/*New York Times*

Robert Trumbull/*New York Times*

...ate diggings on Ocean Island

The *maneaba* (village meeting house) at Bairiki, Tarawa, Gilbert Islands

Inside a *maneaba* in Abaokoro village, northern Tarawa atoll

TWELVE

Smallest and Richest

---

ar below the chalky cliff, a white curve of surf marked the fringing reef that encircled the oval island. An ivory beach shimmered in the heat, but on the hilltop where we stood a cool breeze rustled the palm trees and suffused the broad veranda of State House, the home of the president, with light fragrance from a tangle of flowering vines. I walked down the steps with a short, stocky man whose skin was the color of light mahogany. Hammer DeRoburt, president and "head chief" of Nauru, dug the toe of his shoe into the pale, dry earth. "We are standing on phosphate here," he said. "Eventually this site, too, will be dug up."

It was an eerie feeling to be standing on doomed ground. The gracious State House would be razed, the palms and poinciana trees and vivid bougainvillea would be bulldozed away, and the land would be devoured by great steel shovels. The removed earth would become brown powder and would be poured into the holds of ships, taken across the sea, and mixed with sulphuric acid. The mixture would turn the useless dirt into valuable fertilizer to be sprinkled on distant farms, mostly in Australia, New Zealand, and Japan.

The cool hilltop would then be a glaring waste of ugly white pillars and misshapen gullies, like much of the rest of the despoiled landscape of Nauru. Less than a generation ahead, more than 80 percent of the once pleasing island would look like the surface of the moon, dead and worthless, unless some way could

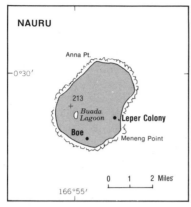

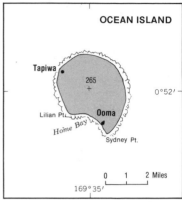

be found to replace the removed material with fertile topsoil.

A scientist from the United States Department of Agriculture, Darnell M. Whitt, whose visit to Nauru corresponded with mine, thought the island might be rehabilitated by spotting the gnarled desert area with pockets of imported soil, and cultivating soil-creating plants such as soybeans. "If we could reclaim only 10 percent of the worked-out land, it would double the present 500-acre arable area," said Doctor Whitt, who was the director of the plant sciences division of the Soil Conservation Service of the United States Department of Agriculture. He suggested a pilot project, using soybeans.

Another proposal was to break down coral pillars and fill in gullies to create an area large enough to relocate the airfield from the coastal strip, where it occupied potentially productive land. These ideas were not just fantasies, for the stalwart, brown-skinned Nauruans had enough money coming in from the phosphate digs to do just about anything short of the miraculous.

Phosphate made Nauru the richest nation in the world, acre for acre and body for body. The annual phosphate shipment of up to 2.2 million tons a year, at an average price of $60 a ton at the time, brought in about $132 million yearly, or approximately forty thousand dollars for every man, woman, and child of the thirty-three hundred Nauruans in terms of per capita gross national product. Not even the wealthiest of the tiny, oil-producing Arab sheikdoms could match that. Of course, only a fraction of this fantastic income was parceled out to individuals, the rest being invested. Nevertheless, poverty was as unknown on Nauru as snow.

Besides being the richest country in the world, Nauru was also the smallest independent republic—eight and a half square miles in area, only twelve miles around by the island-girdling highway, a three-hour hike that the robust Australian girl secretaries for the government and the phosphate company used to take on Saturday nights for exercise. One afternoon, sightseeing in a rented car, I passed a pretty Nauruan girl coming from the opposite direction on a Japanese motorbike; ten minutes later we met head-on again—both of us had driven halfway around the island.

Nauru was not only the smallest and richest republic, but also the remotest—just thirty-three miles south of the equator, one island alone in an empty sea, west of the Gilberts and south of the Marshalls, a tiny dot in the immensity of the central Pacific. I flew in one day from Tarawa by Fiji Airways (later called Air Pacific) and only stayed until the next plane out; but that was a week. Tourism, potentially the second industry on the island after phosphates, was still years in the future. A visitor's visa was tantamount to a personal invitation from the president, and the only accommodation was in the four-bedroom official guest house.

The complex story of Nauru is linked with the history of its neighbor, Banaba or Ocean Island, an even smaller speck on the sea 190 miles almost due east. Each of these islands, which resemble each other in formation as well as history, supposedly originated as a coral ledge that emerged from the sea and attracted countless birds. In the course of centuries, the coral platforms acquired thick blankets of dung. In various natural convulsions, so the theory goes, the two islands sank and rose repeatedly, acquiring in the process coatings of decayed marine organisms that, along with the mass of bird droppings, became compacted between the pillars of coral as phosphatic rock.

Dark-skinned people arrived from other islands, found fertile patches around the sterile areas of hard, putty-colored clay, and stayed to become the ancestors of the present-day Nauruans and Banabans. In the case of Nauru, the permanent inhabitants were considered a mixture of Melanesian, Micronesian, and Polynesian strains, with Polynesian predominating. Where the progenitors of the Banabans originated—they were called by that name even after their island became generally known as Ocean—was to be a subject of debate in British courts, with millions of pounds sterling and the future of thousands of dusky Pacific islanders depending upon the conclusion.

The first white man known to have seen Nauru was Captain John Fearn, of the British whaling ship *Hunter,* in November 1798. He called the place Pleasant Island, which in later years would turn out to be a notable misnomer. Another Briton found Banaba in 1804 and gave it a new name in honor of his ship, the *Ocean.* Ocean Island, to use the better-known name, was only two and a half square miles in area, so small and isolated that it attracted little attention. Nauru, however, became a haunt of deserters from ships' crews, fleeing criminals, beachcombers, and others who found some advantage in settling on an obscure South Pacific island.

At that time, it seems, one of the best-known products of Nauru (phosphate had not been discovered yet) was attractive girls. One became the wife of a young Britain named William Harris, described in an official history as a "remittance man," who settled on the island in 1842 and started a mixed-blood family that stands high in Nauruan society today. Another married the colorful Irish-American sea captain known as His Majesty O'Keefe, the uncrowned king of the Yap Islands.

In those days the island was divided among twelve clans, represented by the twelve-pointed star on the flag of the republic. The clans were frequently at war with each other, and the fighting became bloodier after white men introduced guns. The whole island erupted into a protracted conflict, known as the "Ten-Year War," in 1878 after the Nauruans learned from Gilbert Islanders how to make a highly intoxicating liquor from coconut sap. A small German military force landed from a gunboat in 1888, ostensibly for the purpose of restoring order. The Germans declared the island part of the German empire, banned alcohol, arrested all twelve chiefs, and held them as hostages until the warring Nauruans had turned in every firearm on the island—765 in all, more than enough to arm every adult Nauruan.

Missionaries followed, converted the entire population to Christianity, packed the women into Mother Hubbards, abolished the traditional dances, forbade polygamy, and printed the Bible and other religious works in one of the many Nauruan dialects, which then became the standard language of the island. The German administration, having little interest in the apparently worthless island, let the missionaries handle practically all affairs affecting the Nauruans except the collection of taxes.

With Nauru again worthy of the name Pleasant Island, the scene shifts to the Sydney offices of the Pacific Islands Company, successor to the venerable trading firm of John T. Arundel and Company. The supercargo on one of the company's ships calling at Nauru had found there a curious piece of rock that he brought back to the Sydney headquarters, where it was identified as "petrified wood" and was used for several years as a doorstop. A young New Zealander in the office named Albert Ellis, who had had some experience with phosphates, noticed the object one day. He thought it looked like phosphatic rock and had it tested. When analysis showed the doorstop to be more than 90 percent phosphate, the company acted immediately.

Approaching the Germans, the company offered to exchange its trading stations on Nauru and other islands, along with some plantations, for rights to the phosphate. The Germans accepted, exacting in addition a few shares in the phosphate enterprise and a small royalty. The arrangement lasted until World War I, during which Australia seized the island with sixty-six men a short time before a Japanese force arrived with the same idea.

Had the Japanese been a little faster, South Pacific history would have been different. One may presume that Japan would have added Nauru to the other German holdings acquired by Tokyo, consisting of the Marshall, Caroline, and Mariana archipelagoes. The island would have been included in the group seized by the United States as a result of World War II. Thus, instead of being a separate United Nations trusteeship administered by Australia, Nauru would no doubt have become part of the American-administered Trust Territory of the Pacific Islands, otherwise known as Micronesia, and would never have achieved separate sovereignty as the world's smallest, richest, and remotest republic.

The alert Albert Ellis and his associates in the Pacific Islands Company, noting that Ocean resembled Nauru, landed there in 1900 and found similar rich deposits of phosphatic rock present, as they had expected. The prospectors sought out the "king" of the island and obtained exclusive rights to the phosphate for 999 years in consideration of an annual payment of fifty pounds sterling—then equivalent to two hundred fifty dollars in cash or trade goods. This was the first of many questionable actions with respect to Ocean Island that would later come before the British Parliament and courts. In this instance, it was learned that the supposed king who had bartered away the phosphate for a pittance was only one of many chiefs on the island, and not even a very important one.

Annexation of Ocean Island by Britain followed in the same year, purportedly at the request of the chiefs, and the Union Jack was formally raised on 28 September 1901. In another controversial act that would have severe repercussions long afterward, the British in 1916 incorporated Ocean into the crown colony of the Gilbert and Ellice Islands, a string of atolls of which the nearest was 240 miles to the west.

After World War I Nauru, as a former German colony, became a League of Nations Mandated Territory as a joint responsibility of Britain, Australia, and New Zealand, with Australia handling the administration for all three. The three governments bought out the successors to the Pacific Islands Company on Nauru and Ocean, and replaced it with a new corporation under a tripartite body called the British Phosphate Commissioners, consisting of one representative of each participating nation, to direct the mining, processing, and export of the phosphate.

Little attention, if any, was paid to the wishes of the indigenous people of Nauru and Ocean in any of these arrangements. New agreements, however, provided modest royalties from the phosphate operations to be paid to the owners of the affected lands. The bulk of the phosphate revenue on Ocean went to the support of the perennially impoverished British administration of the Gilbert and Ellice Islands Colony, of which Ocean was officially a part. Natives of the Gilbert and Ellice atolls, and Chinese from British Hong Kong, were brought to both islands to fill out the labor force as contract workers. Meanwhile, collection of the phosphate was made more efficient by the construction of huge cantilevers on shore to load the ships, which had to stand away from the steep-sided islands, moored to buoys.

World War II came to Nauru when two German sea raiders, disguised as merchant ships, sank five freighters congregated around the island. A raider shelled the cantilever and other phosphate installations, but the mines were able to continue operating. Soon after the bombing of Pearl Harbor, Japan seized Ocean, Nauru, and the Gilberts. Britain and Australia had foreseen, however, that the Japanese would covet the phosphate islands and had already evacuated the white community of Nauru except for three administrators, two members of the phosphate staff, and two missionaries, all of whom had bravely insisted on staying behind to give what help they could to the islanders and Chinese. The Japanese sent the missionaries to Truk, along with many Nauruans and Banabans, and killed the remaining five whites following an American bombing raid on the newly built airfield on 23 March 1943—a "war crime" for which the Japanese commander on Nauru was executed after the Allies reclaimed the island.

On Ocean Island the British government official in charge, a radio officer, two phosphate men, and two Roman Catholic missionaries elected to stay with the 700 Banabans and 800 Gilbertese workers, the latter with a number of wives and children. All the whites died from the effects of malnutrition during the first year of the Japanese occupation. Because of the food problem on the barren, sequestered island, the Japanese deported all of the Banabans and Gilbertese to Kusaie, in the eastern Carolines, Tarawa in the Gilberts, and Nauru, except 200 Gilbertese who were retained as fishermen.

Many of the deportees from both Ocean and Nauru died of mistreatment and malnutrition on the islands where they spent the war years. When word of the Japanese capitulation reached Ocean in August 1945, all of the 200 Gilbertese who had been kept on the island were killed except one, who somehow managed to escape. His testimony at a subsequent war crimes trial helped to convict the Japanese commander and quartermaster, who were executed for the massacre.

After the war, the surviving Nauruans were returned to their island, now richer by one Japanese-built airfield. The phosphate plant, wrecked by repeated American bombing on "milk runs" from bases in the Gilberts, was rebuilt and life resumed as before. As for the Banabans, however, very few would ever see their home island again.

A key figure in the modern history of the phosphate islands was to return to Nauru briefly with the Australian warship that arrived to take the surrender of the Japanese garrison on 13 September 1945. He was the New Zealand member of the tripartite British Phosphate Commission, Sir Albert Ellis, whose interest in an unusual doorstop forty-five years before was responsible for starting that history.

In the territorial reshuffle following the end of hostilities, Nauru passed into the United Nations trusteeship system, with Australia remaining in charge on behalf of the three joint administering powers of the old League of Nations Mandate. The change altered the course of history for the Nauruans, who had been given schools, health services, some political education, and a modest share of phosphate royalties by the white rulers, but remained nonpersons in international affairs.

Suddenly, the Nauruans were able to invoke the sympathetic interest of an international community, and the anticolonialist wing in the United Nations was quick to respond. Like the other trust territories around the world, Nauru was visited periodically by a United Nations inspection team whose members, especially those from former colonial countries, were deeply—sometimes emotionally—concerned with the progress of the indigenous people toward self-government. Political advancement, presumably to lead to independence, was a cardinal requirement of the trusteeship compact binding the administering powers, and it applied to Nauru, small and insignificant as it was, as much as to big, important territories like New Guinea.

No such international involvement extended to Ocean and the Banabans, for that island remained a British possession, administrative headquarters of the Gilbert and Ellice Islands Colony, completely beyond the parameters of the trusteeship concept. The British were in charge, and what happened to the Banabans was for London alone to decide. Clearly, it was better to have been colonized by Germany, like Nauru, and be a charge on the international conscience.

The British and their Australian and New Zealand partners in the mining of Ocean and Nauru were sensitive, however, to the impending human problem as the phosphate deposits approached exhaustion and the islands, rendered bleak and sterile by the merciless strip mining, would be abandoned by the diggers. This fate lay only a generation ahead for Ocean at the end of the war, a little longer for Nauru.

Contrary to the popular impression, the environmental aspects of the wholesale despoliation of the landscape were secondary to the economic effect of the closing of the mines. While it was true that the removal of the phosphate would leave four-fifths or more of the surface of the two islands uninhabitable, this would be no real change. Those areas had never been inhabited anyway, for phosphatic earth supports nothing but scrub; phosphate becomes a fertilizer only after the addition of sulphuric acid.

Nauru is shaped like a hat: the crown is a low plateau, composed mostly of phosphatic rock and empty of habitation; the brim is a girdle of fertile soil on which the entire population has always lived, except for the inhabitants of a lush pocket in the interior around the Buada Lagoon, an oasis in a desert of phosphate that I visited often to enjoy the cool village scene in surroundings of luxuriant tropical beauty. The lagoon was divided into individual fish farms. I was told that the fish were a salt-water variety, netted in the sea and kept in conch shells of sea water to which fresh water was added gradually until they became accustomed to the brackish condition that obtained in the lagoon.

Over the years, the Banabans and Nauruans acquired Western habits, wearing the same clothes, living in the same kind of houses, and eating the same food as the whites who ran the phosphate works and administered the islands. The phosphate royalties, though miserly compared to the benefit derived by the Britons, Australians, and New Zealanders from the resource, enabled them to live a largely Western style of life. The Banabans became more or less displaced persons on their own island, being concentrated in four large villages instead of the scattered smaller settlements they had occupied before. As for the Nauruans, their former three-tier class structure had virtually disappeared, but they retained their system of electing chiefs, of whom one was chosen head chief, and retained vestiges of indigenous culture.

The British, Australians, and New Zealanders envisaged no viable future for the two islands after the phosphate ran out. Britain, after moving the capital of the Gilbert and Ellice Islands Colony from Ocean to Tarawa, proposed to solve the problem for the Banabans by simply not sending them back there. From Tarawa, where they had been collected from the various islands to which they had been dispersed by the Japanese, the entire Banaban nation was resettled on the island of Rabi (pronounced ROM-bee) in the Fiji group, which Britain purchased for $125,-000 taken from the Banaban phosphate funds. As will be seen, however, this was not to be the end of the matter, which would in fact become a scandal reverberating in the House of Commons.

The Nauruan case, meanwhile, built up to a denouement in the United Nations, whose inspection missions to the island reported acerbically on the failure of Australia to foster political progress among the Nauruans. By this time, the Nauruans had developed a strong sense of nationhood. An offer of resettlement in Britain, Australia, or New Zealand, with full citizenship in the host country, was rejected; the Nauruans had no desire to become one more small ethnic minority in a larger nation. Australia then offered to give the Nauruans an island to themselves off the tropical northern coast of Queensland. This proposal was received favorably by the Nauruans, but the negotiations broke down when Australia refused to concede sovereignty over the island to its prospective new occupants, an impossible demand for any Australian government to grant in the political climate that prevailed.

Events took a historic turn with the emergence of a remarkable political leader on Nauru in the person of Hammer DeRoburt, a former schoolteacher, educated in Australia, who had been elected to the Nauru Local Government Council, an advisory body, in 1955. His strong character had been molded in the crucible of exile on Truk, the Japanese naval base in the eastern Carolines, where he was the only member of his immediate family to survive. (Of some 1,200 Nauruans removed to Truk, only 737 lived to return to Nauru on 31 January 1946, a date celebrated on the island as "Deliverance Day.")

Becoming head chief in 1965, DeRoburt led a demand for full independence for Nauru, which he felt was the only way Nauruans would maintain a national identity. The proposal of sovereign status among the world's nations for a microscopic island that was being rapidly transformed into a moonscape aroused derision, but DeRoburt persevered. He adopted a strategy, which proved effective, of meeting every counterproposal by escalating his own demands. "Step by step, our message began getting through," DeRoburt said later.

Belatedly, the Australians began to lead the Nauruans gradually toward political maturity. A legislative council of nine members, elected by adult suffrage, was given limited law-making powers. The Nauru Local Government Council, the successor to the old Council of Chiefs, functioned in domestic areas. Finally, in 1967, exhausted by the determination of the doughty Nauruans and the unrelenting pressure of the anticolonialist group in the United Nations, the three administering powers dropped all opposition to independence. Nauru became a sovereign republic on 31 January 1968, a date chosen to coincide with the twenty-second anniversary of the earlier Deliverance Day.

The flag raised over the island consisted of a blue shield, for the sea stretching unbroken to the horizon; a lateral stripe of gold, for the equator; and, at lower left, a white star with twelve points, representing the geographical position of the island and the twelve original tribes. The legislative council was replaced by a parliament of eighteen members, from whom a cabinet was selected, with Head Chief DeRoburt, member of Parliament, as chief executive and head of state with the title of president. In November the infant republic became an associate member of the Commonwealth, with all benefits of full membership except the right to attend conferences of Commonwealth prime ministers.

Meanwhile, the Nauruans arranged to take over the island's phosphate industry, not by nationalization, in the usual manner of emerging countries, but by purchase for twenty million dollars in Australian money, which also was the currency of Nauru. For the Nauruans, who had once received a paltry royalty of half a British penny a pound for their phosphate, fortune had turned around. The same British Phosphate Commissioners took the bulk of the output of the stuff, although the new government of Nauru diversified its outlets by selling smaller amounts to Japan, Taiwan, South Korea, and Mexico. The farmers of Australia and New Zealand never noticed the difference, but the Nauruans certainly did, for now it was they who received the entire revenue. Of the total income after expenses, 7 percent was divided among the landholders as royalties, 58.8 percent went to the government, and the remaining 34.2 percent was invested by the Nauru Phosphate Royalties Trust to insure the future financial security of the Nauruan people. Estimates of the Nauruans' net worth change upward from year to year, keeping pace with inflation.

The phosphate bonanza would run out by the end of the century—although more could be obtained by digging deeper—but the Nauruans need not care. By that time, the accumulated investments and trust funds held abroad would bring in an annual income that might equal the phosphate earnings—"more than enough," said Dennis A. Ferrier, the hired British financial adviser to the government, "to maintain the present standard of living with an increased population."

When I visited the island two years after independence, the standard of living was fantastic by South Pacific norms. It was common to find families with two or more cars and enough cameras, radios, stereo sets, and other toys—some working and some not—to stock a small shop. All these things could be purchased duty-free in the island cooperative stores. For bargains, the island was a vest-pocket Hong Kong.

Machines had a short life in the humid, salty air, but the Nauruans cared little. When an automobile or a stereo stopped functioning, they simply bought another. Since it was usually impossible to obtain competent repairs on the island, this was not so improvident as it may sound. "When you have to send a broken-down car or stereo all the way to Australia to be fixed, it's cheaper just to buy a new one," said Theodore Moses, the manager of the cooperative general store and supermarket. Because of the tax-free economy, automobiles and other imported luxury items cost half the Australian price.

Virtually all the food consumed on the island also came from Australia, since Nauru produced nothing but papayas, breadfruit, coconuts, simple garden crops, and a few fish caught beyond the encircling reef. But that mattered not; imported food was cheaper on Nauru than in Australia, where it came from.

Water was a problem, with the heated updrafts from the glaring, sun-baked phosphate diggings driving away the rain clouds. Reservoirs would have been useless, for the seventy-six-inch annual rainfall was exactly equaled by the seventy-six-inch annual rate of evaporation. Again, no matter: the annual requirement of thirty-six million gallons of water was simply shipped from Australia in tankers.

All the necessities of life, and some luxuries, were free or ridiculously cheap. Government-built houses rented for less than five dollars a month, and the public works department provided free repairs. Medical and dental care, hospitalization, bus transportation, local telephone service, schooling (compulsory between the ages of six and seventeen), and even the fortnightly mimeographed newspaper all cost nothing. And taxes, for Nauruans, were unknown. "Taxation is unsuited to the Nauruan temperament," President DeRoburt explained, apparently surprised that I would ask.

Over-rich living was the island's main problem. Obesity, noticeable throughout the South Pacific, was especially common on Nauru. Too many people, it seemed, had little to do but eat. According to one health survey, diabetes afflicted one Nauruan in every five past the age of thirty, and the incidence of heart disease was rising alarmingly.

While some Nauruans received fortunes in royalties when the phosphate miners reached their lands, other islanders whose holdings had already been worked out, or were to be mined in the future, were getting nothing. The island system of family responsibility, however, and the Nauruan custom known as *bubuji,* which amounted to commandeering whatever one wanted from a friend or relative, assured that no one was in need.

A top cabinet minister explained to me how *bubuji* works. He asked me not to quote him by name, for to seem to complain about the custom would be offensive and deeply resented. "I bought a new car a couple of years ago," he said. "I had hardly driven it before a friend asked me for the keys. I haven't had the car since." Traditionally, when a child is a year old the parents must give a party. Guests are expected to take home anything that strikes their fancy. On such an occasion, even the carpets on the floor may be gone when the festivities end. "If your neighbors don't strip you naked, you feel that they don't like you," said James Bop, the wealthy and well-educated minister of finance.

But as the Nauruans became more sophisticated in the handling of money and realized that the wellsprings of their affluence would one day run dry, some began to look for ways of evading *bubuji* without giving offense. I learned about this when I came unexpectedly upon the Nauruan branch of the far-flung Bank of New South Wales, my own bank in Sydney, and stopped in for a chat with the Australian manager, Jim Belcher. "A woman asked me the other day how she could tie up her money, put it beyond reach of *bubuji,*" he recalled. "I told her about time deposits," he said.

With increasing knowledge of the world beyond the great water, more Nauruans began sending their children to expensive private schools in Australia, whose principals sometimes wrote to parents begging them to go easy on the spending money for the sake of class morale.

The government was generous with employment for Nauruans in the civil service, and not too demanding of time and work. For skilled and manual labor, the Nauruans continued to import Gilbert and Ellice Islanders and Hong Kong Chinese. Some of the Chinese went into business. The one Chinese restaurant and nightclub, called the Star Twinkle because the manager liked the rhyme that begins "Twinkle, twinkle, little star," was capable of putting on a superior Cantonese meal by prearrangement, or if, like me, you were the guest of a cabinet minister.

President DeRoburt, who was astute in business and careful to hire foreign advisers who were even more astute, spent more time in Melbourne than on the island. He was also the republic's one-man diplomatic service, visiting various countries to sign important contracts himself. He acquired a shipping line in the

South Pacific trade and started an airline that eventually connected Nauru with Australia and Japan via many other islands.
In the center of Melbourne he built a forty-five-million-dollar,
fifty-two-story office building, the city's tallest, called Nauru
House. Two floors were reserved for Nauru government missions; the remaining offices, to be rented out, would accommodate four thousand workers, more than the population of the
island.

The South Pacific Conference session held on Nauru in 1975,
at DeRoburt's invitation, provided the motivation for a wholesale
upgrading of the island. The one hotel, on a good beach at an
indent in the coast called Anibare Bay, was enlarged to fifty-eight
rooms. A Honolulu firm built a five-million-dollar civic center,
fully air-conditioned, for the conference. A Japanese contractor
widened and repaved the road around the island, a new Japanese
telephone system was installed, and a fleet of minibuses was
imported to whisk the delegates between hotel and meeting hall.
Air Nauru flew in a jazz orchestra from Rarotonga; dance teams
from Truk, the Gilbert Islands, and the Marshalls; conference
T-shirts from Hong Kong; oysters from Australia; strawberries
from Japan; and steaks from Honolulu. Delegates from twenty
South Pacific governments averred that it was the best conference ever held. Few of the participants were aware that Nauru
was undergoing a serious drought at the time, for President
DeRoburt had chartered a Japanese tanker to bring in thirty
thousand tons of fresh water.

After the two-week conference, life resumed at the old lan-
guorous pace. Men on motorbikes chased pigs and chickens from
the airfield runway before planes took off or landed. Tamed
frigate birds—a hobby peculiar to Nauru—dozed on fourteen-
foot perches along the beach as of yore. (Another pastime for
which Nauru had once been famous in the South Seas, the creation of elaborate figures by passing a length of string around the
fingers—known elsewhere as "cat's cradle"—seems to have
disappeared.) There was talk of an elaborate tourist complex and
the benefits of a tax haven that would eventually make Nauru
"the Switzerland of the South Seas."

One looked in vain for the republic's capital among the clusters
of dwellings that circled the island along the coast road. Except
for the concentration of barrackslike dwellings for the phosphate
workers, called "The Location," and the isolated settlement at
Buada, around the central lagoon, there were no separate towns,

only district designations for voting purposes. The government of the republic was housed in a group of clapboard buildings just off the airport. Having assembled in the parliament there, many of the same people then drove a few miles down the road to another building to take their seats in the Local Government Council, which administered various public projects financed by phosphate. A dispute between the two bodies, a frequent occurrence, virtually amounted to people arguing with themselves. The seemingly carefree, slightly zany atmosphere pervading Nauru masked the actuality of shrewd management behind the scenes. The shipping line kept adding vessels. The airline—once known, appropriately, as the world's smallest—grew from a single eight-seat "executive jet" to a fleet of forty-passenger machines. Hired experts of the Nauru Phosphate Corporation undertook research and experimentation that eventually improved the quality of the product to 91 percent purity, making it the highest grade known and opening an entirely new market for use of the material in the manufacture of soaps and detergents. A few years after independence, the Nauruans were selling phosphate at more than the world price, belying the confident predictions by departing Australians that the industry would fall into ruins after the islanders took over the ownership from the British Phosphate Commissioners. "Nauru has a future as a trading nation," said Dennis Ferrier, the British financial adviser.

Also to the surprise of skeptics, the toy republic turned out to be a viable political entity despite its minuscule size, with a functioning parliamentary democracy. Though little noticed in international affairs, since it lacked the people to maintain embassies, the Nauruans succeeded in preserving a distinct identity among South Pacific peoples. "We have a motto in Nauruan," said Finance Minister Bop, uttering a phrase in his mother tongue. "It means, 'Tomorrow will take care of itself.'"

The political independence and prosperity of Nauru caused envy and bitterness among the two thousand Banabans living unhappily on Rabi, sixteen hundred miles from their ancestral home on Ocean Island. Although the Banabans had become citizens of Fiji, they too yearned for a national identity.

When I visited Ocean in a Gilbert Islands trading vessel from Tarawa, the destruction of the island was well advanced. The sea front was a bustling panorama dominated by the giant phosphate crushing plant and the four-hundred-foot cantilever arm that poured the powdered earth into the holds of ships standing offshore. At one time the islanders had had to bring the phosphate to the waiting vessels by canoe. Now the whole operation was mechanized, and the pulverized phosphate slid into the holds from the cantilever at a rate of fifteen hundred tons an hour. The only Banaban present was the official representative of the Rabi community. My requests to see him were blandly ignored by my Australian host at the phosphate plant.

"This island is the tropical British equivalent of the old-fashioned company town," Tom Ainsworth, the courteous British district commissioner for Ocean, remarked over a cool drink on the veranda of his comfortable bungalow overlooking the sparkling sea. "The phosphate commission provides virtually everything there is, except the government's few police and schools and a couple of small shops run by Chinese."

The island's shoreside slopes, which rose gradually to the 265-foot height of the central plateau, were covered with the cottages and apartment buildings occupied by the twenty-seven hundred residents, nearly all of whom were connected with the phosphate works. There was a forested area in the unmined central section of the island, an oasis in the sun-baked desert of misshapen coral pillars and deep, twisting gullies where the phosphate had been removed by the usual strip mining. Banaban leaders whom I interviewed later on Rabi insisted that this jungled area could be the nucleus of a new settlement, although the British viewed the island as hopelessly uninhabitable once the phosphate reserves were exhausted and the plant shut down. According to the Banabans, their ancestors settled on this inhospitable rock long before the beginning of the Christian era.

The British, in an effort to give legitimacy to the attachment of Ocean to the Gilbert and Ellice Islands Colony, maintained that the Banabans were really Gilbertese, the descendants of migrants from Beru atoll. The Banabans, though acknowledging a common Micronesian ancestry, cite linguistic and other differences, and point out that when the British came they had a separate kingdom whose existence was unknown to the Gilbertese atoll dwellers.

From the beginning, the Banabans had received a niggardly recompense for the despoliation of their once-pleasant island. Early in the story, their shabby treatment at the hands of the colonial authority had been the subject of sharp questions in the House of Commons. The payment improved, but taxes also were increased, and the Banabans never ceased to feel that they were being milked for the benefit of strangers. As the end of the mining approached, the Banabans were receiving collectively a royalty of 15 percent of the profits, which came to something less than half a million dollars a year. At the same time, 84 percent—or around 2.5 million dollars a year—was paid into the British administration of the Gilbert and Ellice colony.

The Banabans became symbols in the South Pacific of the unequal struggle of a weak island people against white colonial might. The postwar wholesale transplanting of the entire Banaban population to Rabi, sixteen hundred miles from their home island, had been intended to improve their condition. In fact, however, they were ill-fitted to cope with an entirely new way of life in a completely strange environment.

Rabi was a run-down coconut plantation, unsuited for any kind of livelihood except raising copra and fishing. Neither of these occupations fell within the experience of contemporary Banabans. Although they were given Fiji citizenship, they remained an isolated racial minority in a foreign country. Getting to Rabi from Suva was a tortuous process, requiring first a flight to Vanua Levu by the Fijian internal airline, then a two-hour taxi ride to Buca Bay, and finally a wet, bumpy trip by boat that took one to three hours, depending upon the kind of craft available.

The Banabans met me on the wharf at Rabi with a welcoming committee that conducted me to the frame bungalow where the ten-man Island Council was holding a meeting around a plain wood table. Over the years, a neat little town had grown along the shore, with a school, a hospital, and several churches. The island was run by the council as a municipality, with autonomy in local affairs but taxes paid to Suva for such services as public health and education. A company, Rabi Holdings, Ltd., had been set up to channel the phosphate royalties into business enterprises in which the Banabans could find employment. The businesses would also insure the self-reliance of the island as the income from Ocean dwindled and finally stopped. Because of their inexperience, however, the Banabans saw one hopeful venture after another turn out disastrously.

The Island Council, with a stalwart elder named Rotan Tito as chairman, was mounting a legal and political onslaught against the British government when I visited the island. With the help of sympathetic British advisers, the Banabans calculated that they were owed 25 million dollars to compensate for gross underpayment of phosphate royalties over the decades. Lawyers discovered an old, forgotten contract in which the British Phosphate Commissioners agreed to rehabilitate and plant a 250-acre plot on Ocean—a sixth of the entire area—or compensate the islanders. Since neither the replanting nor payment had been carried out, the Banabans asked another 27 million dollars in fulfillment of the obligation. To these demands they added another: independence for Ocean Island. Rabi, said Rotan Tito, would be kept as a "garden" island and the new country would be associated with Fiji, a proposal that found favor with the government in Suva. "We know that becoming independent is the only way for us to get the benefit of the phosphate that is left," Tito told me on Rabi.

A British journalist friend, Bertram Jones, who had helped the Banabans as an adviser on public relations, observed that Marshal Josip Broz Tito of Yugoslavia would cease to be the only "President Tito" in the world if Ocean Island became independent, although the Banaban leader's name was pronounced "seeto."

The Banaban position was heatedly contested by the government of the Gilbert Islands, a British colony that was progressing toward independence with Ocean as an economically vital part of its territory. Gilbertese leaders viewed with great alarm any move to divorce their impoverished atolls from the rich Ocean Island phosphate deposits. To the Banabans, however, the Gilbertese attitude was sheer exploitation of a weaker population. The sympathies of the British government, which wished fervently to be rid of the costly fruits of earlier imperialism, were wholly with the Gilbertese.

In the end, however, classic British justice prevailed. The Banabans hired top-grade London lawyers to argue their case, and the courts rejected the pleas of the government to quash the suits. The judge of the High Court hearing the case, Sir Robert Megarry, accepted the Banabans' premise that the devastated island itself had to be Exhibit A in the proceedings. He prevailed upon the government to pay the air fares for himself and the lawyers involved to travel to Ocean for a firsthand look, having exchanged the traditional black robe for shorts and knee socks.

The ensuing 226-day trial was the longest in British history, as was Sir Robert's 100,000-word decision, which took him four and a half days to read. The judgment was a devastating indictment of colonial perfidy and broken promises. Sir Robert ruled that the phosphate company must pay compensation in lieu of restoring the island to its original condition, with the amount to be agreed upon. The Banabans' claim for reparations from the British government was dismissed, however, on the ground that the court lacked jurisdiction.

The dauntless spirit of the Banabans, and their ultimate triumph, lifted morale among exploited peoples throughout the Pacific. It also inspired new respect for the judicial process bequeathed by the former colonizing powers. Thus a handful of Micronesians on a tiny, remote equatorial island, lost in the immensity of the Pacific, left their mark on history.

THIRTEEN

The Problem Atolls

HE strong identity consciousness of Pacific peoples, epitomized in the numerous independence and autonomy movements that flowered after World War II, led to the eventual break-up of an unwieldy political anachronism called the Gilbert and Ellice Islands Colony, a collection of several groups whose Micronesian and Polynesian ethnic elements proved incompatible.

These widely dispersed dots on the map, straddling the equator about midway between Hawaii and Australia, had a colorful history. The early white contacts included whalers and blackbirders, as well as missionaries. On several occasions the ruthlessness of the blackbirders so incensed the warlike Gilbertese that they attacked their ships and massacred the crews. Doctor Hiram Bingham, of the famous Hawaii missionary family originally from New England, launched the Christianization of the group in 1857 and compiled the first dictionary of the Gilbertese language. Other well-known personages who became temporary residents of the Gilberts included such disparate figures as Captain Bully Hayes, sometimes called "the last buccaneer," and Robert Louis Stevenson, who lived for a time on Abemama, once the seat of the Gilbertese kingdom.

Before the colony split in 1975 along predictable ethnic lines, it had comprised forty-two scattered islands and atolls with a total land area of about 360 square miles, more than half of it on Christmas Island, the isolated site of several nuclear weapons

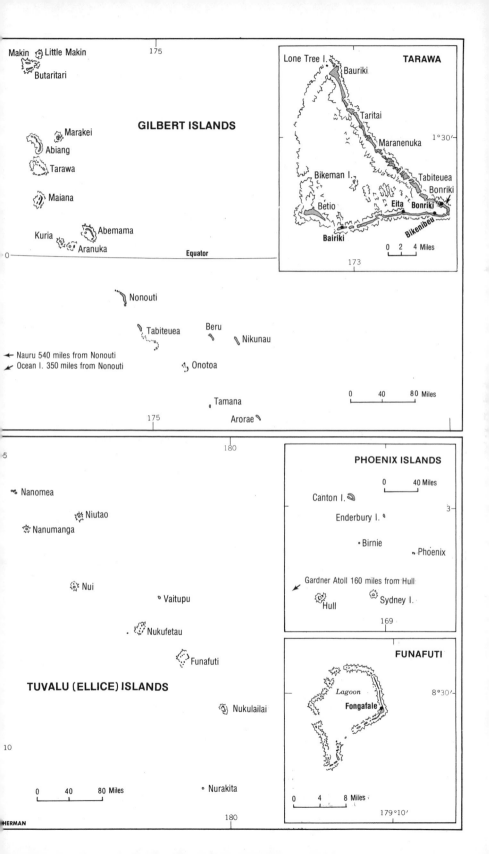

Makin ⌾ Little Makin   175
 ⌕ Butaritari

                    GILBERT ISLANDS

       ⌕ Marakei
   ⌔ Abiang
   ⌔ Tarawa

   ⌔ Maiana

Kuria ⌕ ⌕ Abemama
       ⌕ Aranuka   Equator
0

              ⌕ Nonouti

            ⌕ Tabiteuea   Beru
                              ⌕ Nikunau
◄ Nauru 540 miles from Nonouti
◢ Ocean I. 350 miles from Nonouti   ⌕ Onotoa

              ⌕ Tamana   0   40   80 Miles
       175   Arorae ⌕

TARAWA

Lone Tree I.
           Bauriki
              Taritai
                 Maranenuka   1°30'
           Bikeman I.
                          Tabiteuea
                            Bonriki
              Betio   **Eita Bonriki**
                      Bairiki **Bikenibeu**
                   0   2   4 Miles
         173

180
5

⌕ Nanomea

       ⌕ Niutao
⌕ Nanumanga

       ⌕ Nui
              ⌕ Vaitupu

         ⌕ Nukufetau

              ⌕ Funafuti

TUVALU (ELLICE) ISLANDS

              ⌕ Nukulailai

10

   0   40   80 Miles
              ⌕ Nurakita
         180

HERMAN

PHOENIX ISLANDS

              0   40 Miles
Canton I. ⌕
                              3
   Enderbury I. ⌕

       • Birnie
                 ⌕ Phoenix

   Gardner Atoll 160 miles from Hull
◄   ⌕   ⌕ Sydney I.
         Hull
              169

FUNAFUTI

         Lagoon   8°30'
              Fongafale

   0   4   8 Miles
              179°10'

tests by Britain and the United States (the American explosion at the U.S.-owned Johnston Island, the first in the upper atmosphere, lighted the sky from Hawaii to New Zealand and was not repeated). Britain acquired the colony piecemeal beginning in the latter part of the nineteenth century, bringing one island after another under British protection with the agreement—so it was said—of the local chiefs. A protectorate over the entire Gilberts group was established in 1892. The Gilbert and Ellice island chains together were converted to a crown colony in 1916. The colonial office kept extending the boundaries of the "G.E.I.C.," as it was called for short, until 1972, when the five uninhabited specks known as the Line Islands were added.

Nationalist aspirations of two minority peoples hit the G.E.I.C. from two sides at the same time. While the two thousand Banabans of Ocean Island struggled to become independent partly on ethnic grounds, but mostly to keep their island's phosphate revenue for themselves, the other separatist agitation came from the seven thousand Polynesians of the Ellice group, south of the Micronesian Gilberts. Their fear of political and economic domination by the fifty thousand Gilbertese to the north grew acute as the prospect of self-government for the colony came nearer. The Polynesians wanted not independence but to become a separate British colony.

The Gilbertese were quite willing to let the Polynesians go, but the British were far from happy to take on another deficit colony. London reluctantly permitted a referendum on the issue in 1974, and the separatists won—as expected—by a vote of 3,799 to 293. Three days of celebration, with swaying dancers in grass skirts, chants to the accompaniment of wooden drums, and gorging on oven-cooked pig, bananas, taro, breadfruit, coconut, chicken, and fish hailed the birth of the new South Pacific territory of Tuvalu, which would thenceforth replace the name of Ellice, a nineteenth century British member of Parliament, on the map of the Pacific.

Tuvalu, the ancient name of the chain, is translated as "group of eight," or "eight together," meaning eight atolls. Actually there are nine atolls involved, but one of them, Niulakita, at the southern end of the archipelago, was not counted because it has never been permanently inhabited. "Nobody regards himself as coming from there," an official explained. Funafuti, the main atoll and center of the government, had been an American air base in World War II.

While the Polynesian Tuvaluans are the same race as the natives of Samoa and may have come from there, the shorter, chocolate-colored Gilbertese resemble their fellow Micronesians in the nearby Marshall Islands, the eastern wing of the American-administered Trust Territory of the Pacific Islands. There have been occasional informal expressions in favor of a political union of the Gilberts and Marshalls (named after two British naval commanders who explored the groups in 1788), but no serious move toward that end.

The war came early to the Gilberts. Japanese marines raided Tarawa on 10 December 1941, three days after the attack on Pearl Harbor, but the invaders left after wrecking the radio station and some boats. The alarmed British administration evacuated all the whites, except twenty-two who elected to stay at their posts to help the Gilbertese. These were interned when the Japanese returned and occupied the atoll, and on 15 October the same year, following a punishing American air raid, all were executed by their enraged captors.

An American commando-type raid on Butaritari, the main island of the Makin atoll, with Marines landing in rubber boats launched from two submarines, alerted the Japanese to the weakness of their defenses in the Gilberts. They thereupon proceeded to convert Tarawa, an atoll south of Makin, into a strongpoint. Meanwhile, the Americans built up Funafuti as an advance base to support the coming drive into the Central Pacific. On the morning of 20 November 1943, combined United States naval, air, Marine, and army forces simultaneously attacked Tarawa, Makin, and Abemama. As a *New York Times* war correspondent, I accompanied the army unit that landed on Butaritari in the invasion of Makin. It was the first atoll I had ever seen; I would discover that all atolls are very much alike.

After a sharp fight that lasted three days and included one of the first of the famous night suicide charges, known as *banzai* attacks, by the beaten Japanese, Major General Ralph Smith of the 165th Infantry radioed the victory message, "Makin taken." (The play on words misfired, for Makin is pronounced "muggin.") I proceeded to Tarawa, where the battle was still going on, in a battleship with General Howland M. (Howlin' Mad) Smith, the renowned Marine commander (there were three generals named Smith on the expedition, causing the war correspondents to call the invasion "Operation Coughdrop," after the Smith Brothers product).

Betio, the island of the Tarawa atoll on which most of the fighting took place, is shaped like a bird with a long beak. Its area of 347 acres is less than half the size of New York's Central Park and was the scene of one of the historic battles of the war. More than one thousand Americans and the entire Japanese garrison of fifty-six hundred men died, exclusive of 146 Korean laborers taken prisoner, in the fighting that raged over this confined space for seventy-six terrifying hours. We could smell the dead, rapidly decomposing in the fierce equatorial heat, as we clambered from the battleship into a boat and headed for a battered pier.

Betio (pronounced BAY-show) was an unforgettable sight that day. Although the peak of the fighting had passed, the crack of rifles and thud of hand grenades in the cleanup phase made the eardrums ring. Smoke lay over the flat, sandy island from countless fires. Corpses lay everywhere among the shattered trees. Some bodies of Marines were so bloated that the swollen flesh burst the tough fabric of the green jungle uniforms. Many Marines had died doubled over the barbed wire barricades in the shallow water a few yards offshore, where they had been caught by enemy fire as they struggled forward on foot after their flat-bottomed landing craft had grounded on the fringing reef in an unexpectedly low tide. Dozens of Marines lay dead in the shallow wavelets lapping the beach, their outstretched arms rising and falling with the gentle motion of the light surf. The Marines had made a beachhead only by coming on and on, stepping over their fallen comrades as man after man went down.

Inland, where the airfield lay like a white gash on the green face of the island, more of the dead wore the khaki uniforms of the Japanese Special Landing Force, their counterpart of Marines. Many of the Japanese lay in clusters, blown apart by high-explosive shells. Many had been burned to a black crisp by that fearful Marine weapon for close fighting, the flamethrower.

The military said at the time that the battle of Tarawa had opened the Central Pacific "road to Tokyo." Later there were doubts that the costly battle had been necessary. Critics asked, could not the island have been bypassed? There was much criticism of the military planners for having failed to heed warnings that the morning tide at that time of year might be too low to permit a landing by assault boats, as turned out to be the case. When I returned to Tarawa twenty-five years later, to do a special story for the *Times* on the silver anniversary of the battle, the tides were behaving exactly the same way.

The airfield for which the Marines had fought no longer existed twenty-five years later. Neat rows of coconut palms now covered the central flat, where countless warplanes had once taken off on grim missions to islands farther west. Tarawa was now served by another airfield, built by the Americans on Bonriki islet at the southeastern end of the atoll. Passengers went through customs under a canopy of thatch with a wooden sign, "Bonriki International Airport," where they were greeted by smiling, flower-decked girls singing high-pitched Gilbertese songs.

Although the famous airport was gone from Betio, other relics of the war were everywhere. A naval gun originally obtained by Japan from the British Vickers company for the Russo-Japanese War still pointed a broken, rusted barrel seaward, but wave action had so changed the contour of the island that the installation now sat some fifty yards inland from the position I remembered. A landing boat that had been abandoned on the beach was now surrounded by a village, and its crumbling bow ramp was being used as a rack for drying coconut husks for fuel. In the shallows just offshore, American tanks and landing craft still stood awash where they had been put out of action by Japanese gunners twenty-five years before. Amphibious tracked vehicles—the famous "amtracks" or "Alligators"—moldered where they had been grounded and left on the reef. Villagers fished from the broken ribs of the *Saida Maru,* a Japanese freighter wrecked in its berth by American bombs two months before the invasion.

Of some five hundred fortified positions counted after the battle, many remained intact. Dozens of Japanese pillboxes, covered with sand for camouflage and protection from bombs and shells, dotted the island like dunes. One huge blockhouse with sturdy concrete walls was now part of the administration's social club. Another blockhouse had been converted into a squash court, having been found to have the right dimensions. Japanese dugouts had become hideaways for lovers. Still the most conspicuous landmark on the island was the immense, two-story concrete fortification that had been the headquarters of the Japanese commander, Rear Admiral Keiji Shibasaki, who was believed to have died on the second day of the battle, some say by suicide.

Walking around in the sand, one could still kick up a corroded cartridge case that had been emptied in the battle. It might be a live cartridge, too; only a year before my twenty-fifth anniversary visit, a Gilbertese using an old Marine rifle for a cooking bar was killed when a cartridge in the breech exploded. Two years earlier, a team from the British Royal Engineers had removed 140 tons of live ammunition from the island, a risky job for which the commander, Major Henry Qualtrough, received the George Medal, the military award for heroism in peacetime.

With Guy Slatter, the young English information officer, and Isakala Paeniu, his assistant from the Ellice Islands, I went by canoe to Buariki, in the northern part of the atoll, where Lieutenant Colonel Raymond L. Murray had led a Marine force against Japanese defenders hidden in pits, behind coconut logs, or in the tops of palm trees. Thirty-two Marines and 175 Japanese had been killed in the ensuing fire fight. My companions and I collected a handful of spent cartridges on the site.

Many heroes of Betio, both American and Japanese, had never gone home. "Every time anyone digs a ditch, we discover skeletons of men killed in the battle," said R. B. (Robby) Beets, the Dutch-born head of the electrical division of the public works department on Betio. C. S. Loades, the white-haired chief of the post and telecommunications department, found two human arm bones while digging up soil in his garden to fill a flowerpot. By arrangement, any remains identified as American were sent to the United States War Graves Agency. Japanese remains, in accordance with instructions from Tokyo, were put in bags and buried at sea beyond the reef.

Two simple monuments honored the fallen on both sides in the battle of Betio. At an intersection of coral streets near the island social club, a simple wooden post with an inscription in Japanese (which no one on the island could read) had been installed by a delegation from Tokyo; the British had placed the battered turret of a Japanese light tank around it for protection. The other war memorial on the island was a plain granite cross and a tablet inscribed with twenty-two names and the statement: "In memory of twenty-two British subjects murdered by the Japanese on Betio on the 15th of October, 1942. Standing unarmed to their posts they matched brutality with gallantry and met death with fortitude."

Aboard one of the ships lying off Betio during the battle was Colonel Vivian Fox-Strangways, who had been appointed resident commissioner (equivalent to governor) of the British colony just before the Japanese attack. In his gear he had a Union Jack, which he took ashore. And when the battle had ended and the island was declared "secure," the American and British flags were raised simultaneously on adjacent bullet-scarred palm trees. The American flag had departed with the last GI's.

Many postwar changes had come to Betio, too. The island, with two new stone piers near the site of the Marines' first narrow beachhead, had become the urban center of the G.E.I.C., where people gathered from far-off atolls for work and diversion. The built-up area near the piers bustled with machine shops, the radio communications center, Chinese-run stores and restaurants, the cooperative department store, two movie theaters, and a dance hall where teen-agers in shorts or *lavalava* gyrated to the rock tunes of a quartet of Polynesian musicians from Funafuti who called themselves The Brown Boys.

"Betio swings!" a Gilbertese friend exclaimed. The urbanization of Betio had brought the attendant evils of idleness and juvenile delinquency, which went together in the South Seas as elsewhere. Gilbertese police watched outside the dance hall nightly, ready to break up the fistfights that frequently enlivened the soft tropical evenings, fostered by the volatile combination of alcohol, music, and girls.

Physically, Tarawa was divided into two worlds. The atoll is shaped like a sail, with the north-south reef line as the mast. On the northeastern islets, along the sail's slanted trailing edge, the dreamy villages of thatched huts had changed little since the first white traders introduced tobacco and canned goods. The southern islets, along the bottom of the sail, were the administrative and industrial heart of the colony. This would no doubt surprise the wartime American residents, who knew them by their navy code names: Helen (Betio), Cora (Bairiki), and Ella (Bikenibeu).

Since the war, the islets from Bairiki to Bonriki had been connected by man-made causeways of rock and coral, which made travel easier but altered the wave action in unforeseen ways that affected fish movements and changed shorelines, causing some economic dislocation. Nevertheless, still another causeway, connecting Betio and Bairiki, enabling the completion of a road from the airport on Bonriki to the population center on Betio, was a cherished dream of the administration. Till its realization, the lifeline of southern Tarawa remained the Bairiki-Betio ferry, a chugging, smelly vessel always packed with merry Gilbertese families.

The administrative headquarters for the colony was on Bairiki, a typical low, flat atoll island, so narrow that one could drive a golf ball from one shore to the other at any point. Guy Slatter

could step out one door of his house for a swim in the lagoon
—or go out the other side and plunge into the open sea. Nearby
lived the resident commissioner, or "rescom" in official jargon,
in a large, airy bungalow called The Residency—later changed
to Government House when the office was upgraded to governor
and "His Honor" became "His Excellency."

A few yards from The Residency stood the "secretariat," a
neat, blue-painted, boxlike wooden building with a gleaming
metal roof. Here the business of government was carried on by
the expatriate staff—many recently arrived from defunct British
colonies in Africa and the Caribbean—and their brown-skinned
local aides, all in the standard tropical work dress of the British
colonial service: white or plain-colored open, short-sleeved shirts
tucked into sober shorts, and white knee socks.

Nearby stood the Legislative Building, a pleasing combination
of masonry and thatch befitting the dignity of British law in a
remote place. Besides housing the legislature, the graceful structure was also the scene of the solemn proceedings of the colony
High Court. The inside was impressive, with a tasteful ceiling of
split bamboo, huge photographs of Queen Elizabeth II and her
consort, Prince Philip, and the colony crest of an albatross above
a rising sun bursting out of the sea. It was a lovely building.

Dwarfing the government buildings, and contributing to the
atmosphere of a genuine South Sea island, was the giant *maneaba,*
or meeting house, the center of community life in every Gilbertese village. The thatch-covered, V-shaped roof sloped steeply
from a ridge pole sixty feet high. The eaves extended over the
open sides to within five feet of the ground to protect the spacious interior from blowing rain. The inside was always cool, and
a scene of activity day and night. Every able-bodied person in the
village helps to build a new *maneaba,* each family having an assigned task—one gathering the material for the roof, another
putting the thatched panels in place, others cutting the trees for
the side poles. There is an assigned space for each family to sit
in at formal meetings.

The Residency at Bairiki, where I stayed for a few days as a
house guest during the term of Sir John Field, was the focus of
social life for the senior officials and their wives. The rooms were
high and broad, with ceiling fans and mixed Pacific and colonial
British decor. Sir John, a short, ruddy, informal man with long
experience in Africa, had also been governor of Montserrat, in

the West Indies, and Saint Helena, in the South Atlantic, whose most famous resident had been the exiled Napoleon. Dinner at The Residency called for long dresses and "Red Sea rig"—formal evening trousers with cummerbund (a traveler could get by with dark slacks and belt), white shirt, and black bow tie.

One evening, just after the ritual toast to Her Majesty with the port, the sounds of song and laughter wafted on the trade wind from the direction of the *maneaba*. There followed a demonstration of the camaraderie developing between the British administration and the islanders. Led by Sir John, we trooped across the village green in brilliant moonlight, found a village festival going on, and were immediately invited to become part of it. It may have been the first time a knighted British colonial governor in full Red Sea rig was seen dancing in a *maneaba* with tawny Gilbertese girls in grass skirts.

The stirring Gilbertese dances have a distinct form that seems to combine Polynesian hip movements with the hand and arm motions of Indonesia, accompanied by rhythmic clapping and chanting. The end of the female dance is dramatic and provocative, as the girl abruptly advances several long, swift strides toward the audience with arms extended.

Sir John had been assigned to the G.E.I.C. to help work out a new constitution as an interim step toward self-government and eventual independence. "This will be my ninth constitution," he said. "It is not exactly a trail-blazing exercise, though," said the future first chief minister, Naboua Ratieta of Marakei atoll.

"We have come to this stage later than other territories," he added. At any rate, by May 1974 the colony had a House of Assembly, elected by universal suffrage except for three official members—the deputy governor, attorney general, and financial secretary—who were appointed by the governor. The elected members voted for a chief minister, who then appointed a cabinet.

With the establishment of the House of Assembly, replacing the former Legislative Council, the G.E.I.C.—soon to be reduced to just the Gilberts, with such distant and inconsequential adjuncts as the deserted Line Islands—became virtually autonomous in internal affairs. Each of the cabinet ministers was made fully responsible for a department of the government; the cabinet together, including the three official members and the governor as chairman, constituted a Council of Ministers that met weekly and carried out the day-to-day policy of the country. Full self-government was set for 1 November, 1976, with independence to follow in 1978 if the islanders agreed.

"Have the British trained enough islanders to take over?" I asked Reuben Uatioa, a senior Gilbertese politician. "To that I answer a flat no," he said. "In many of the outer islands the people are unaware of the changes taking place in the rest of the world and are completely ignorant of the advantages and disadvantages of constitutional advancement. Actually, they are quite content to let matters go along as they are."

Uatioa (pronounced oo-WAH-see-OH-a), mission-educated on his home island of Beru, had founded one of the two functioning political parties in the Gilberts and had long held the post of chief elected member, or leader, of the legislature under the old system. His way of life probably was a preview of the future in South Tarawa, if not in the less acculturated remoter atolls of the group. He and his wife lived in a completely Western style in a frame house overlooking the Tarawa lagoon. On the wall hung a framed certificate signed by Queen Elizabeth II, showing that Uatioa was a member of the Order of the British Empire, entitled to put M.B.E. after his name. Mrs. Uatioa, in a blue frock, served a guest coffee and egg sandwiches—an honor, as eggs were in short supply at the time.

You step back into the South Seas of literary renown at the border of the Uatioa front yard. The slender shadows of the coconut trees across the coral road grew longer in the waning daylight. A white heron waddled off the powdery beach and drank from a clam shell filled with rain water. A bronzed fisherman sauntered by with a spear over his shoulder on which he carried his family's dinner, an octopus.

The Central Pacific has the most chromatic sunsets in the world, and it was nearly time for one. Half the sky would soon turn glaring red with streaks of somber violet and light green, and the glassy lagoon would suddenly look afire, with canoes standing out as black spots. Minutes later the calm water would reflect the stars, which seem to be closer here. A giant moon would turn the coral road along the narrow causeways to a glowing white ribbon, and the palm fronds would be dappled with soft silver tones. In the cool tropical night, the sound of waves blended with laughter from the *maneaba*.

"The sun sets on the British Empire with style," I reflected.
Bikeman is an islet in the lagoon where the British establish-

ment people go, by sailboat or slim outrigger canoe, for picnics. Bikeman looks like a cartoonist's idea of a South Sea island, tiny and round, all sand with a clump of palm trees in the center. It is possible to have the whole island to one's self and to play at being Robinson Crusoe. One day I went with Guy Slatter and his wife. Shortly another British couple arrived. They nodded politely, and then repaired to the other side of the tiny islet, to be seen no more. It was an illustration, said Guy, of the curious social cleavage in the tiny white community of Tarawa, perhaps 120 persons among 15,000 Gilbertese.

The expatriate community of southern Tarawa was divided along work lines. The Betio people, connected mostly with the operation of the port and related activities, considered themselves the "doers" of the colony and disparaged the rest. Bairiki residents, who worked for the administration, were referred to as the "bureaucrats." The white colony at Bikenibeu, concerned principally with the medical establishment and the schools, comprised the "intellectual" sector of the British community. The three groups mingled only marginally. Betio wives resented to a woman the regular forays of wives from Bairiki and Bikenibeu into the cooperative one-story department store near the port, which apparently had first choice of incoming trade goods and offered far more variety than the rather mean establishments at the other two expatriate settlements. Tarawa was a place of recurrent shortages because of its isolation: one month no eggs, another month no oranges, and so on. Any disruption of the sketchy shipping service brought real consternation to the colony.

When Fiji Airways (later renamed Air Pacific) extended its Gilbert Islands service from Tarawa to Makin with a twice-weekly flight to Butaritari, I went back for the first time since I had landed there with the Third Battalion of the 165th Infantry in the second wave. Butaritari was a beautiful island, as lovely as its lilting name, when I first glimpsed it in the cool dawn as battleships pumped 2,000-pound shells into the innocent palm groves. Fleets of bombers blasted the villages before we headed for the beach in flat-bottomed assault boats, and for a time the island was less pretty. But recovery is fast in the tropics.

My boat had grounded on a coral head, and we jumped from the lowered bow ramp into water to the armpits to struggle ashore on Red Beach 1, a steeply slanted stretch of coarse, bright sand. Just inland were the thatched, open-sided huts—the first I had ever seen that were really meant for living in—of Ukiangang, code-named Hen Village on the maps for "Operation Galvanic." The soldier in front of me flung himself prone behind a coral rock, whipped his carbine to his shoulder, and snapped off a shot at a crouching figure under a palm tree. His movements were very professional. Fortunately the shot missed; the other man was one of our own.

In the three days that it took to overcome the 800 Japanese on the island, killing 700, 66 Americans were killed and 152 wounded. (How many were shot by fellow Americans I never knew.) The Japanese evened the score by putting a torpedo into the aircraft carrier *Liscombe Bay*, which went down with a loss of 644 officers and enlisted men. Meanwhile, the frightened Gilbertese began to straggle back from the neighboring island where they had taken refuge when the shelling and bombing of Butaritari began. Among them were the first genuine grass-skirted, bare-breasted South Sea island girls most of us had ever seen.

Butaritari before the war had been the commercial center of the Gilberts, with frequent calls by freighters at the main port, which had the same name as the island. Even the deserted Butaritari town we entered in 1943 had a look of importance. Landmarks included two major wharfs, the big On Chong store, and the shop and warehouses of Burns Philp and Company. A huge, shot-up Japanese four-engined seaplane, the reconnaissance type code-named Emily, listed in the water near the piers.

The Seabees bulldozed a coral-surfaced airfield out of a palm grove. A forest of GI tents appeared on the island. Where the white coral paths intersected on the way to Butaritari town from Red Beach 1, homesick soldiers from New York nailed two signs to a palm tree, with "Broadway" on one and "W. 42nd St." on the other. A strait-laced American officer distributed army T-shirts to the local girls, who customarily went topless. The girls were delighted, but found the strange garments too confining around the bosoms and wore them with two holes cut out of the front.

Returning to Butaritari after a quarter-century, I was met at the simple shack that served as an airport terminus by Tataua Kauriri, who had watched the troops swarm ashore on Red Beach 2 as a frightened eighteen-year-old boy. He drove a dented, run-down truck, the only automotive vehicle functioning on the island, with a body badly frayed by the effects of humid, salt-laden air. The open truck bed soon filled with laughing, scantily clad

Bonriki International Airport, Tarawa, which is typical of atoll airports in the Gilbert Islands

old *Emily,* a Japanese warplane still at ·itari in 1970

Pit on Tinian airstrip, from which the first atomic bomb was loaded into the *Enola Gay,* bound for Hiroshima. Mayor of the island, Jose R. Cruz, stands at the memorial in 1969

A classic South Seas panorama, from Moen Island, Truk, Micronesia

Tin roofs and palm trees on Moen Island

Gilbertese boys and girls of school age, who sang steadily in high, sweet voices as we bumped along a rutted track that showed only traces of the hard surface laid down by the long-gone Americans. We stopped every hundred yards or so to refill the leaking radiator with swamp water.

Time had erased most of the thin Western veneer acquired by Butaritari in the busy years before the war. Gone also were most signs of the American presence, now only faintly remembered by islanders younger than Kauriri's generation. The town of Butaritari, which I recalled as a small but solid-looking tropical port, had become a simple, almost primitive South Sea village, slumbering in the sun, although the population had doubled in the intervening years to four thousand. Such wartime landmarks as the barnlike On Chong store and the Burns Philp branch had vanished. The once-busy On Chong dock, and next to it the King's Wharf, named for a local high chief, had gone out of use and were so deteriorated that they almost blended into the ragged shoreline of coral rock and rubble. One weatherbeaten frame building, the only Western structure left among a collection of traditional houses of reed and thatch, was the government office. But the shot-up old Emily, now little more than a skeleton with most of the covering weathered away, lay where I had last seen it in 1943; it was Butaritari's only conspicuous relic of the war.

"The business never came back to Butaritari," said Kauriri. Kauriri was the president of the Island Council, the elected self-government organization that exercised legislative, executive, and judicial functions in local affairs. The traditional system of government by chiefs had withered away in the Gilberts under the influence of white missionaries and civil officials. The high chief of Abemama, alone among native nobility, still headed an Island Council because of his rank; the other chiefs were considered aristocrats, but had no special power or wealth. When the high chief of Makin died in the 1960s, there was no clear succession and the British never recognized an heir to the position. But "The Ellice," as the British called the Polynesian atolls to the south until they became Tuvalu, retained a hierarchy of high chiefs and talking chiefs similar to the Samoan system. This was another significant cultural difference from the Micronesians of the Gilberts that helped make the political separation of the two peoples inevitable.

The loss of its former commercial importance had left

Butaritari like a picture-book island of the South Seas. The healthy-looking people were cheerful and laughing, and invariably greeted a stranger with a hearty "Kanamauri," the Gilbertese equivalent of "hello." Lightly clad and barefoot, they lived happily in the shade of countless palm trees and groves of papaya, banana, and breadfruit.

And the living, they said, was easy. At a *batere,* or feast, in the *maneaba,* eating mats were piled high with baked reef fish and stewed pandanus fruit. The plentiful coconuts, exported in the form of copra aboard colony trading ships, and government employment were the principal sources of cash to purchase the cloth, soap, matches, tobacco, and canned goods stocked by the locally owned cooperative stores. The South Seas custom of taking whatever one wanted from the possessions of a friend or relative, known in the Gilberts as *bubuji,* spread the wealth. (*"Bubuji* bleeds us down to equality," said a Gilbertese.) "We see very little cash money here, but we don't need much," Kauriri said.

As idyllic as life might seem to a Western visitor in a beautiful and tranquil place like Butaritari, the pressures of the times were being increasingly felt even in these balmy scenes. The people of the Gilbert Islands, and the companion Tuvalu group, faced in an acute form the quintessential problem of the atoll dweller: environment.

An atoll, being a narrow rim of barely habitable land around a lagoon, usually broken into a series of *motu,* or reef islets, is a circumscribed, meager place by definition. Its only resources, besides a restricted subsistence agriculture, are coconuts and fish. More often than not, the coconut groves are neglected and unscientifically cultivated. Nor, as a rule, are atoll people great fishermen. Their fabricated goods are limited to handicrafts of woven ware—mats, baskets, and souvenir items like the wicked Gilbertese fighting swords of wicker studded with needle-sharp shark's teeth, and the fake "stick charts" of the Marshall Islanders, made for sale to tourists. The possibilities for a tourist industry are limited by space and the paucity of ground water, which lies beneath the porous covering of sandy soil in a narrow lens, easily contaminated. An atoll has no streams—though there may be brackish ponds, as on Butaritari—hence the commonest source of fresh water for drinking is rain water drained off corrugated metal roofs into large storage tanks, the well water being suitable only for washing and flushing. Droughts are common on some atolls, such as Tarawa, where water is often rationed during dry periods.

The British government, in its last years, undertook a coconut replanting program, hoping to maximize the production of copra. Fisheries resources were also being studied, in the hope that an export trade in tuna might be developed. There was small scope for expanding the agricultural sector of the atoll economy beyond coconuts, however. Once the economic development section sent a soil sample from Tarawa to a German laboratory for testing. "They thought we'd made a mistake or were playing some kind of British joke," said Mike Allen, a finance officer, "and wrote back that the sample was not soil but sand, unsuitable for being cultivated with plants."

Tourism, considered a peripheral industry in the Gilberts, was being promoted desultorily. "All the material needed to develop and support a tourist industry has to be imported," said Allen, referring not only to building material but also to food, vehicles, furnishings, and skilled personnel. Some of the Gilbertese employed at the only hotel in the Gilberts, the Otintai ("sunrise") on the beach at Bikenibeu, had never heard of a hotel a year before they went to work. (The name is pronounced oh-sin-TAI, "ti" being "si" in Gilbertese; school children sing "It's a long way to Sipperary.")

Officials pressed a family planning program and reported optimistically that it seemed to be taking hold. With a population growth of 3 percent a year, the Gilbertese would double in number before the end of the century unless couples went in for fewer children. With manpower to spare, a major export from the Gilberts was people. Whole communities were transplanted, with British help, to the uninhabited Phoenix Islands (a part of the G.E.I.C.) and to underpopulated areas of the Solomons, and some Ellice Islanders were resettled on Kioa Island in the Fiji group.

A merchant marine training institute on Betio, assisted by the Maritime Consultative Organization of the United Nations, turned out several hundred Gilbertese graduates every year and placed them with British and West German shipping lines as qualified seamen, engine room personnel, and stewards—a new, humane form of blackbirding. "When the men go to sea," said Captain Michael Drew, the British director assigned by the United Nations agency, "it means less drain on the food reserves here, the money they send home is an important source of foreign income, and it helps the population problem because, being away most of the time, they have fewer children."

What does the future hold for the atoll people? The limited economic expectations on their tiny, sparsely endowed islets, coupled with expanding awareness of a larger world, unquestionably dictate a steady emigration of the young to lands of greater opportunity, like the blacks from numerous small Caribbean islands whom one meets in Miami, New York, and Montreal.

Hopes for a new and permanent major source of revenue in these deprived backwaters grew from the movement in the South Pacific, emulating the bigger maritime powers, to establish exclusive economic zones extending 200 miles offshore, thus enabling the island governments to charge licensing fees to the countries whose fishing fleets operate in those rich waters. Cheered by this development and the promise of continued grants by Britain, Tuvalu planned to celebrate full independence within the Commonwealth on 1 October 1978. The Gilberts, intent on coming to terms with the Banabans, looked forward to sovereignty in 1979, or a little later, by which time they hoped also to find a more Micronesian-sounding name for their country than that of an 18th-century English discoverer, Captain Thomas Gilbert.

FOURTEEN

The Rusted Trust

EOGRAPHICALLY, Micronesia is the home of the sturdy people whose ancestors migrated deep into the central Pacific from Malaysia, an origin that still shows in the high cheekbones, slightly tilted eyes, and fair skin of many members of the race today. Politically, the name has been appropriated for the three sprawling archipelagoes of the Marshall, Caroline, and Mariana islands, ruled successively by Spain, Germany, Japan, and the United States. As a United Nations trusteeship administered by the United States, the islands and atolls became, in formal parlance, the Trust Territory of the Pacific Islands. After a generation of benign neglect by the American authorities, critics called it the "Rust Territory." For years, exporting scrap metal left from the war was the second industry, after copra.

Economic progress was desultory, but the Americans fostered striking advances in education and responsible government. In the classic pattern of emerging colonies, these gains were counterproductive for the white mentors. Young Micronesians, whose fathers had been limited to a grade-school education by the former Japanese masters, were sent to American universities on government scholarships and promptly became politicized. Many returned to the islands to agitate against continued United States rule. The sophisticated political processes introduced by the Americans enabled the new generation to carry the rebellion against foreign authority into elected legislative bodies like the

251

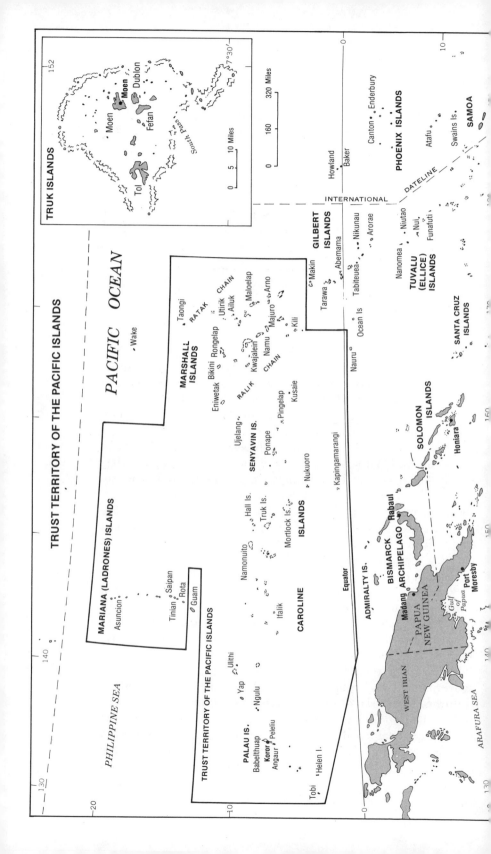

Congress of Micronesia, the central organ through which the islanders exercised the law-making powers granted to them in steadily increasing measure by the American administration.

The political maturing of Micronesia is especially noteworthy because of the high strategic importance of these way stations along the sea lanes between North America and East Asia. Throughout their modern history, the political shape of the islands has been determined by the outcome of foreign wars in which the Micronesians played little or no part.

How many islands there are in Micronesia depends on the answer to the question, what is an island? The number keeps changing anyway, as bits of land emerge from the sea or are washed away in the restless Pacific tides, but a figure commonly used is 2,141, of which only 96 are listed as permanently inhabited. Most of the islands, like nearly all of the Marshalls, are typical low, flat, sandy atolls, with a meager economic base in coconuts. The so-called high islands of the Carolines and Marianas, often rising to a thousand feet or more in steep volcanic peaks covered with matted rain forests, have greater possibilities for development in agriculture, fishing, and tourism. Flecks of green in an azure sea, they speckle an expanse of ocean as big as the continental United States in a belt extending 2,400 miles from east to west and 1,000 miles northward from the equator. The land area adds up to only 706 square miles, about half the size of Rhode Island.

The cultural variety among the 115,000 or so people of Micronesia is immense, as the vast distances between the groups prevented any substantial interchange. The physical appearance also changes markedly as one moves from the western groups, where the people have a distinct Mongol look, to the eastern extremity, where they resemble Polynesians.

Spain laid claim to all three archipelagoes by right of discovery, but the first sighting of various individual islands is attributed to dozens of navigators of various nationalities over more than three centuries following the arrival of Ferdinand Magellan at Guam, in the Marianas, on 6 March 1521. That island became a United States possession as a result of the Spanish-American War in 1898. Spain, following her defeat, liquidated her Pacific empire by ceding the rest of the islands to Germany for four million dollars. Japan ousted the Germans early in World War I, then lost the islands to the United States in World War II. Through all these colonial permutations the bulk of the islanders remained under the authority of their traditional chiefs for ordinary affairs.

The American period opened bloodily. Japan had closed the islands to outsiders in the 1930s and began fortifying key points, in violation of the terms under which Tokyo administered the territory as a League of Nations Mandate. Meanwhile, however, the Japanese had quit the league in order to pursue a course of untrammeled imperialism in Asia. Truk, in the eastern Carolines, was transformed into the major forward naval base for the war against the United States that began with the attack on Pearl Harbor. Other major strong points were constructed in the Marshall Islands and the Palau group of the western Carolines. At that time the name Micronesia scarcely existed except as a vague geographic concept of interest only to Pacific scholars. Soon after Pearl Harbor, the exotic names of previously unheard-of islands became household words in the United States.

After carrier-based bombing forays against various Japanese bases in the Marshalls, American amphibious forces seized Kwajalein atoll in February 1944, following up with the capture of Eniwetak atoll (formerly spelled Eniwetok), also in the Marshalls, Peleliu and Angaur islands in the Palaus, and Saipan and Tinian in the Marianas. There was a devastating effect on the landscape, which quickly recovered in the manner of all tropical places, but the "natives" mostly escaped injury by staying away from the areas under assault.

Meanwhile, Truk and other key Japanese outposts were held down by incessant bombing. Later in the war, these bypassed islands were cut off from supplies by American submarine operations that virtually cleared the seas of Japanese shipping. It was during this period, with the food situation desperate and the military outlook hopeless, that the Japanese officers reversed the normally considerate policy toward the island people and inflicted untold cruelties upon the helpless Micronesians in their charge.

The invasions in the islands were milestones in the American progress toward ultimate victory. The loss of Saipan, bringing Tokyo within range of land-based bombers, caused the fall of the Tojo Cabinet. The capture of Iwo Jima and Okinawa, considered part of the Japanese homeland as much as Hawaii was regarded as an integral part of the United States, was staged from the Marianas. Finally, it was from Tinian that the atomic bombs were delivered on Hiroshima and Nagasaki, ending the war.

American knowledge of Micronesia before World War II had been scanty, depending mainly upon accounts of missionaries, whalers, traders, and a few others. Proselytizers of the American Board of Commissioners of Foreign Missions in Boston had set up stations on many of the islands of the Caroline and Marshall chains, and converted large numbers of natives to Protestantism. The first tour of all the major islands by an American journalist, so far as I have been able to determine, was my own reporting trip for *The New York Times* in March and April of 1946.

American servicemen, arriving as conquerors, had no mass contact with the local people on the islands captured during the war. The policy was to segregate the "natives" in a place removed from troop concentrations, preferably on another island. The United States Navy made the rounds of the bypassed islands following the Japanese surrender, repatriating the Japanese and establishing American control under military government.

In the "navy days," as the Micronesians call that period, the islands were administered by cadres of officers who had been trained for the job at a navy military government school in the United States. "Language officers," who spoke Japanese, used that language to convey the orders of their commanders to the bewildered and docile local chiefs, who had learned Japanese under the previous rulers. Navy doctors inoculated the entire population of various islands, and eradicated the endemic disease of yaws. "Education officers" taught all the school children to sing *God Bless America,* in the hope that they would thus learn English and a proper attitude toward the occupying power. Americans fraternized with the island girls, often after thoughtfully checking their health records in the files compiled by the medics.

The period of administering the islands like captured territory—as some islands indeed were—was a prelude to a lasting American involvement with Micronesia, although the United States had disclaimed any desire to acquire territory as a result of the war. The borders of American sovereignty had not been extended since the annexation of Swain's Island as part of American Samoa in 1925. But Swain's would not be the last territorial acquisition by the United States in the Pacific.

Military government in Micronesia nominally ended on 18 July 1947, the date of President Harry S. Truman's formal approval of an agreement with the United Nations making the former Japanese Mandated Islands a trust territory, like Nauru, Western

Samoa, and eastern New Guinea in the South Pacific, and a host of other former colonies in Africa. To the embarrassment of Americans, all would become free states before Micronesia, the only United States responsibility in the trusteeship system.

Unlike the others, the Trust Territory of the Pacific Islands was designated as a strategic trusteeship, of interest to the Security Council as well as the Trusteeship Council of the United Nations. The United States, as the sole administering power, was specifically authorized to use the islands for military purposes. The trusteeship compact also obligated the United States to foster social and economic improvement in the islanders, and to prepare them for eventual self-government or independence, in accordance with the wishes of the inhabitants. In later decades, the interpretation and implementation of this seemingly straightforward compact would embroil the United States in endless controversy both at home and abroad.

The navy stayed on till President Truman transferred the administration to the Department of the Interior, the agency traditionally assigned to insular affairs, on 1 July 1951. The Department of Defense, however, exercising the military rights granted by the trusteeship agreement, used Bikini and Eniwetak atolls in the Marshalls for test explosions of nuclear weapons, and Kwajalein atoll became a permanent missile range. Such operations had a devastating effect on the lives of sundry displaced Marshallese.

Navy rule returned to the Northern Marianas—Saipan, Tinian, and a string of small, mostly uninhabited volcanic islands stretching northward toward Japan—in January 1953. There ensued a bizarre period during which a large part of Saipan, a forty-seven-square-mile island shaped like a seahorse, was a guarded security area that no Saipanese and few Americans were permitted to see. When I visited the island in 1958, I was escorted everywhere by not one but two navy officers, both with the rank of full commander. All questions about the sizable area that our sightseeing tour ignored were brushed aside with a vague reference to "security." It came out later that the Central Intelligence Agency was using the forbidden zone for the training of Nationalist Chinese troops for infiltration and commando operations against the Communist mainland. On arrival at the airfield, the Chinese were put in windowless buses so they would not be observed on the drive through Saipanese towns.

The C.I.A. constructed a twenty-five-million-dollar model town for its people, laid out like a middle-class American suburb on a secluded, landscaped hilltop with a magnificent view of the blue sea and a garland of lovely reef islets far below. There were administration buildings, workshops, and ranch-type homes, all stoutly constructed to weather the typhoons that periodically raked the Marianas, plus a well-appointed club and other recreational facilities. Until Guam became a center of tourism and light industry some years later, this hidden subdivision on a raised plain hacked out of the Saipan jungle was the most American-looking place west of Honolulu.

When the C.I.A. eventually terminated the Chinese project and the navy handed the Northern Marianas back to the Department of the Interior in 1962, the administrative headquarters of the trust territory moved to these relatively luxurious surroundings from tattered Quonsets on Guam. For the first time, the center of government for the trusteeship was located inside the Trust Territory itself. The former C.I.A. installation was named Capitol Hill.

For administrative purposes, the three great archipelagoes had been divided into six districts. These had been delineated by the trust territory government more or less arbitrarily for logistical convenience, in the manner of colonial regimes the world over. From the eastern extremity westward, the districts were the Marshall Islands, Ponape, Truk, the Marianas, Yap, and Palau. Tiny Rota, visible from Guam, had district status when the navy was on Saipan. No two districts spoke the same language, and there were other differences.

Linguists disagree on the number of languages spoken in the islands, the question being what is a language and what is a mere dialect, but it is generally accepted that there are at least nine major languages. I have met, or heard of, only a few Micronesians who spoke more than their own island's language, though many also spoke English or Japanese. Since the beginning of European times the common means of communication among people of different groups, if any, has been the language of the current ruling power. I knew one elderly chief in the Truk group who spoke them all—Spanish, German, Japanese, and English.

Theoretically, at least, future generations of Micronesians will all be able to speak English, the Language of instruction under the American administration from the fourth grade onward. The supposition assumes that education is universal; but in fact, according to education officials, the schools were reaching only about three-fourths of the school-age children. There was a time when the one teacher on a remote island might be a Micronesian who had never gone to school. Classes were often held under the palm trees, or in a shelter consisting merely of poles holding up a roof of thatch, with a blackboard. An education officer from headquarters was seen only every three months or so, when a field-trip vessel called for a few hours during which the teacher, as likely as not, would be occupied loading copra.

The belated coming of the Peace Corps to the trust territory in the 1960s brought a badly needed expansion in the teacher force. The Peace Corps volunteers in Micronesia numbered more than seven hundred at peak strength. Every inhabited island had at least one, who lived with, and like, the local people and spoke their language. "They are the only Americans who eat in native restaurants," a touring anthropologist said admiringly of the volunteers. They were also the only Americans who could converse with Micronesians in their own language, with the exception of some missionaries and a few dedicated trust territory officials like Robert Halvorsen, who had come out to the islands as a navy officer in the military government and stayed on. Halvorsen headed the civilian administration in several districts and studied the language in each. On retirement he made his home on Ponape, his last post, an island that many consider the most beautiful in the Central Pacific. Halvorsen died there in 1976, and was buried beneath the palms he loved.

Normally the Peace Corps volunteers were young, but there were also some gray-haired retirees. All were equipped with some kind of special skill and were full of good intentions. Many were newly married couples just out of university, who would complete their two or four years in the corps with a tidy accumulation of compulsory savings withheld by the government from their modest stipends. Their ranks included nurses, x-ray technicians, civil engineers, radio operators, surveyors, architects, lawyers, business specialists, and "generalists" who could be found engaged in all kinds of community development work in their assigned areas. The great majority taught English; if not always particularly qualified as instructors, they at least did better than just teaching their pupils to bawl *God Bless America.*

Many of the Peace Corps workers were astonished to find most Micronesians wholly devoid of nationalism, a deficiency that some of the young Americans fresh from the campus set out to remedy. The youthful Peace Corps journalists, assigned to turn out mimeographed newspapers on main islands as the beginning of an indigenous press, became crusading editors on behalf of the Micronesians. At the request of the administration, the journalist category was dropped from the program. "Your equipment does not include a soapbox," later volunteers were told.

Gradually, government high schools appeared in all the districts, and the mission schools also expanded. All the public high schools had Micronesians on their staffs, many as principals. The ideal combination was thought to be a Micronesian teacher with an American degree, qualified academically by western standards but able at the same time to interpret the curriculum in terms of a Pacific island environment from personal experience.

The mixture of cultures produced anomalies. The high school girls of Yap appeared for their graduation ceremonies in modish American-style dresses, usually ordered from a mail-order catalogue; after solemnly receiving their diplomas, they joyously changed to the traditional grass skirt, with no top, for the graduation party (at the Roman Catholic high school the nuns, unlike their austere missionary predecessors, thought the custom charming). At the Outer Islands High School on Falalop Island in the Ulithi Atoll, a distant attachment to the Yap district, barebreasted girls learned to use microscopes in the biology class.

Post-secondary education, virtually unknown to Micronesians before the American era, became commonplace among the elite. Hundreds of young Micronesians went every year to the University of Guam, the University of Hawaii, and mainland institutions on scholarships. Many finished their education with bachelor degrees, and a few even earned doctorates. "There's just no comparison between the Japanese and Americans in education policy," a pleased Micronesian school official told me when I visited a high school in Majuro, the administrative center of the Marshall Islands.

The Americans were even more assiduous, from the beginning, in fostering democratic political forms in Micronesia. The islands were organized into municipalities, each under an elected magistrate (called a mayor in the case of a town) with an elected council. Eventually each of the six districts had a legislature, and all were represented in the elected Congress of Micronesia. This central legislative body consisted of a House of Representatives and a Senate, with a speaker of the House, a president of the Senate, and an array of committees, in faithful imitation of the Congress in Washington. Its powers were gradually increased as the Micronesian legislators grew in experience, although the high commissioner, being responsible to the Department of the Interior rather than to the people of Micronesia, retained a veto.

Acceptance of the American electoral system had been slow and cautious among islanders accustomed to a more monarchial form of government, under traditional chiefs who held their rank by a combination of heredity and acceptance by the people. When the first Americans set out to change the ancient pattern in accordance with western ideas, the bewildered islanders went along politely. Since the Americans insisted on elections, they elected the traditional chiefs, or their chosen protégés in instances when the chiefs considered the holding of elective office to be unseemly. Campaigning for lesser offices was desultory at best, for the islanders considered it a breach of manners to compete openly for honors. As time went on, however, spirited American-style politicking took hold throughout the islands. A milestone in Micronesian political development was passed when an able and energetic young man named Lazarus Salii, with no noble rank in his background but with a degree from the University of Hawaii, defeated a high chief of Palau, a bastion of conservatism, for election to the Senate.

The Congress of Micronesia met in a neat, air-conditioned building constructed for its use on Capitol Hill, with a sweeping view down to the sea. Some members traveled more than two thousand miles from the Marshalls to attend the sessions. Except for the formal opening, when an official photograph was taken for posterity, they wore the South Seas uniform of gaily patterned Hawaiian shirt, slacks, and sandals. Men from islands separated by vast reaches of the central Pacific got to know each other at the bars of the local tourist hotels, chatting in American-accented English with fluent use of Stateside slang. Here they seemed to be not Yapese or Palauan or Marshallese or Ponapean or Trukese or Mariana men, but Micronesians together.

Driving around Saipan in the Japanese car that I had rented from the agency owned by Joe Tenorio, a one-time bus boy in the navy mess who had since become the wealthiest businessman in the Northern Marianas, I gave a lift to Richard Towai of Palau, a recent high school graduate now working on Capitol Hill as a clerk. We talked about the "unity in diversity," as a popular saying had it, that might emerge in a Micronesian nation. "You can go to any district center from Palau to the Marshalls and find people from all the other districts working together, speaking English," he said.

Dwight Heine, a distinguished Marshallese whose name came from a German ancestor, was less confident of the prospects for a unified Micronesian nationality. Heine was a personal friend whom I had first met in Majuro in 1946. He spoke mission English and worked for the navy commander, who had assigned him to me as an interpreter. Later he held many responsible posts in the Trust Territory administration. I found him back in Majuro twenty-one years after our first meeting, this time as the district administrator ("distad" in the jargon of the trust territory bureaucracy) of his native Marshall Islands, and the first Micronesian to hold such a position. Now he was a special adviser to High Commissioner Edward E. Johnston on Micronesian affairs, and it was his job to be in touch with political thinking in all the districts. "Remember that the people of the various groups, generally speaking, had no contact with each other until the Americans brought them together," he said. "It will take time to create mutual understanding."

The idea of Micronesia as a single political entity was a creation of the United Nations, which the U.S. State Department and the Department of the Interior endorsed until the concept became clearly nonviable. The cleavages between the districts left little in common among the different groups beyond a vague sense of sharing a Pacific island identity.

The thirty-four low, flat, verdant atolls of the Marshalls are distributed in two approximately parallel groups, the western Ralik (Sunset) and eastern Ratak (Sunrise) chains, running diagonally from southeast to northwest for some six hundred miles beginning one hundred fifty miles north of the equator. The old-time Marshallese voyagers traveled among the far-flung atolls in canoes, navigating by "stick charts," an arrangement of thin reeds bent in shapes duplicating the wave patterns on the approaches to various islands, which were represented on the chart by small shells tied in place with coconut fiber. Together the Marshalls produced more than half the total coconut crop of the trust territory. Thus, to the dissatisfaction of the Marshallese, these relatively lush atolls accounted for a share of the agricultural income and tax revenues out of proportion to their numbers (some 25,000 out of a total trust territory population of 115,000, as counted in the last census in 1973), while their return was proportionately less.

Being such a profitable source of copra, the Marshalls had been a commercial battleground between German and Australian interests through much of the nineteenth century. Even during the period of nominal Spanish sovereignty, Spain had paid little attention to the Marshalls, and affairs in the islands of concern to Europeans were actually administered by Germans until the Japanese took over. It was New England missionaries, however, who induced the Marshallese women to cover their lithe brown bodies with ungainly Mother Hubbards; since they were worn even when swimming, respiratory ailments and skin diseases became endemic.

The American period has been the darkest chapter in the history of the Marshalls. Two atolls, Bikini and Eniwetak, were evacuated by their inhabitants at the behest of the navy to accommodate nuclear tests, while the population of Kwajalein was redistributed to clear the famous missile range. The results were disastrous for the Marshallese in each instance.

The reluctant migration of the 167 unhappy Bikinians took them first to Rongerik, then to Kwajalein, and finally to Kili island, a lonely outcropping at the southern end of the Ralik chain. Kili, being but a single island without a lagoon and lacking even a sheltered boat anchorage, presented a shattering adjustment for atoll dwellers, along with their other misfortunes. The island was rainier than Bikini and significantly smaller, without the fish resources of a lagoon. To cultivate the strange soil, the Bikinians had to learn how to grow food plants that had not existed in their previous environment. Violent seas completely isolated the island for many months in the year.

The 137 Eniwetakese were moved to remote Ujelang atoll, far to the west of the main Marshalls groups. There they found themselves confined to a dry land area a quarter the size to which they had been accustomed. The 25-square-mile Ujelang lagoon seemed tiny compared to the majestic sweep of the 388 square miles of tossing water, rich with fish, enclosed by the necklace of islands comprising Eniwetak. Crops were sparse and poor. Eniwetakese whom I met on Majuro, where they had come to protest to the administration, told me that the forlorn little community—swollen to more than three hundred by then—had been hungry on occasion for weeks at a time.

Meanwhile the main islands of Bikini and Eniwetak were wracked by repeated nuclear explosions. In 1954 a hydrogen bomb blast over Bikini raised a cloud of radioactive coral dust that drifted on an unexpected wind, enveloping Rongelap and Utirik atolls and the Japanese fishing vessel *Lucky Dragon*. As a result of this mishap, a Japanese fisherman succumbed to illness attributed to radiation. Rongelapese were undergoing operations for thyroid disorders many years later, and a young man died of leukemia, possibly induced by the exposure. More fortunate Rongelapese suffered loss of hair and changes in pigmentation caused by the noxious fallout.

The Bikinians received consolation payments from the United States of $3,000,000, the bulk being safely invested in a trust fund; they were also given the use rights to Kili and three unoccupied islets in the Jaluit atoll. The Eniwetak natives were paid something over $1,000,000 in trust. Following the conclusion of the nuclear program, the government embarked on a lengthy and expensive project to rehabilitate Bikini and Eniwetak so their people, sacrifices to the atomic age, could go home at last.

Kwajalein is one of the world's largest atolls, with some ninety islets around a 650-square-mile lagoon. The main island, also called Kwajalein, is the site of a billion-dollar installation from which missiles are fired to knock down other missiles coming some five thousand miles from Vandenberg Air Force Base in California. When my wife and I passed through in 1967 en route to Majuro and were forced to stay overnight because the plane did, the security was so tight that our military host escorted us to our seats on departure and made sure that we were buckled in. Civilian jurisdiction stopped at the nearby island of Ebeye, a bedroom community for Marshallese employes of the base, who were brought to "Kwaj" in the morning by ferry and returned at night.

With its huge airstrip, enormous radar domes, and model American-style town with tax-free supermarket, movies, television, daily newspaper, schools, and every kind of recreational facility, Kwajalein was indeed a changed island from the ravaged battlefield where I had slept in foxholes while covering the bloody invasion by American forces in 1944. Kwajalein was the first Japanese territory taken by the Allies. The elaborate housekeeping operation for the postwar defense establishment was run by a California company on contract to the government. This was unquestionably the most efficient way to administer a tiny Pacific island overcrowded with foreigners, but it took money.

The missile operation, which periodically lit up the atoll with the most spectacular fireworks display ever witnessed by man as one missile collided with another, required the evacuation of islets on the so-called corridor where the range passed overhead. There was the usual disorientation of the Marshallese separated from his land. To add to the confusion, according to Dwight Heine, the Americans sometimes unwittingly paid the agreed monetary compensation to the wrong party in the complex settlement of claims.

High wages on Kwajalein, three to four times the rate for similar work elsewhere in the trust territory, were an irresistible lure to the Marshallese in other atolls. The worker settlement built by the Americans on Ebeye was soon overwhelmed, and the spillover of humanity collected in a squalid community of makeshift tin hovels described by one official as "a slum in paradise." Doctor William V. Vitarelli, of New York, the trust territory representative on Ebeye at the time, estimated that at least one thousand Marshallese who had come to the island with hopes of making a fortune, by Micronesian atoll standards, had been unable to find jobs and were sleeping on the sand. An effort called "Operation Exodus," aimed at getting the unemployed Marshallese to return to their home atolls, had been a failure. By 1967, when Ebeye was jammed with some four thousand restless Marshallese, the U.S. Army put up a $7,000,000 housing project, with water and sewage service, that was supposed to take care of most of the people on the island, if not all. My last report was that the population of Ebeye, already overswollen, had doubled again to 8,000.

According to Doctor Vitarelli, the historic significance of Kwajalein in the lives of the Marshallese was "the stunning social revolution," as he called it, wrought by close contact with the American PX civilization. "It's astonishing," he said, "how quickly the Marshallese have learned to want such twentieth-century appliances as electric refrigerators, automatic toasters, and tape recorders. And they want them right now." On the positive side, he said, was the swift training of hundreds of Marshallese on Kwajalein in myriad vocational skills previously unknown on islands that had slumbered in the sun till the coming of the Americans with their miraculous machines. Where the Marshallese would use these skills was another question.

Kwajalein belonged to the space age. The simpler administrative center housed in Quonsets at Majuro was also a busy place, though on a much lesser scale. Majuro was a crossroads of shipping and air travel with hotels and picturesque club decorated in Micronesian style, the Coconut Grove, where an American caller found it impossible to keep up with the drinks shoved in front of him by hospitable Marshallese. But among the thirty-four atolls were many where the rare visitor from outside stepped backward in time.

Such a place was Arno, said to be the site of the legendary "University of Love," where Marshallese girls are taught the art of pleasing men. (Or so the story goes. Everybody in the Marshalls seems to have heard of this supposedly ancient institution, but the location is a well-kept secret— if it exists.) The seven hundred people of Arno's dozen islets, with a total land area of five square miles, lived happily in traditional thatched houses, contentedly harvested rich groves of coconuts, and sang, mostly Protestant hymns, half the night. The villages, kept scrupulously clear of the fallen palm fronds and other debris that litter many Micronesian settlements, are connected by roads paved with flat slabs of scrubbed stone. As we strolled through one such village, a smiling, gray-haired woman appeared and silently handed my wife a beautifully woven basket containing a collection of marine shells found on Arno's beaches and reefs.

Micronesia is dotted with unspoiled atolls. Kapingamarangi and Nukuoro in the Ponape district of the eastern Carolines, Polynesian enclaves believed to have been settled by castaways hundreds of years ago, are two such places. Kapingamarangi is the more famous of the two, probably because a model Polynesian village of Kapingamarangian expatriates on the district's main island of Ponape is a tourist attraction known throughout the trust territory. Every American who spends any time in Micronesia hears of Kapingamarangi and yearns to go there. Few ever make it, for the atoll's only contact with the outside world is a small trading ship that calls once every four to eight weeks and seldom takes nonofficial passengers.

I flew down from Guam in a two-engine Albatross, the amphibian plane that the navy used when it was necessary to go to an island where there was no airfield, with a scientific team investigating the mysterious proliferation of the crown of thorns starfish, which was ravaging Pacific coral reefs. The pilot, Lieutenant Commander John K. Trimble, took the plane in a wide circle as we neared the equator and finally spotted the atoll where it lay like a shadow on the sea, the only land in sight. We slid to a landing in the broad lagoon and watched the approach of a flotilla of outrigger canoes that would take us ashore in this westernmost outpost of Polynesia.

"This is the first airplane we've seen in more than four years," siad Eresin Habuet, the chief of the atoll's two-man police force, who was the first to bring his outrigger canoe to the open door of the plane. He and his fellow policeman, he said later, had little to do except break up fights following excessive imbibing of a local brew made from yeast and coconut sap. Like many of the 500 Kapingamarangians, who were all Christians, he had a Western name that had probably been adopted from some long-gone missionary. His first name, Eresin, was a Japanese corruption of Elison.

Life was simple and seemingly happy in "Kapinga," as the atoll was called for short. The trading ship brought all the population's material needs—sugar, coffee, kerosene, tobacco, cooking fats, cloth, Japanese thonged slippers, and other simple supplies —and took away a few hundred sacks of copra, the only cash crop, on each trip. An islander estimated that the exhange left the atoll richer by four to eight dollars a head. This added up to a per capita income of less than fifty dollars a year, one of the lowest in the world. "We don't need to buy much, anyway," said Samuel Charles, the atoll's elected representative in the Ponape district legislature that met in Kolonia, the former Japanese town on the main island. "What we eat comes mostly from the coconut and breadfruit trees, the taro patch, and the sea," he explained.

A square of printed cotton, wrapped around the waist like a sarong, sufficed as clothing for both sexes. The neat houses had walls of native reeds, roofs of palm-frond thatch, and floors of white coral pebbles that were never allowed to become muddy. The toilets were sheds built on stilts over the water on the ocean side of the island. There were no electric lights except battery flashlights; kerosene lamps lit the houses. The small generator that ran a two-way radio for communication with the administrative center in Ponape was the only piece of machinery on the atoll. The wheel was all but unknown, the only two being on the bicycle belonging to the medical aide, Welsin Radford, who tended the one-room clinic that served the entire population. "We had another bicycle, but it got broken," the policeman said.

Without wheels, there was no need of roads on the two inhabited islets of Touhou and Weru, which together had an area of less than twenty acres. The two streets, one on each islet, were mere coral paths between rows of houses. One Western-style building was the common meeting hall, another was a cement church in which Sunday services were held, for which the female parishioners covered up in voluminous dresses. The wooden bridge between the two islets was being replaced by a concrete span less vulnerable to the occasional heavy seas that pounded the two islands.

The beach was lined with low, thatched sheds in which the islanders kept their fleet of outrigger canoes, said to be the finest vessels of their kind in the Pacific. The canoes were vital to the community for fishing and for travel to the outlying islets used as coconut plantations. The two inhabited islets were virtually indistinguishable except that Weru, slightly smaller, had a six-teen-foot hillock in the middle—the highest point in the atoll.

In one of the canoe sheds I found an English-speaking Kaping-amarangian listening to the news on a battery-powered transistor radio. Isolated as they were on their tiny atoll only 60 miles north of the equator, with the nearest neighbor, Nukuoro, 200 miles to the northeast, the Kapinga people kept abreast of the world's happenings. We fell into conversation about a recent moon mission. What, I wondered, did a resident of a virtually wheelless Polynesian atoll think of men being rocketed to the moon? The canoe-maker was unimpressed. "Was it worth all that trouble just to bring back some dirt?" he asked.

The name of the atoll is believed to be a Polynesian corruption of "Captain Mariano," the commander of a Spanish vessel that once called there. There were nearly as many Kapingamaran-gians living in their expatriate village of Porokheit on Ponape as on the home atoll. The Porokheit people, who supported themselves by catching fish to sell to the Ponapeans, tried to duplicate the Polynesian habitat in their Micronesian surroundings, and were hosts periodically to the traditional chief of Kaping-amarangi, named Duiai, who was sometimes called a "king" and also held the title, under the Americans, of chief magistrate.

Ponape, one of the most luxuriant and beautiful islands in the Pacific, had a strong culture of its own. The principal island of the Senyavin group, named for the ship in which a Russian survey party explored the Carolines in 1828, Ponape is famous for the mysterious stone ruins of the abandoned city of Nan Madol, also known as "The Venice of the Pacific" because it was built on about one hundred partly man-made islands. Massive structures of shaped basalt blocks, each weighing tons, indicate the presence of an advanced race of builders hundreds of years ago. Carbon tests have indicated that the site was inhabited as early as the twelfth century. Similar ruins exist on nearby Kusaie island.

According to Ponapean tradition, Nan Madol was the capital of a ruling dynasty called the Saudeleurs, who reigned over the entire island. The last Saudeleur, the story goes, was overthrown by a chief from Kusaie, leader of the progenitors of the present Ponapean race. Ponape was then split into five principalities, each under a hereditary ruler called a *nanmwarki* (the "w" is silent). These divisions became "municipalities" under the Americans, with an elected local government headed by a magistrate or mayor. The *nanmwarki* continued to command immense prestige among his people, who honored him with a fixed number of feasts every year at which there was prolonged consumption of the Ponapean version of *kava*, called *sakau*. His judgment was generally accepted in disputes involving local custom, such as land questions.

Ponapeans, a relatively light-skinned people with facial features suggesting an Asian strain, had a history of intractability under the former Spanish and German rulers. There were several uprisings, all unsuccessful. The Japanese concentrated on the agricultural development of the island, introducing new crops such as sugar and pepper. The old town of Kolonia (spelled with a "C" by the Spanish, changed to "K" by the Germans) became a bustling city of eight thousand residents, with streets laid out in a rectangular pattern and a main avenue of shops. Old-timers remember a famous geisha restaurant called the Sun and Moon. Japan planned to ease population pressure in the homeland by resettling eight thousand Japanese farmers in Ponape, but World War II brought an end to these ambitions.

After the war, in which Ponape was an air base frequently bombed by the Americans, little remained of Kolonia but charred foundations, a few gutted brick business buildings, the partly destroyed cathedral, and the old Spanish wall. Rebuilding under the American administration has been a slow process. A belated awakening to the possibilities in tourism, with the brooding ruins of Nan Madol as a ready-made attraction, has led to a gradual proliferation of small hotels of picturesque native design. Visitors spread the fame of Ponape pepper, acclaimed by the head of the American Culinary Federation as "truly a gourmet product."

Major Japanese towns, expanded from Spanish and German beginnings, were also obliterated in wartime operations against

Japanese bases in Truk, Yap, Saipan in the northern Marianas, and Koror in the Palau group. All but one of these sites would become, after the war, a trust territory district headquarters. The exception, left to molder in the swiftly growing jungle, was the elaborate Japanese naval settlement on Dublon island of the Truk group, the wartime forward command post of the Imperial Combined Fleet. Since a large Japanese garrison remained on Dublon at the time of the surrender, not as prisoners of war but as "disarmed military personnel" awaiting repatriation to Japan, the U.S. Navy established itself on Moen island, in the usual makeshift Quonset quarters. There the later civilian government of the Truk district remained, since the facilities—such as they were—were already in place. The Truk district jurisdiction extended to a dozen other scattered Micronesian atolls.

Truk, discovered by the Spanish navigator Alvaro de Saavedra in 1528, is a scattering of towering green volcanic islands (the highest, Tol, rises to a 1,427-foot conical peak) within a magnificent 500-square-mile lagoon enclosed by an encircling ring of coral islets on the great surrounding reef. The effect, stunning and unique in my experience of Pacific scenery, is that of a group of "high" islands within an atoll. A few minutes in a motor boat are enough to transport a traveler from the urban surroundings of Moen, which has a jet airport and several air-conditioned hotels, to smaller islands hardly touched by the twentieth century.

As headquarters of the Combined Fleet, Truk had been an awesome bastion of Japanese power when the American forces began their drive into the Central Pacific in the Gilberts in November 1943. I saw the dark green peaks of Moen, Dublon, Fefan, and Tol, and their low outriders covered with fleecy palms, for the first time one dazzling day the following February from the bridge of the battleship *Iowa*, part of a task force sent to neutralize Truk while amphibious forces assaulted Eniwetak, some 400 miles to the northeast. With carrier planes and naval gunfire, the naval force destroyed or damaged at least 265 Japanese planes and most of the 50 enemy warships and transports caught in the great lagoon. Vice-admiral Raymond A. Spruance, in his flagship *New Jersey*, took *Iowa* and a pickup team of cruisers and destroyers on a sweep around the reef in which our guns sank the fleeing Japanese vessels that had escaped the carnage in the lagoon. From being a feared forward base of the Japanese, Truk became an insignificant backwater in the war.

The hulks in the lagoon, some so near the surface that they can be viewed in the clear water over the side of a boat, have become one of the principal tourist sights in Micronesia. Skin divers with Trukese guides can be found photographing the wrecks with underwater cameras any fine day beneath the schools of flying fish that constantly ripple the surface of the clear, blue water. The district legislature, meeting in a new building of simulated Micronesian architecture near the Moen airport, declared the collection of hulks a protected underwater park. Divers are forbidden to remove material from the sunken ships as souvenirs.

"Truculent Trukese" is a hackneyed trust territory pun with much truth in it. The 20,000 people of Truk proper, not counting another 10,000 residents of the district on outlying atolls, are known as individualists. At a time when most Micronesian politicians were advocating a permanent union with the United States, Trukese rallied to a minority party called the Micronesian Independence Coalition, which called for complete sovereignty for the islanders. Some of the Trukese leaders have Japanese surnames, a heritage of the days when the Japanese military complement numbered some 35,000 men.

In the villages on the outskirts of Colonia, capital of the Yap district (not to be confused with Kolonia, on Ponape), the traditional South Seas come to life as in no other administrative center. Yapese men, considered the most conservative of all Micronesians in their resistance to amelioration of local customs by the American influence, routinely appear in town wearing only the scanty *thu*, a minimal loincloth decorated with strands of hibiscus fiber. Women may cover their breasts in Colonia but never in the villages, where they wear only a bulky grass skirt.

In Yap proper, a cluster of four hilly islands that the Germans connected with stone causeways and improved with roads paved with slabs, the traditional chief is supreme in village affairs. A complex caste system is observed, including a form of untouchability. In earlier times the young men's clubhouse was graced by a communal mistress called a *mespil*, an honored position that usually led to a distinguished marriage. All Yapese are addicted to chewing betel nut, carried in a large woven bag suspended from the shoulder. An ancient practice of magic survives, as does the segregation of menstruating women in a small hut in each village.

The famous stone money of Yap, called *rai*, disks up to twelve feet across with a hole in the center for carrying on a pole, still serves ceremonial purposes and is displayed outside Yapese houses as status symbols. Many specimens, quarried in Palau, were brought to Yap by the Irish-American mariner and trader Captain David Dean O'Keefe, who traded it for copra and beche-de-mer or trepang, prized by Chinese for soup, which he sent as far as Hong Kong and Malaya in his own schooners. "His Majesty O'Keefe," as he was called, lived on the lagoon island of Tareng, or Terrang, where the remains of his house can be seen, till he disappeared at sea in one of his ships, presumably lost in a storm. O'Keefe's stone money can be distinguished by its regularity and chisel marks, missing from older examples towed from Palau by sailing canoe.

Also strongly traditionalist, yet keenly attuned to modern life in occupational pursuits, were the sophisticated elite of Palau, at the western extremity of Micronesia. A chain of lush, wooded volcanic islands with fertile soil, dazzling white beaches, and some of the most spectacular underwater coral parks in the world, Palau was once known as the "Japanese Riviera" and is making a modest comeback in tourism under American development. Koror, the main town and administrative center for the district, which includes several outlying atolls, was once a Japanese city of 20,000 with up-to-date amenities for its time. An American commanding officer who had lost a son in the war is blamed for the senseless destruction of the town with bulldozers during the early period of navy rule.

Koror had been the center of a strong Japanese navy complex, which the advancing American forces bypassed after seizing Peleliu and Angaur islands, at the southern end of the chain, in bloody fighting. Peleliu had been largely denuded of vegetation in the bombardment preparatory to the Marine landings, but when I returned a few months after the end of the war the island was again covered with dense jungle.

More than any other Micronesians, the Palauans were attuned to Japanese ways. The Japanese language was spoken widely, shops were stocked with Japanese magazines, records, clothes, canned goods, and other consumer items, and Palauans used their Japanese-made transistor radios to listen to Japanese broadcasts.

At the same time, the entrenched indigenous institutions flourished. The peak-roofed men's clubhouse called an *abai*, the architectural inspiration for tourist hotels all over the Pacific, and the women's age group clubs remained the center of Palauan social life. Souvenir collectors prize the Palauan "story boards," with pictorial carving retelling an ancient legend, usually erotic.

Considerable residual authority rested with the two traditional hereditary high chiefs, the *ibedul* of Koror and southern Palau, and the *reklai* of Melekiok, a district on the main island of Babelthuap, and the north. When Ibedul Ngoriyakl died, the thirty-day investiture ceremonies had to be postponed until the heir, a moustached young man named Yutaka Gibbons, obtained an early release from his enlistment in the U.S. Army, which had sent him to Germany.

Unquestionably, the most Americanized of the Micronesians were the fourteen thousand hybrid people of the Northern Marianas, whose flimsy homes were periodically destroyed by the typhoons that whirled out of the Central Pacific, leaving a trail of disaster until they finally dissipated after a climactic fling at Japan. Frequent exposure to American luxury on nearby Guam, the gateway to the outside world, brought to the Marianas a consuming thirst to share these delights.

The Mariana Islands are one of the few examples of successful genocide, a difficult thing to bring off. When Magellan landed on Guam in 1521, the first European to lay eyes on the chain, he called the islands Ladrones (Spanish for "thieves") because of the light-fingered proclivities of the dark-skinned inhabitants. The name survives, appearing on maps in parentheses. According to carbon dating of archeological finds on Guam, that island was inhabited as early as 500 B.C., by Malayo-Polynesian migrants believed to have come in stages from Southeast Asia. Estimates of the number of inhabitants in Magellan's time go as high as one hundred thousand.

The Spanish Roman Catholic missionaries who arrived in 1868 renamed the islands Mariana, after their patroness, Queen Maria Anna of Spain. Efforts to convert the islanders to Christianity were violently resisted. The Spanish then embarked on a campaign of systematic extermination of the Chamorro people, as they were called after the name of their common language, and by the beginning of the eighteenth century there were only five thousand left, mostly women. The Spaniards collected these survivors on Guam, leaving the northern islands uninhabited for the next 150 years.

Guam became a provisioning stop for the treasure-laden Spanish galleons plying between Manila and Acapulco, Mexico, and a hangout for the British buccaneers, notably the famous Captain

Woods Rogers, who preyed on these tempting prizes. Meanwhile the Chamorro women intermarried with Spaniards, Mexicans, and Filipinos. Their offspring were brought up as good Roman Catholics, with Spanish surnames. Carlos Taitano, a Guamanian political leader and businessman with one of the few Chamorro surnames left, told me that the last pure-blooded Chamorro had died early in this century. So far as I know, the obliteration of an entire race has seldom been duplicated, the aborigines of Tasmania (who differed from the aborigines of Australia proper) being one the few other familiar examples.

The annexation of Guam by the United States following the Spanish-American war artificially separated the people of that island from their kin on Saipan, Tinian, and the other Northern Marianas, which by that time had been repopulated. The Germans who took over the Spanish holdings did little in the Marianas, preferring to concentrate on developing the rich copra plantations of the Marshall Islands, where they were already entrenched, and the more inviting commercial prospects of the Carolines (which the Spanish had originally called Carolina, after King Charles II of Spain). But the Japanese, after ousting the Germans from the Central Pacific, turned Saipan and the neighboring islands of Tinian and Rota into prosperous sugar plantations. All that remains to recall the German presence is the old lighthouse at Garapan Heights, a post-World War II housing development.

United States Marines landed on the western side of Saipan on 15 June 1944 and met strong Japanese resistance. In the ensuing three-week battle, more than three thousand Americans and the entire Japanese defending force of thirty thousand men lost their lives, plus an unknown number of Saipanese. Relics of the war, such as the abandoned cannon in the last Japanese command post and the two tanks hanging on the reef where they were stopped by enemy fire are photographed by Japanese honeymooners at the nearby hotels. Japanese tourists flock to Suicide Cliff, at the northern tip of the island, where thousands of Japanese soldiers and civilians leaped 800 feet to their deaths rather than surrender.

The former Japanese capital of Garapan, which once boasted more than six thousand buildings, and other towns of the busy prewar era have vanished, as has the once-thriving sugar industry. But reminders of the former Japanese rule abound, such as the giant statue of Shunji Matsue, the one-time "sugar king" of the island, who had been a graduate of Louisiana State University. Nearby sits an old-fashioned locomotive that once pulled railroad cars loaded with sugar cane from field to factory. There is an abandoned Japanese jail, where some believe that Amelia Earhart and Fred Noonan, the lost American aviatrix and her navigator, were imprisoned and died. The story has many adherents but has never been confirmed.

Across a three-mile channel lies the steep-sided, thirty-nine-square-mile island of Tinian, where the vanished Japanese grew sugar, pineapples, and vegetables for the home market. Once, for a few hours, Tinian was one of the most important places in the world. There, on a great limestone airstrip long overgrown with creeping green vines, the first atomic bomb dropped on man was hoisted inside the belly of a B-29 called *Enola Gay*.

At 2:45 A.M. on 4 August 1945, with Colonel Paul W. Tibbets, Jr., at the controls, *Enola Gay* lifted off for the twelve-hundred-mile flight to Japan, where the bomb was detonated over Hiroshima. Three days later the second atomic bomb was loaded from another pit on the same runway and was taken to Nagasaki. Five days after that, Emperor Hirohito broadcast Japan's surrender. The two pits, filled with earth, were planted with decorative palm trees and flowering shrubs by the Tinian municipal government "as a symbol," said Mayor Jose Cruz, "that the forces of nature, which can destroy man, can also give life."

The seven hundred farmers and fishermen of Tinian, which had had no permanent population before the war, longed for the American military to come back and reactivate the deserted wartime port complex and the four big bomber strips. The silent runways had long been abandoned to the birds, lizards, and wandering cattle from the ranch started by Ken Jones, a former Seabee who saw war service on Guam and returned to the islands with "a hatful of junk jewelry" as capital and became a multimillionaire businessman. After four hundred years of foreign rule, which saw the complete extinction of indigenous culture, the Saipanese longed for an identity. As political leaders saw it, the best chance of the Saipanese for self-expression lay in merger with the United States. In my many visits to the island, I continually heard pro-American expressions of an intensity that had long been out of fashion in the United States itself.

The sentiment of the majority was summed up in a statement to a Congressional subcommittee by Eddie Pangelinan, a Saipanese legislator and chairman of the Marianas Political Status

Commission, which was then negotiating for a permanent link to the United States.

> For over four hundred years, the people of the Mariana islands have been ruled by foreign powers. By conquest came the Spaniards, then the Germans, then the Japanese. Without consultation or consideration, our lives, homes, land, culture, and tradition were crushed. We had no opportunity to speak out on matters of importance to us, such as the nature of our government, the development of our economy, and our future destiny. But now we have this opportunity, for after twenty-five years of American administration our people have come to understand and appreciate the American system of government. The spirit of two hundred years of democracy, of individual liberty, of equal justice under the law, of a country that has historically been a refuge for the oppressed and a land of opportunity for all people, was brought to the Marianas by the United States.

The image of the United States on Saipan had been burnished by the efficiency of the navy administration, which left the pleasant little island a network of well-made motor roads and other material amenities lacking elsewhere in the trust territory. The administrative center for the Marianas district at Susupe, across the road from a flossy hotel named the Royal Taga after a legendary Chamorro chieftain, reflected a progressiveness conspicuously absent in the other districts, where the Americans in charge seemed to absorb the easygoing nature of their Micronesian wards.

In contrast to the manicured appearance of Capitol Hill and Susupe, a quarter of a century after the arrival of the Americans the other district centers presented a depressing vista of rusting Quonset huts and other dilapidated buildings of corrugated metal, with muddy, rutted tracks for roads. Micronesian villagers, flocking to the district center for work with the government, which furnished most of the wage-paying employment in the trust territory, huddled in shanties of salvaged wood and rusted metal sheets. Visitors, appalled by the spectacle, went away muttering about "tropical slums" in the midst of some of the most spectacular tropical scenery on earth. "The most beautiful scrap heap in the world!" a recently arrived American official exclaimed, recalling his first impression of the scene.

For years the American administration in Micronesia had scraped along on miserly annual budgets, cannibalizing wornout machinery and replacing hopelessly broken-down equipment with secondhand military stores discarded by the previous users at bases around the Pacific. Instead of the "Can do" motto of the

Seabees who preceded them, the slogan of the trust territory engineers was "Make do."

"It would not be good to bring the Micronesians along too fast," officials explained. This was an attitude known as the "zoo theory," leaving the islanders to develop at their own pace. In time the "zoo theory" was abandoned as Micronesians themselves returned from colleges in "the States" in increasing numbers. The appearance of modern tourist hotels built by Continental Airlines, replacing the abominably managed makeshifts that had served for years, set the pace for a higher standard of construction in the official establishment. Gradually, long past time, the Quonset image began to fade from the trust territory as successive administrations persuaded Washington to increase the yearly budget to a respectable figure.

With the investment in education paying off in a pool of qualified local personnel, the administration began to look less American and more Micronesian as islanders moved into higher echelons. A milestone in "localization" was reached in January 1976, when that month's edition of *Highlights*, the official news bulletin from Capitol Hill, appeared with a banner line on the front page: "Six Distads Are Micronesians." This meant that each of the six administrative districts now had a chief executive native to the place, born into the local culture, and able to talk to the people in their mother tongue. Four of the six held bachelor of arts degrees from the University of Hawaii, and the other two had attended colleges in Hawaii or Guam. None of the earlier fears by American officials that giving the highest posts to local people would result in nepotism and the exploitation of clan connections came true.

Meanwhile, however, the growing sophistication of the Micronesian people was accompanied inevitably by a shift from the easygoing South Seas subsistence economy to a dependence upon work for wages. As new standards of living made imported goods indispensable, the islanders discovered the need for cash earnings. The old way of life was clearly over. Government remained the biggest employer, generating 60 percent of the economy. Development of agriculture, fisheries, tourism, and other cash-producing enterprises became the top priority.

Equally inevitable in the evolution of Micronesia was the accelerating pace of transition from a United Nations trusteeship to a more advanced political stage. The islands were now on the threshold of self-government, if not independence. Many leading Micronesians were thinking in terms of full independence, but not necessarily as a united country with a central government in Saipan. Separatist sentiments appeared in the Marianas, the Marshalls, and Palau. Undoubtedly, according to many of my well-informed Micronesian friends, the bulk of the 115,000 islanders gave little or no thought at all to high politics, being content with a more or less easygoing life from day to day. But the Future Political Status Commission set up by the Congress of Micronesia, under the chairmanship of Senator Lazarus Salii of Palau, leaned toward continuing a link with the United States, at least for some years to come, under a formula called "free association." In principle, the plan provided for a unified state of Micronesia that would be self-governing in local affairs but under the protection of the United States, and receiving financial assistance from Washington in return for American rights to exclusive military use of the islands. Washington would retain control over foreign affairs. The arrangement was formalized in a document called a "compact," following protracted negotiations between representatives of the Congress of Micronesia and an interdepartmental American team headed by a representative of the president. The political viability of a unified Micronesia, artificially created, remained a question for the future.

The Marianas district legislature did not doubt that the overwhelming majority of the fourteen thousand people in those islands wished ardently to become American citizens, as attested by dozens of resolutions, petitions, and statements to that effect by the legislature and municipal bodies going back nearly a quarter of a century. Discussions with the Americans led to a plebiscite on 17 June 1975, in which the islanders voted to accept an offer of American citizenship, with the bow-shaped archipelago becoming a full commonwealth of the United States. Ninety-five percent of the registered voters went to the polls, and 78.8 percent of those voted for the commonwealth arrangement. The agreement was subsequently approved by the United States Congress and President Ford, but would not take effect until the termination of the American trusteeship over Micronesia as a whole, a step that Washington hoped to complete by 1981. Meanwhile the district was renamed the Northern Mariana Islands, in recognition of the exclusion of Guam, already an American possession. On 1 April 1976, the Northern Marianas were removed from the trust territory administration and were placed under a separate jurisdiction headed by an American official to be known as the resident commissioner.

The accession to the United States, though still incomplete, was celebrated with jubilant singing, dancing, and feasting on all of the inhabited islands. At a ceremony on the beach where the Marines had made their first landing on Saipan, the covenant signed by President Ford was put on display under a palm tree, with the pen that he had used. The Saipanese finally had a nationality. "It is such a good thing to have a permanent political status," said Francisco Ada, who had been elevated from Distad to acting resident commissioner. "We have had the Japanese, the Germans, and the Spanish here. Now we are no longer insecure. We feel we belong to something."

But not everyone was happy with the move, even on Saipan. An expatriate minority community of about one thousand descendants of migrants from the Caroline Islands, who had retained their ethnic purity and lived in their own villages apart from the Chamorros, felt further alienated from their ancestral roots. There was sadness and irritation in the remaining five districts of the trust territory (which became six again when the major island of Kusaie, in the Eastern Carolines, was detached from Ponape and was made a district on its own), but any sense of loss was ameliorated by a feeling that the intense pro-Americanism of the Mariana people would have made them permanent misfits in a larger Micronesian state.

International critics of the United States denounced the acquisition of the Northern Marianas as "colonialism." Critics at home questioned the wisdom of taking on additional territorial obligations in the Western Pacific, suggesting that the defense of the islands would be an onerous responsibility. Washington was accused of having influenced the overwhelmingly favorable vote by promising enormous amounts of financial aid. It was said that the people of the Northern Marianas would be receiving only "second-class" citizenship in the United States, since they would have no vote in Congress and would not vote in the presidential elections—all of which was true, of course, in the case of citizens in other offshore American territories, such as Guam.

Micronesia in the other districts accepted the loss of the Northern Marianas either in sadness or with renewed determination to push their own sectional interests. The Congress of Micronesia made plans to move the capital to Ponape. Critics seemed to overlook the American obligation, under the trustee-ship agreement, to respect political self-determination on the part of the Micronesians. It had apparently been forgotten that the people of the Northern Marianas, now suspected of having voted to join the United States under inducements by Washing-ton, had voted the same way in numerous polls during the years when official policy was strongly opposed to a territorial division in Micronesia. In a plebiscite taken in 1969, which the American administration refused to recognize, the northern islands over-whelmingly endorsed a proposal to rejoin Guam. A week earlier, however, a plebiscite on the American island had rejected a merger with the Northern Marianas. Officials ascribed the nega-tive vote on Guam, although the proposition was favored by Guamanian political leaders, partly to apathetic organization of the poll (only a third of the eligible voters turned out) and partly to lingering wartime resentment of the Saipanese, who had served the hated Japanese occupiers of Guam as interpreters. In later years, with old animosities fading, the reunification of the Marianas has been discussed on Guam as a possibility. Meanwhile the Guamanians talk of political fulfillment for that island as a county in the state of Hawaii, as a state in its own right, or as an independent country, although the latter idea has little appeal for most Guamanians, who have taken great pride in their Ameri-can citizenship.

Historically, bringing the Northern Marianas under the same flag as Guam is at least a partial rectification of the artificial separation of the islands by the United States following the defeat of Spain in the Spanish-American War. The Marianas chain should have been taken over as a unit at that time, but the navy wanted only the natural harbor at Guam. That facility, inciden-tally, remained sadly neglected until after American forces had recaptured the island from the Japanese occupiers, a step that had to await the bloody seizure of Saipan and Tinian first. Since then, the lush island has become a major base of the United States Strategic Air Command and the nuclear submarine fleet in the Pacific, and seems destined to be a keystone of American defenses on the outskirts of Asia for the foreseeable future. From the military point of view, the addition of Saipan and Tinian as permanent American outposts in the same waters could only be considered a gain.

An American naval commander on Guam, Rear Admiral Philip P. Cole, once made the defense position clear in a speech to a gathering of Micronesian political leaders on Saipan. "Whatever form your individual future governments may take," he said, "the United States will be responsible for this area." A Micronesian attitude had been expressed to me by the multilingual chief on Truk many years before. "I wouldn't want the United States to lose a war in the Pacific," the old chief had said. "I might have to learn still another language."

FIFTEEN

The South Seas Community and the "Pacific Way"

WHILE touring the Pacific with a British official mission many years ago, a New Zealand journalist named Robert William Robson was surprised to find how isolated the island peoples were from each other. "Everywhere I went," he recalled many years later, "people begged for news of the other islands I had visited. They often knew what was going on in London, Paris, Washington, or Sydney, but had no idea what was happening on the next island." So he founded in 1930 the *Pacific Islands Monthly,* a magazine that was to have a profound influence on South Pacific affairs by making the islanders aware of common interests. The South Pacific community has come a long way in mutual involvement since "Robby" Robson supplied a catalyst with his wide-ranging, often astringent publication.

In their subsequent development, the islanders have followed the paths that they have considered most suitable for their individual needs. Economic and security considerations have impelled the smaller, weaker territories to retain political links with the metropolitan—or colonial—power. Many reject the idea of independence, confounding anticolonialist zealots in the United Nations who confused freedom with sovereignty. Some South Pacific peoples are proud of their right to carry a British, French, American, or New Zealand passport. The tie with a larger country is valued. Nevertheless, even the smaller island entities have come to identify in spirit with the emergent regional community of the South Pacific. The result is a new bloc on the international

281

scene, led by young, eager states destined never to carry great weight in world councils through any inherent strength, but still asserting a distinctive character and hoping to influence events in the gentle "Pacific way."

How powerfully the philosophy of conciliation and consensus embodied in the "Pacific way" may sway affairs of state on a wider scene is undoubtedly questionable. At least Sir Albert Henry, speaking as premier of the Cook Islands, was heard with respect —if not to great effect at the moment—when he argued the views of the archipelagic states of the South Pacific at an international conference on the law of the sea in Caracas, Venezuela. The "Pacific way" does work in South Seas regional conferences, and those are deliberations of potential importance in maintaining stability and balance in a strategic area whose health is of consequence to the powers bordering on the largest of the oceans.

All of the island territories have shared assets and aspirations, as well as liabilities. Most have at least a superficial homogeneity, although larger groups like the Solomons, Fiji, and Papua New Guinea experience deep internal cultural cleavages and are not free from racial sensibilities that pit brown against white (not vice versa any more). The communal ownership of land, besides providing a stabilizing built-in social security system lacking elsewhere, also relieves many new island states of the land redistribution problems that plague former colonial countries in Asia and Africa. There is a general willingness among South Pacific leaders to accept innovative ideas in government, especially any that blend modern concepts with traditional values. Finally, the leadership class already existing under ancient custom is being expanded in depth everywhere by the spread of education, and I have found no significant disposition among the conservative oldsters to stifle the progressive young, despite the generation gap that obtrudes in family life.

The shared problems are numerous and deep-seated. Except in mineral-rich New Caledonia and possibly Papua New Guinea, the economy is based on such thin foundations that on many islands, especially the numerous atolls, any expectation of eventual self-sufficiency must be considered unrealistic even in the long term. Urbanization, the inevitable by-product of modernization, has produced corrosive social dislocation and environmental damage. On some islands, overpopulation is approaching the classic Malthusian stage.

Cook, in one of his journals, set down his conviction that the

South Pacific islanders would have been better off if they had never been exposed to the Western "arts that make life comfortable." The same thought has occurred to others. "It may be too late to go back to their old less perfect contrivances," Cook observed in an astute afterthought. The time has long passed when there could have been any going back; but the islands were never a paradise anyway for the lower classes, hagridden by superstition and tabus.

Many thinking islanders, however, have found themselves losing the good in their traditional way of life—the mutual caring, and so on—without compensating benefit from the new technology that has been injected into their lives. The resulting dissatisfactions leave the islands vulnerable to social agitation, which has not been slow to enter from the seedbeds of the universities. "In many cases," said Frank Palacios, a senator in the Congress of Micronesia from Saipan, at one of the island conferences I attended, "the products of modern technology have entered before the islands were ready to absorb them." Adjusting to a strange money economy, he added, is a complicated process in "a culture based less on materialism than on family and kinship ties." (The reverse of the problem has been observed among young American women who have married island men and found themselves plunged into the bewildering world of communal sharing, in which individual ownership carries with it the obligation to relinquish possessions and money to others within the group, more or less on demand.)

If the adjustment to Western concepts was difficult for a man like Palacios, who came from a relatively highly acculturated island in the Northern Marianas where most people wanted to be Americans, how much more painful it must have been for such as Gordon Siama, who was a graduate of modern schools in New Zealand but had been brought up in the timeless backwater of his native island of Choiseul, in the Solomons. "To meet those changes," he said, speaking of demands for economic development, political advancement, and social services, "we must also change our ideas, our customs, even our way of life. We must try to keep what is best of the old, but we cannot avoid shifting our ground and accepting the best of the new."

Said a Marshallese, writing in the trust territory magazine, *Micronesian Reporter:* "There is a whole new class of people whose point of orientation is now different. This group would rather have a Coca-Cola than a coconut." At numerous conferences in which South Pacific leaders discussed their mutual problems, the implication was clear that responsible islanders were willing to entertain the idea of change. At the same time, they yearned to retain as much as possible of the way of life that had endeared the South Seas to countless visitors in the past two centuries or more.

Increasing familiarity with Western forms of government, instead of advancing the adjustment to foreign versions of democracy, often encouraged uneasiness and doubts as to the adaptability of alien systems to the island temperament. The urge to modify imported systems was strong after islanders had experimented with power. Somare's early determination to create what he called an "original society" in Papua New Guinea, with tribal customs molded into the law code inherited from Australia, was symptomatic. Mara of Fiji, among others, wondered whether power struggles between rival political parties in an adversary relationship was seemly in a Pacific island context, and his reservations became stronger after an official tour of black African countries that had rejected the party system.

"Is the Western pattern of government necessarily the one best suited to us in the Pacific?" he asked in a lecture at the East-West Center in Honolulu. "Or are those African countries right who have tried the Western democratic pattern only to find that the real answer to their problems, and the way to progress, was through one-party government? After all, what is called full parliamentary government only came to pass in Britain after hundreds of years of parliamentary and political experience and in a homogeneous society. . . ."

"But in the Pacific many of us have widely differing cultures within a country," said Mara, whose own background as a Lau Islander had been influenced by both Polynesian and Melanesian backgrounds. "It is not only a matter of racial differences. Some countries have people who appear to be very similar throughout, and yet from island to island there are very great differences of custom, culture, and language. To expect a minority to feel themselves adequately represented in an assembly composed entirely of people widely different from themselves implies a degree of integration which takes very many years to achieve."

As noted in the Solomons, well-meaning efforts to marry features of the British system with the "Pacific way" of consensus can prove to be impractical. Possibly, however, the attempt in the Solomons had less chance of succeeding because it had never been a genuine response to Melanesian thought so much as an idea of some imaginative British administrator in those islands. It was a bogus adaptation, suitable to neither culture, and thus foredoomed. And perhaps the experiment was tried too early in the political evolution of undeveloped isles.

The village-council concept governed island politics, and the idea that elected law-makers bore a responsibility to the nation, not just to their own constituencies, was slow to catch on. Thus, South Sea parliaments tended to have swinging doors. Many hard-working politicians, conscientiously toiling long hours in their offices and following the most tedious and trivial parliamentary debate with close attention in the capital, were rewarded with defeat in the next election simply because their faces had not been seen often enough in their home districts. "Most people are not interested in politics and they just want you to do practical things for them," said Ekpap Silk, a successful legislator from the Marshall Islands. In the tiny, coconut-growing atolls that he represented in the Micronesian legislature, people looked to their congressman for help in such matters as "problems with companies not returning empty copra sacks," he declared.

Reverence for customary ways survived even under the relentless Americanization of education and politics in the cultural mosaic of Micronesia. The constitution for the proposed self-governing nation, to be called the Federated States of Micronesia, contained an article preserving the special status of the so-called traditional leaders, or chiefs. The clause even provided for the establishment, when and if desired, of a Chamber of Chiefs as an adjunct of the government, with unspecified powers. The constitutional convention, consisting of elected representatives of the six districts, attached a resolution affirming that nothing in the charter of the new Micronesia was intended "to affect adversely any of the relationships which prevail between traditional leaders and the people . . . not to diminish in any way the full honor and respect to which they are entitled."

Notable young men like Lazarus Salii of Palau, the principal Micronesian spokesman in the negotiations with Washington, were amenable to modification of American democracy in the islands. But Dwight Heine, of the Marshalls, believed that time would remove any anomaly. "Eventually," he told me, "the new legislative forms will overtake the old customs."

Continued Americanization of Micronesia seemed inevitable. Although the conservative Palauans opposed a proposal by the

United States to militarize the airfield on the main island of Babelthuap, along with a 2,000-acre area to be used for amphibious training exercises, and the harbor of Malakal, the Micronesians were in a weak position to refuse this concession in return for needed economic development assistance, involving huge gifts of money from Washington. There was opposition also to a proposed commercial "superport," with a huge international oil storage depot and transshipment point, on environmental grounds.

The prospect of a sizable American military presence in the Northern Marianas, at air bases and harbor installations on Saipan and Tinian, was welcomed by all but a small minority of the local people because of the employment and money that the projects would inject into the slender island economy. Although there were no plans for immediate militarization of Saipan and Tinian when those islands became American territory, a build-up was expected eventually and it would inevitably speed Americanization. Americanization was what they had voted for in the plebiscite. In any case, the people of the Northern Marianas and Guam were already the most Westernized of the Micronesians, with little left of an indigenous culture except the Chamorro language, the legends of the *taotaomona,* or ancestral spirits, and the mysterious tall, mushroomlike pillars of coral rock, called "latte stones," probably used as building supports. What passes for a local culture in the Marianas actually came from Spain, with modifications added in the Philippines. Yet the Guamanians' deep love of their home island—as shown by its name, which comes from the Chamorro *guahan,* meaning "we have"—is typical of Pacific people.

The major threat to South Sea culture and customs, as many island leaders saw it, was tourism. The appearance of hotel complexes and the package tour was viewed with deep alarm, although it was clear that the visitor industry offered the only hope for significant economic expansion in Pacific territories dependent upon the uncertain market for coconut products and one or two other items of tropical agriculture. Not that tourism was much more reliable as a money producer, as many island enterprisers learned when an economic recession curtailed foreign vacations.

Officials from various relatively unspoiled islands, attending a session of the South Pacific Conference in the luxurious Guam Hilton Hotel on Tumon Bay, outside Agana, had a glimpse of their possible future and reacted with mixed feelings. At Tumon Bay, the virgin jungle came down to the sand when we used to go there in jeeps from Cincpac Hill (now Nimitz Hill), the headquarters of Fleet Admiral Chester W. Nimitz in the latter part of World War II, to swim in the tepid surf that lapped the shining sands of Ipao Beach. The visitors from the South Pacific now eyed a forest of masonry towers where formerly the landscape that curved around the sapphire bay had been all green. Battalions of tourists, mostly Japanese, debouched from the buses that picked up passengers from the jumbo jets that landed several times a day at the airport a few miles away. Most would never meet a Guamanian socially.

The then Prime Minister Tamasese of Western Samoa, thinking of the still uncluttered green vistas of his jungled homeland, eyed the concrete jungle of Tumon Bay with distaste. "Western Samoa isn't ready for this," he said. But George Kalkoa, a delegate from the New Hebrides, looked around with admiration. "Tourism is a real money-spinner," he said enviously, using an Australian expression. Mara, accustomed to mass tourism in Fiji, thought that travelers had helped to preserve vanishing handicrafts with their insatiable appetite for curios, even if most of what they bought was of the spurious variety known to insiders as "airport art," of a standard fit only for souvenir counters.

Apart from the intrinsic instability of a luxury industry subject to the shifting winds of the international economic climate, tourism benefited fewer island residents than might appear. Much of the revenue flowed outward to foreign hotel owners, airlines, and travel agents. The jobs provided for local people were mostly at the menial level, offering moral temptations and destructive of pride.

Unlike Guam, Fiji, and Tahiti, with their rapidly multiplying resort complexes, most of the islands were still in the beginning stages of major tourism, if even that advanced. To their representatives at the Tumon Bay conference, experiencing an international chain hotel for the first time, the spectacular growth of the industry on Guam in a few years was a breathtaking prospect, whether for good or bad. "Wouldn't it be fine," a Micronesian from tranquil, seldom-visited Kusaie Island mused, "if the tourists would just stay home and send us their money?"

Americanization and tourism—developing in twain on islands where the preponderance of visitors were from the United States —also speeded modernization where it was needed. The requirements of hotel keepers and the duty-free merchants in the resorts and towns on Viti Levu between Suva and Nadi spurred the long-delayed construction of an improved road connecting those two main population centers of Fiji. The appearance of modern hotels on the principal islands of the trust territory, in place of the shabby, badly run establishments that had served before, inspired other overdue improvements. The brisk competitiveness learned by young Micronesians in contact with Americans on United States campuses, though at variance with the easygoing spirit of the South Seas, promised to help put the islands on a more progressive course than they had ever known before.

Probably the most far-reaching social development I observed in years of reporting from the Pacific was the development of a conscious regional identity in common among South Seas people disparate in culture but similar in outlook. From the Marianas to the Solomons, one sensed a feeling of belonging to a single community of different families with shared interests, thinking more or less the same way, considerate of opposing views when opinions diverge, inclined toward compromise to achieve a collective approach on questions of mutual concern, with able individual spokesmen acceptable to the group.

The community spirit of the South Seas, remarkable considering the short space of time in which leaders of the different island groups have been able to maintain direct contact with each other, grew out of the identity of interests discovered in forums such as the South Pacific Conference. From these meetings, encouraged by the South Pacific Commission, came such regional development organs as the South Pacific Bureau for Economic Cooperation, or SPEC, the Pacific Islands Producers Association (PIPA), and various proposals for pooling of resources in airline and shipping operations among the islands.

Mutual pride in common regional identification has been honed in such popular new area institutions as the colorful South Pacific Festival of Arts, held in different island centers in turn, in which the territories proudly demonstrate the haunting beauty of their native songs, dances, and crafts. Transistor radios throughout the South Seas are tuned to broadcasts of the South Pacific Games, the interterritorial sports competition held every third year in a different island capital. The development of common interests has been a significant by-product of higher education for island youth at the University of the South Pacific, in Fiji, and the University of Papua New Guinea.

The foreseeable outcome is a South Pacific counterpart of the European Economic Community, in which the South Pacific countries will forge positions to be taken by the group. No longer would the West participate in South Pacific affairs except as donors of economic aid and technical assistance, a more or less permanent need of all the islands.

The mood of the emergent South Seas community was summed up at a South Pacific Conference session in Suva by Oala Oala-Rarua, the future diplomat from Papua New Guinea. "Change must come, and is coming, where Pacific islanders must have their place in the world of today," he said. "Collectively, the entire Pacific is a relatively big nation and should be paid more attention by the great powers of the world."

This was the voice of the new South Pacific, demanding to be heard. Interest abroad was desultory, or routine at best. An American ambassador took up residence in Port Moresby, but most foreign envoys were accredited concurrently to Canberra, and the Papua New Guinea government deplored the practice as an unwanted reminder of Australian colonial rule. The People's Republic of China opened an embassy in Suva under a charge' d'affaires, Chang Ying, but that great Communist power's rival, the Soviet Union, gave the South Pacific to its ambassador in Wellington as extra duty. "The Russians do not come here to help but to control," Chang Ying warned in an interview with the *Samoa Times.* An eight-man Communist Chinese embassy set up shop in Apia in the new Hotel Tusitala, on the site of the old Casino (Tusitala, Samoan for "teller of tales," was the affectionate local name for Robert Louis Stevenson). The Western Samoan head of state was received in Peking with all honors, as was Michael Somare. (It was at an official banquet for Somare that the Chinese disclosed important changes in the government, and the Papua New Guinea leader's picture was published in newspapers around the world; it was the first time that a South Pacific personality had figured in news of major international importance.) Tonga, always disdainful of trends, opened diplomatic relations with the Soviet Union but allowed the embassy of the Nationalist Chinese government on Taiwan to stay. Nobody cared, or not much, and it seemed that the era when the South Pacific was a cockpit of international power rivalry had passed.

But the South Seas were still important, it seemed. Interest in the new Communist presence in the area was awakened as if by a thunderclap when it became known that King Taufa'ahau was carrying on serious negotiations with Moscow on the Soviet offer of economic aid in return for a fisheries base in northern Tonga. There was consternation in Wellington, where Prime Minister Robert Muldoon had recently referred to Tonga as a collection of islands of little worth to anybody. Canberra, already apprehensive of Soviet naval power in the Indian Ocean, now saw a Communist menace closing in from the Pacific side as well; shortly afterward, Canberra set up a fund of sixty million Australian dollars to be dispensed to South Pacific islands in economic aid over a five-year period. Admiral Noel Gayler, the commander-in-chief of United States forces in the Pacific, warned that the proposed fishing facilities could readily be converted to military use and undoubtedly served intelligence purposes. Admiral James L. Holloway III, the United States chief of naval operations, stated during a Pacific tour that Washington, dependent upon sea lanes for oil deliveries, would be looking at the Pacific "with a much broader perspective than perhaps ever before." The people of Guam, he added, would presently be seeing more of the United States fleet. A high state department official said that if the United States did not assist needy South Pacific governments, others would do so for political and military objectives.

Among the South Pacific peoples upon whom the international spotlight so suddenly shone, being a center of world attention in a military context brought mixed reactions. The Soviet offer of economic aid was welcome, as was the prospect that other countries would follow suit in their own interest. Many islanders thought that the new awareness of their needs was long overdue in the great capitals. The government of Western Samoa, to whom Moscow offered a fish cannery among other largesse, promptly decided that the time had finally come, after fourteen years of independence, to join the United Nations and "speak with its own voice in international affairs," as the first Samoan delegate to that body, Tupua Tamasese Lealofi IV, told Kathleen Teltsch of *The New York Times.* (On his first appearance in the General Assembly to take Western Samoa's seat as the 147th member, he solemnly tapped one shoulder three times with his ceremonial fly whisk, a 200-year-old implement made of human hair; the purpose of the gesture, he explained, was to ward off evil and instill confidence and wisdom in the wielder.) With Fiji, Papua New Guinea, and now Western Samoa in the United Nations, and other new island states probably to follow, the old isolation of the South Seas from world councils had ended. Islanders with painful memories of having been the object of attention by big powers in times past had reservations, however, like the Micronesian who said whimsically, "Here we go again!"

An era of change lay ahead as the peoples of the South Seas matured in political methodology. New leaders would take over, and fade away in their turn. In the process of self-determination, some Pacific territories would assume different shapes; in Micronesia, for example, Palau and the Marshall Islands followed the lead of the Northern Marianas and entered into separate negotiations with the United States on future political status. Some islanders reached into their past for classic names to replace the ones bestowed by whites (thus Kusaie, in the Eastern Carolines, became "Kosrae," and the Marshallese called themselves the "Ralik Ratak nation"). The seeds of change fell on ground made fertile in the dynamic generation following the historic watershed of World War II.

Index
